Scott Basham

Word 2010

in easy steps

In easy steps is an imprint of In Easy Steps Limited
Southfield Road · Southam
Warwickshire CV47 0FB · United Kingdom
www.ineasysteps.com

In Easy Steps Limited supports The Forest Stewardship Council (FSC), the leading international forest certification organisation. All our titles that are printed on Greenpeace approved FSC certified paper carry the FSC logo.

MIX
Paper from
responsible sources
FSC® C020837

Printed and bound in the United Kingdom

ISBN 978-1-84078-403-9

Contents

6 The References Tab 123

7 The Mailings Tab 139

8 The Review Tab 151

1 Finding Your Way Around

This chapter quickly gets you started with Word 2010. It shows you how to launch Word, and explains all the main areas in its screen layout. You'll learn some basic text editing, as well as how the main controls are organized and accessed.

Introduction

Word processing was one of the first popular applications for the modern personal computer. In the early days, it provided little more than the ability to enter and change text on the screen. Today, many more people have computers at home and in the office, and virtually all of these use a Word Processor regularly. As the years have passed, the capabilities of the computer and its software have dramatically increased, far beyond the expectations of the first generation of users back in the 1970s and 80s.

Almost since the beginning, Microsoft Word has been acknowledged as a leader in its field. It is one of the best selling software applications in any category. It grew in complexity, from a program with a handful of menu commands, to the sometimes bewildering array of features we see today.

In creating Word 2010, Microsoft have logically built on the foundation of the previous version. Rather than relying on complex menus, Word 2010 works with tabbed visual controls that reconfigure themselves to suit what you are currently doing. Accordingly, this book works as a graphical teaching guide – wherever possible, pictures and worked examples are used to demonstrate the concepts covered. It's not intended to replace Microsoft's documentation; instead, you should view it as a way of getting up to speed quickly on a wide range of useful techniques.

The full range of Word's features is covered in this and the following chapters – from creating and editing simple text-based documents, to tables, graphics and research tools, as well as more advanced techniques, such as viewing and editing documents on the Web.

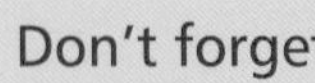

It's very important to experiment using your own examples – trying techniques a few times on test documents will give you the fluency and confidence you'll need when working for real.

How to use this book

To gain maximum benefit from this book, make sure you are first familiar with the Windows operating environment (using the mouse, icons, menus, dialog boxes, and so on). There are a number of books in the Easy Steps range that can help you here.

It is a good idea to start off by going through Chapters One and Two fairly thoroughly, since these introduce basic concepts on which later examples depend. Once you've done this, you can then freely dip into the other chapters as you like. There is a chapter for each of the Command Tabs in the Word interface, so this book is organized in the same way as Word itself.

Starting Word 2010

On some computers Word may have been set up with a desktop shortcut. If it hasn't, here's how to start it up.

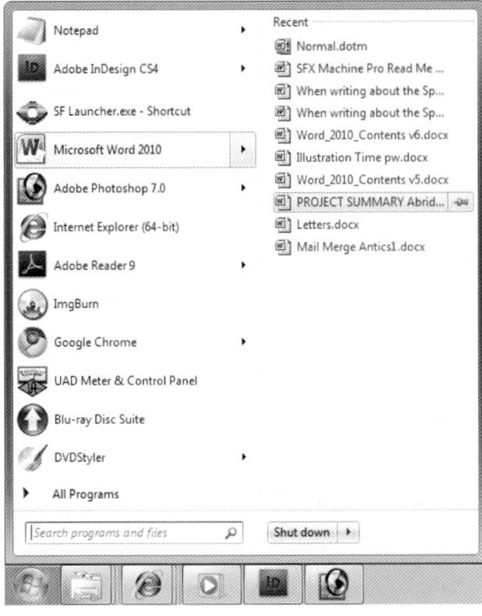

1. Click the Start button in the bottom left corner of the screen
2. If Microsoft Word appears in this menu, you can select it straight away
3. If it isn't in the menu then click All Programs

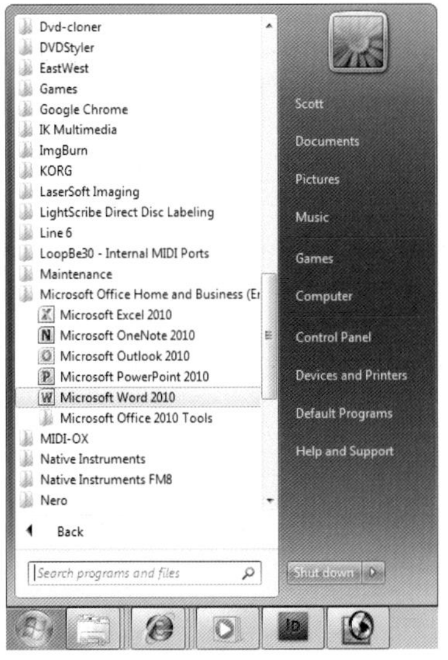

4. The menu expands to show you a list of programs and program groups represented by small folder icons
5. Click the Microsoft Office folder to expand its list of programs
6. The list of Microsoft Office applications you see will depend on what has been installed on your computer
7. Click on the small icon for Microsoft Word

Hot tip

Next to the Word icon you may see a list of recently-opened documents. Clicking on one of these will start up Word and also open the document automatically.

Hot tip

If you right-click on the Word icon a pop-up menu appears. Choose "Pin to Taskbar" or "Pin to Start Menu" to make it permanently appear in the Windows Taskbar, or the main part of the Start Menu.

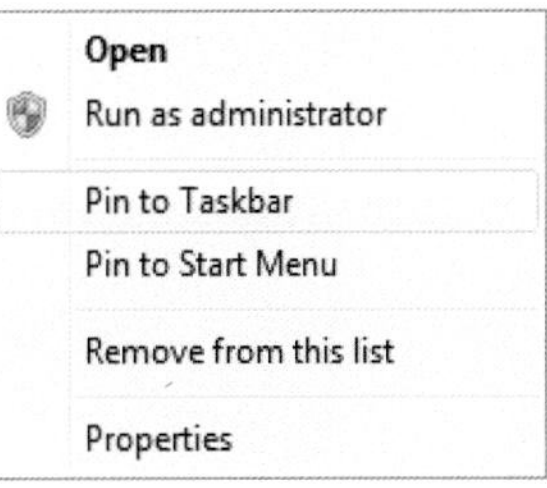

The Main Screen

Don't worry if your screen doesn't exactly match this illustration. Word's display is highly customizable and most visual elements can be switched on or off according to your own preferences. You will find tips on how to do this throughout the book.

Once Word is up and running, you should see the following screen – with all the elements illustrated here:

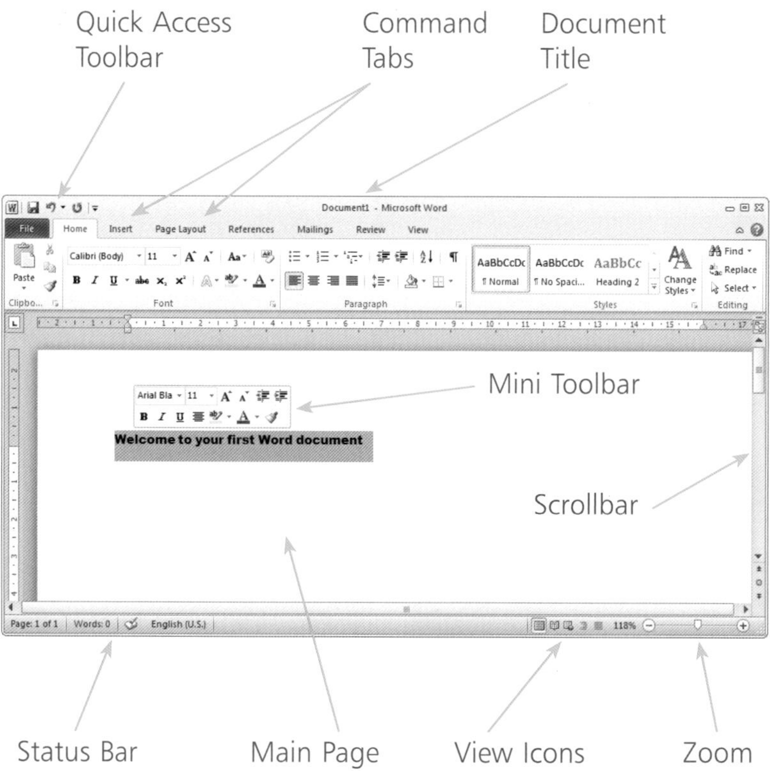

You can resize Word's window in the normal way, by dragging on its border (if it's maximized then you'll need to click the Restore Down button first).

As you can see from the two illustrations on this page, Word automatically resizes and reconfigures its workspace and controls to make the best use of the space available. If you can't see the icon or control you want, simply make the window larger or click the symbol to see what's been hidden.

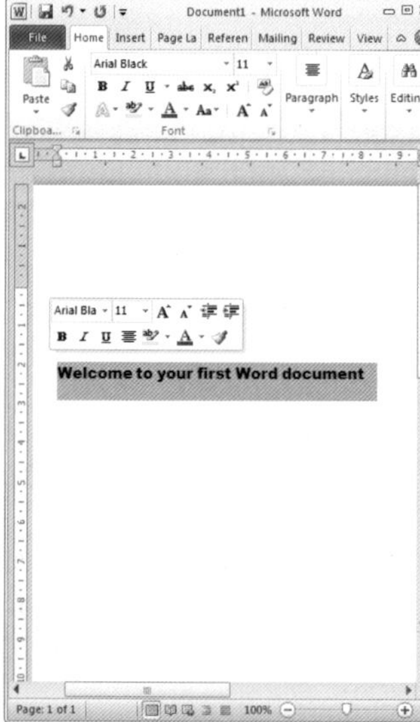

The Ribbon

Near the top of the screen is the Ribbon, which gives you access to most of Word's controls with a few mouse clicks. It's divided into a number of Tabs, only one of which is active at any one time. In the example below, the Home Tab is showing basic text editing and formatting features.

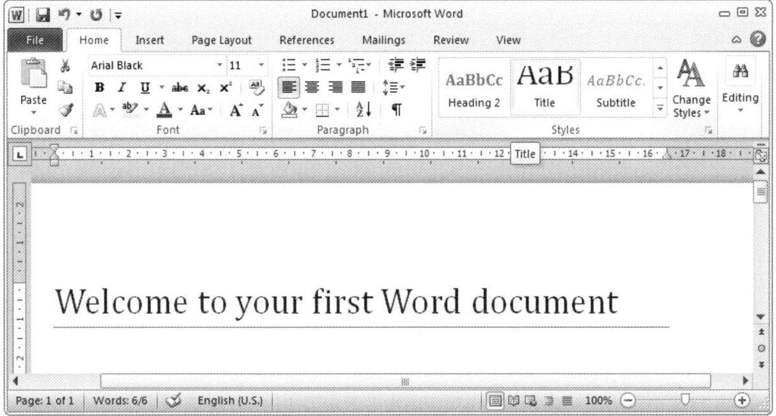

Using different Tabs in the Ribbon

1. Click on the Insert Tab's title to activate it. You will see that it's subdivided into seven sections

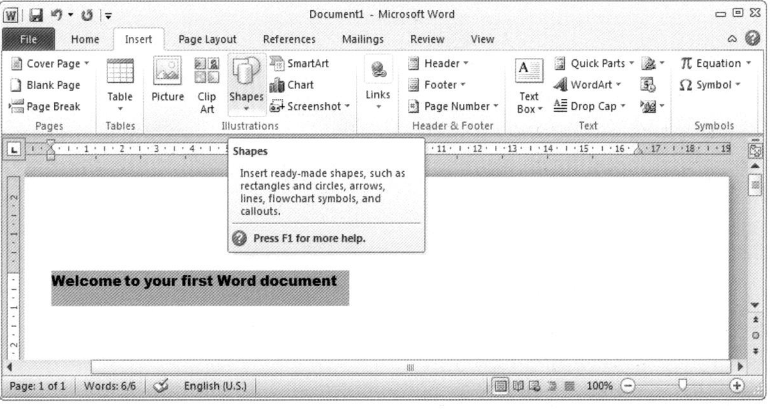

2. Each section contains groups of related controls. Let your mouse hover over one of these to see a brief explanation of its function

Hot tip

In this example, the highlighted text changes its appearance as the controls in the Ribbon are used. It is currently formatted using the style "Subtitle". As the mouse hovers over the style "Title" the text temporarily changes its format to preview this style. For more about text styles, see Chapter Two.

...cont'd

3. Double-click on the currently active Tab to hide the Ribbon temporarily. This is useful if you want to maximize the amount of screen space available for viewing and editing your document

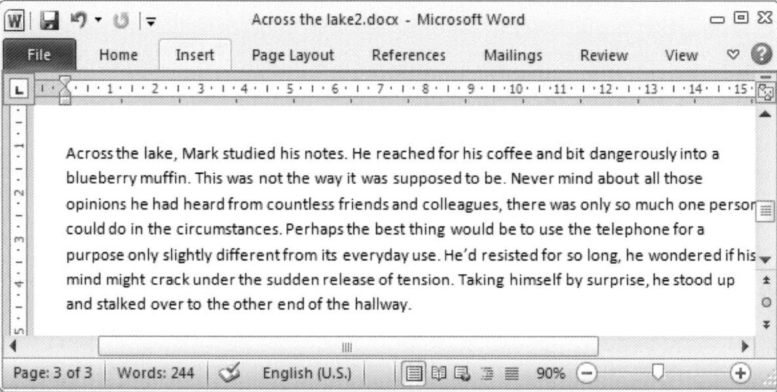

4. When the Ribbon is hidden in this way, clicking on a Tab heading will temporarily reveal its contents. Double-click on a Tab to restore the Ribbon permanently.

5. Click on the File Tab to see Word's new Backstage View. This lets you save and load documents, print and manage files, together with a range of global options and tools.

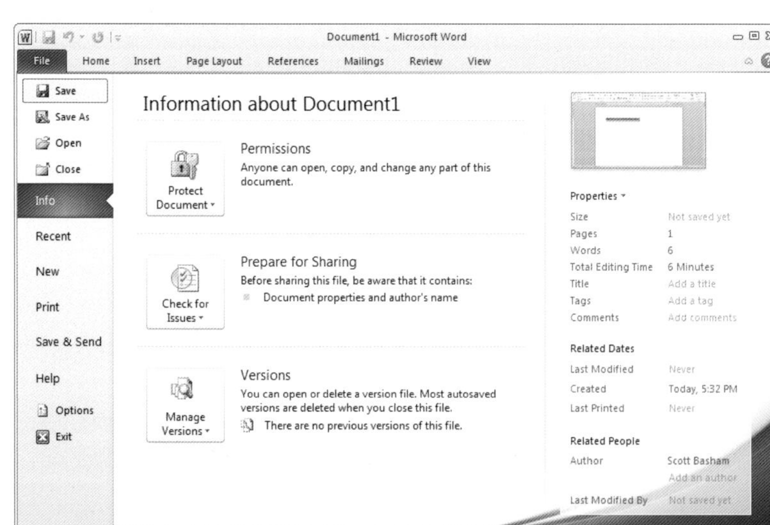

Don't forget

Each of the main Ribbon Tabs has its own chapter in this book. The Backstage View (File Tab) is covered in detail in Chapter Ten.

The Mini Toolbar

Whenever you have some text selected, the Mini Toolbar will appear nearby. It gives you immediate access to the most commonly used text formatting options.

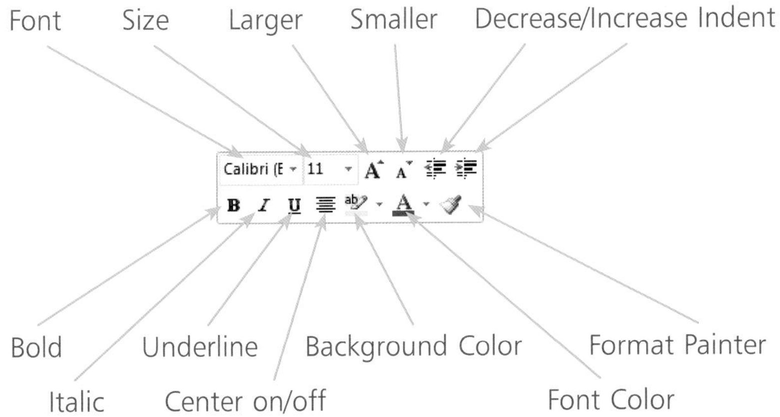

Using the Mini Toolbar

1. Type some text and then select it, by dragging across it with the mouse

2. Drag the mouse directly over the selected text, and then gradually move upwards. The Mini Toolbar will fade into view just above the text (see illustration below). As you move up towards the Mini Toolbar, it will become more solid

Jasper took a long look at his shoes' reflection and decided to call it an afternoon. Swaying slightly with the unfamiliar extra weight he ploughed a silent unwelcome furrow through the still-damp concrete and made it to the municipal buildings. He allowed himself several lungs of cold air then turned around

3. Click on one of the controls within the Mini Toolbar to change the appearance of your selected text

Hot tip

Some of the Mini Toolbar's controls have keyboard shortcuts. For example, Bold can be set on and off by typing Ctrl+B, and Italic with Ctrl+I. To find out if a control has a shortcut simply hover over it with the mouse pointer for a few moments. There is a handy reference table of keyboard shortcuts in the inside front cover of this book.

Hot tip

If the Mini Toolbar fails to appear when you hover over selected text with your mouse, try right-clicking. A pop-up context menu will appear with the Mini Toolbar immediately above.

The Quick Access Toolbar

The Quick Access Toolbar is the small collection of tools at the top of the screen, above the File Tab.

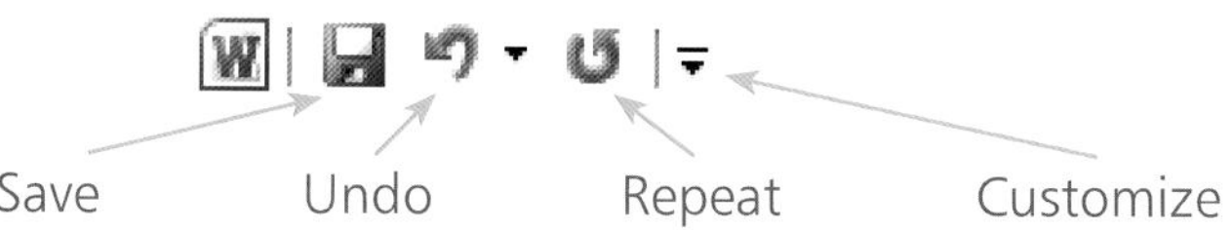

Customizing the Quick Access Toolbar

Hot tip

You can also access this dialog by activating the File tab (also known as Backstage view), choosing Options then selecting Quick Access Toolbar.

1. Click the Customize icon on the Quick Access Toolbar and select a command, or choose More Commands... to see the full list

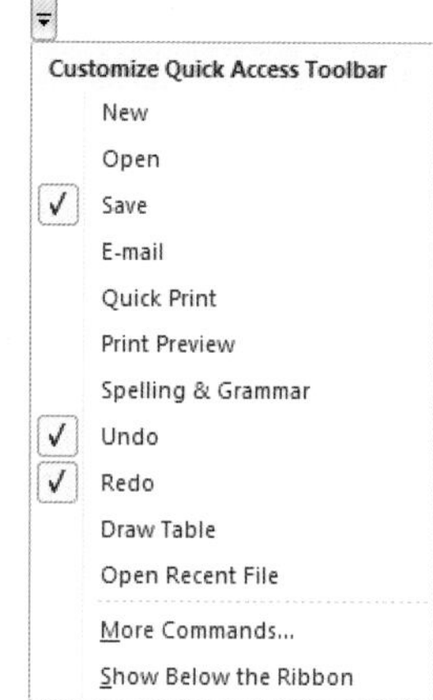

2. In the dialog that appears, select the "Choose commands from" value to see a list of Word commands

3. If you want your customizations to be global, make sure "For all documents" is selected under Customize Quick Access Toolbar

Hot tip

If you use the Quick Access Toolbar's Undo button, then a Redo button becomes available. Undo and Redo together allow you to step backwards and forwards through your actions.

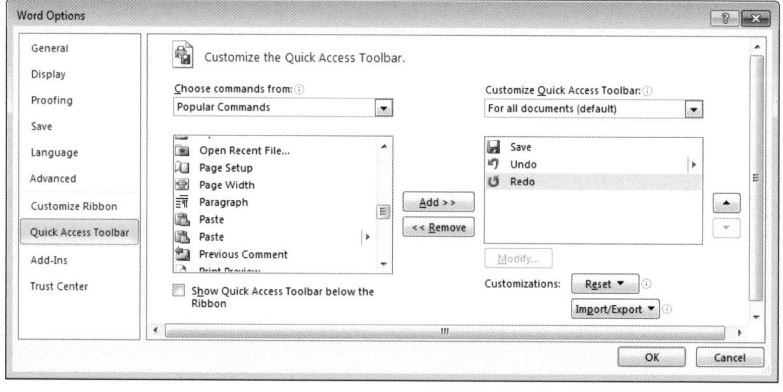

4 Add icons by double-clicking in the left-hand list, or click once to select and then choose Add>>

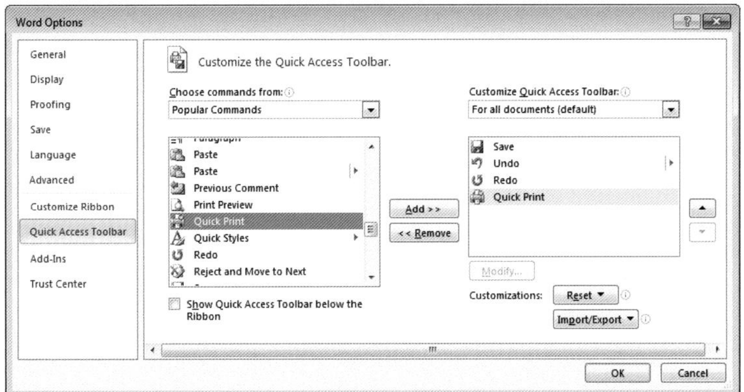

5 Remove icons by double-clicking in the right-hand list, or click once to select and then click on the Remove button

6 You can control the order in which the icons appear in the toolbar. To do this, select a command from the right hand list then use the up and down buttons to change its position. The top item in the list will appear as the first icon at the left of the toolbar

7 Click OK when done, or Cancel to abandon your changes. The Quick Access Toolbar will now show the icons you selected

From the Customize Quick Access Toolbar dialog, you can reset the Toolbar to its initial state by clicking the Reset button. It's also possible to Import and Export your customizations to a file on disk. This might be useful if, for example, you want to migrate your customizations to another computer.

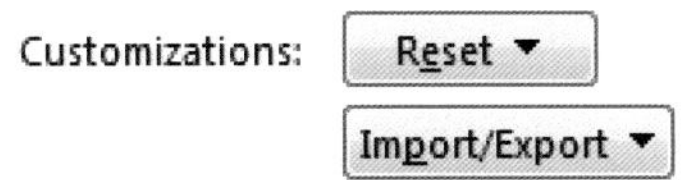

Hot tip

In this illustration you can see that Quick Access Toolbar is the highlighted item at the left of the dialog. If you select the Customize Ribbon option directly above then you will have the opportunity to completely redesign Word's layout of controls.

The Status Bar

The Status Bar is the horizontal strip at the bottom of the Word screen. It normally shows details of general settings and display options, and can be used for adjusting the zoom level.

Customizing the Status Bar

1. Right-click anywhere on the Status Bar to call up the Customize Status Bar menu

2. All the Status Bar options are listed, along with their current values. For example, in this illustration we can see that the Vertical Page Position is 3.2 inches – even though this is not normally displayed in the Status Bar

3. Click on a menu item to add it to or remove it from the Status Bar

4. Click anywhere other than the menu to close it when you have finished

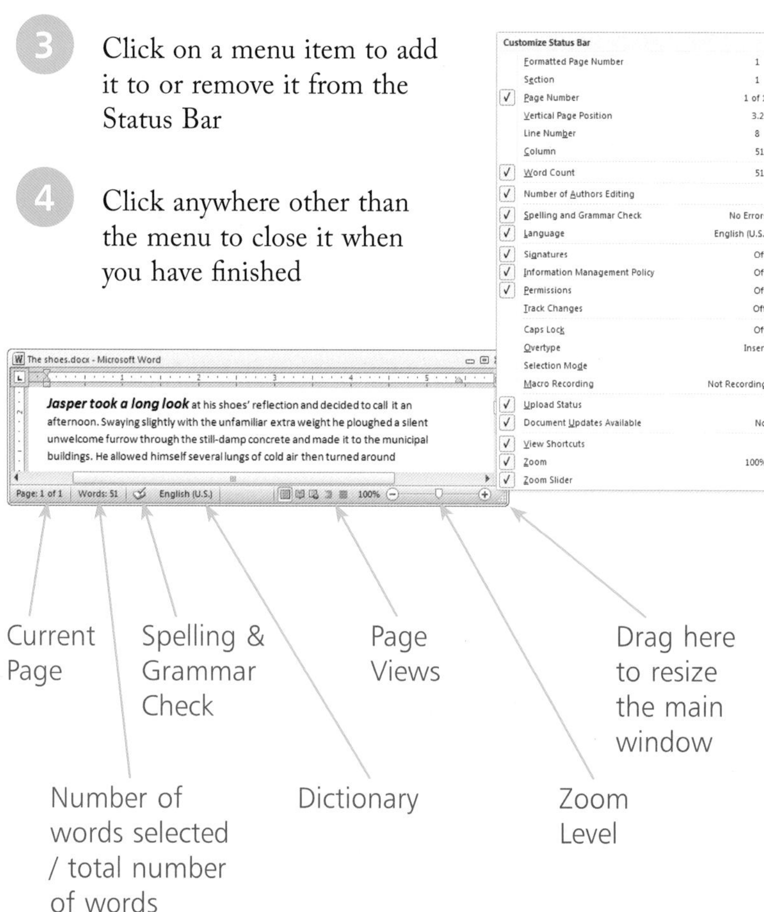

Getting Help

1. Move your mouse over a command in the Ribbon. After a few moments, a Super Tooltip appears, showing you the name of the command (useful if it's displayed only as an icon in the Ribbon). You'll also see an explanation of its function

2. The icon indicates that a dialog box will open if you click on it. If you just hover over it with the mouse, however, the Super Tooltip will include a preview image of the dialog – as in this example

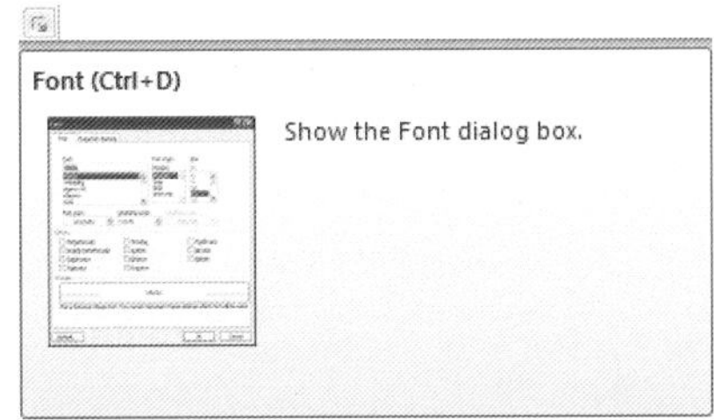

3. For more online information about any of Word's features, press the F1 key, or click on the icon in the top right corner of the screen

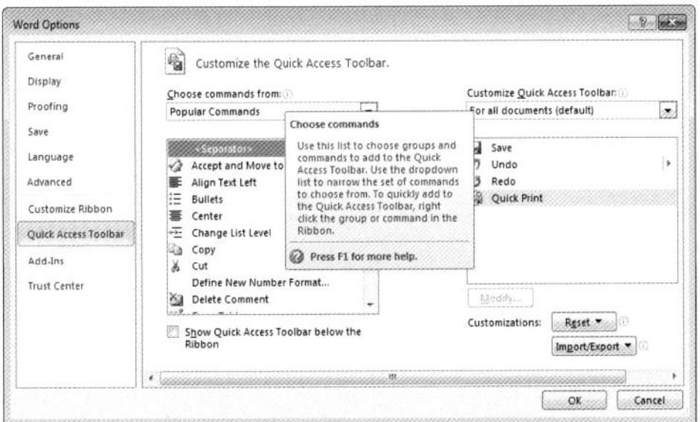

4. You'll see an explanation of the control in question. If your mouse was not pointing at any controls when you pressed F1, then a general searchable Help window appears

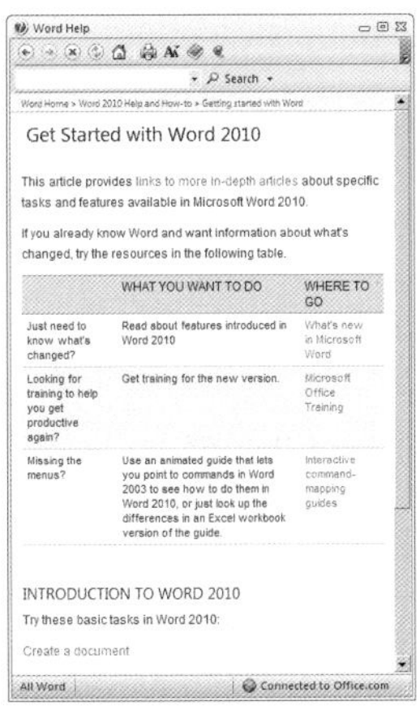

Hot tip

If you have an active Internet connection you can also access Microsoft's online help content. If the indicator in the lower right corner of the Help window is set to Offline, then click directly on it and select "Show content from Office.com".

Text Editing

Text editing in Word is no different to other programs, such as Notepad, Wordpad, Outlook or PowerPoint. If you're already familiar with the basic skills, then you might want to skip ahead to the next section.

Getting Started

1. Start up Word so that you have a new blank document. If Word is already open, then click on the File tab, and choose New, then "Blank document" and click Create

2. Enter some example text, enough for a line or two. Don't worry if you make mistakes, as these will be easy to correct later on. Note the flashing vertical line (known as the Insertion Point) which indicates where new text will appear.

3. You can easily move the Insertion Point anywhere in your text by clicking with the mouse. The arrow keys will also let you move up, down, left and right within the existing text. Move your Insertion Point so that it is somewhere in the middle of your text.

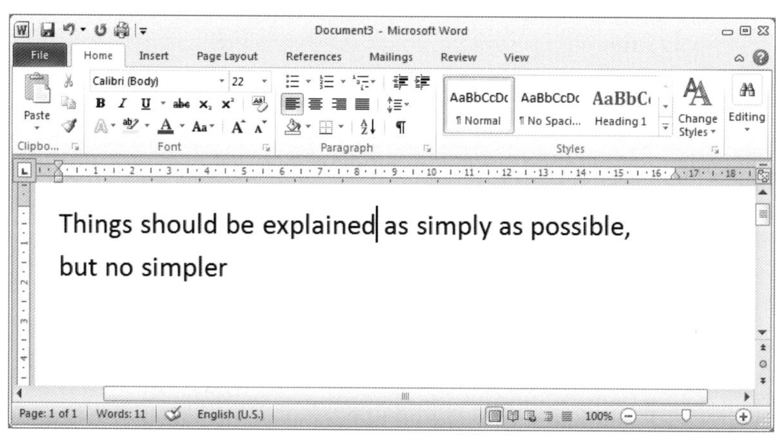

4. If you type more text now, it will be inserted at your current position. To remove text, use the Backspace key to delete the character to left of your current position, and the Delete key to remove the character to the right.

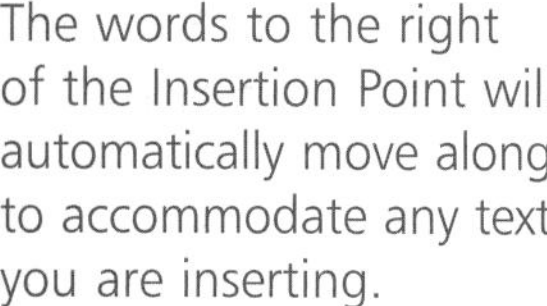

The words to the right of the Insertion Point will automatically move along to accommodate any text you are inserting.

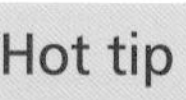

Hot tip

Word automatically works out when to start a new line, without breaking words. If you want to force a new line, to begin a new paragraph for example, press the Return or Enter key.

Selecting Text

Basic Techniques

Selecting text is almost always the first step when formatting or editing, so it's worth knowing all the different techniques.

1. Click and drag over the text you want to select. This is quick and easy for small amounts of text

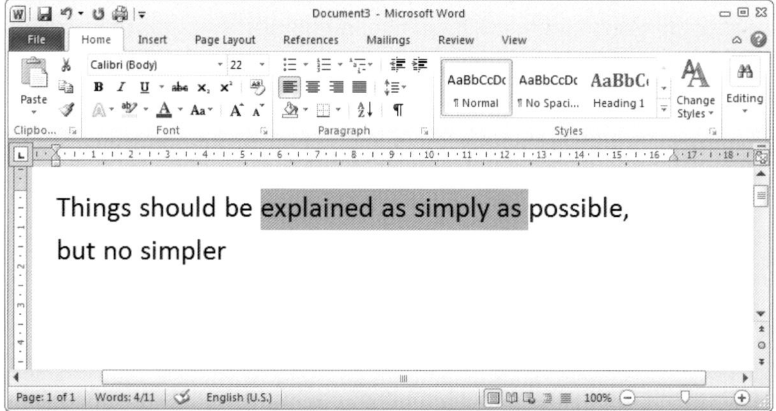

Document3 - Microsoft Word
File
Home
Insert
Page Layout
References
Mailings
Review
View
Calibri (Body)
22
Paste
Clipbo...
Font
Paragraph
AaBbCcDc
¶ Normal
AaBbCcDc
¶ No Spaci...
AaBbC
Heading 1
Change Styles
Styles
Editing
Things should be explained as simply as possible,
but no simpler
Page: 1 of 1
Words: 4/11
English (U.S.)
100%

2. If the wrong text is highlighted, click anywhere in the text editing area to cancel the selection, then try again

3. Double-click directly on a word to select it. Triple-click to select an entire paragraph

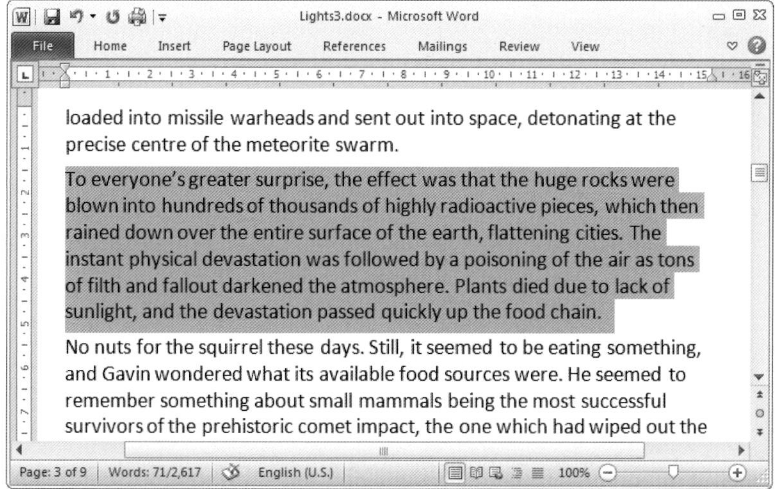

Lights3.docx - Microsoft Word
File
Home
Insert
Page Layout
References
Mailings
Review
View
loaded into missile warheads and sent out into space, detonating at the precise centre of the meteorite swarm.
To everyone's greater surprise, the effect was that the huge rocks were blown into hundreds of thousands of highly radioactive pieces, which then rained down over the entire surface of the earth, flattening cities. The instant physical devastation was followed by a poisoning of the air as tons of filth and fallout darkened the atmosphere. Plants died due to lack of sunlight, and the devastation passed quickly up the food chain.
No nuts for the squirrel these days. Still, it seemed to be eating something, and Gavin wondered what its available food sources were. He seemed to remember something about small mammals being the most successful survivors of the prehistoric comet impact, the one which had wiped out the
Page: 3 of 9
Words: 71/2,617
English (U.S.)
100%

Don't forget

Using the arrow keys, or a mouse click, allows you to reposition your Insertion Point anywhere within the text. If you try to move beyond the existing text, you'll find that the Insertion Point refuses to move. One way around this is to move just to the right of the last character and then add more text.

Beware

Don't be tempted to add extra spacing by pressing the spacebar many times. Although this will work to a certain extent, it's not the most flexible way of controlling spacing. You'll learn much better techniques for this in the next chapter.

...cont'd

More Advanced Techniques

It's worth experimenting with these. Once you've practised for a while, you'll be able to instinctively choose the best method each time you need to select text.

Hot tip

You can quickly select all the text in your document by clicking on the Select option in the Editing section of the Home Tab, and choosing Select All. The keyboard shortcut for this is Ctrl+A.

1. Move your mouse into the left margin area. You can tell that you are in the correct area when the cursor turns into an arrow pointing to the right instead of to the left
2. Drag vertically to select whole lines of text

Start dragging here

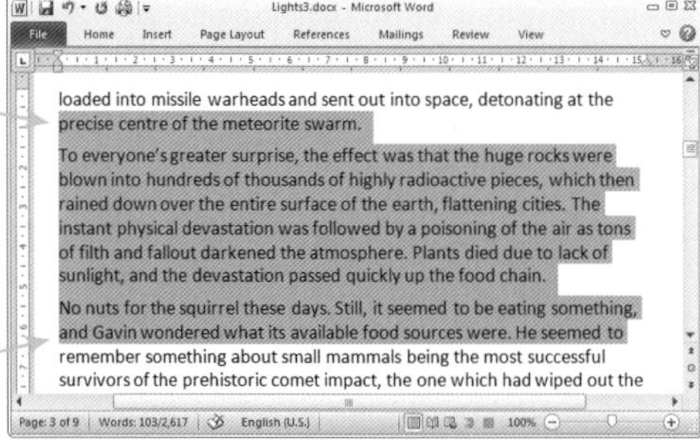
Lights3.docx - Microsoft Word
File
Home
Insert
Page Layout
References
Mailings
Review
View
loaded into missile warheads and sent out into space, detonating at the
precise centre of the meteorite swarm.
To everyone's greater surprise, the effect was that the huge rocks were
blown into hundreds of thousands of highly radioactive pieces, which then
rained down over the entire surface of the earth, flattening cities. The
instant physical devastation was followed by a poisoning of the air as tons
of filth and fallout darkened the atmosphere. Plants died due to lack of
sunlight, and the devastation passed quickly up the food chain.
No nuts for the squirrel these days. Still, it seemed to be eating something,
and Gavin wondered what its available food sources were. He seemed to
remember something about small mammals being the most successful
survivors of the prehistoric comet impact, the one which had wiped out the
Page: 3 of 9
Words: 103/2,617
English (U.S.)
100%

Finish dragging here

3. The easiest way to select larger amounts very precisely is to click the mouse at the start of the text
4. Locate the end of the area, scrolling if necessary
5. Hold down the Shift key and click. All text between the start and end will be selected. If you accidentally clicked at the wrong endpoint, simply Shift + click again

Hot tip

If you hold down the Shift key when clicking in the left margin area, the current selection will be extended up to the point where you clicked.

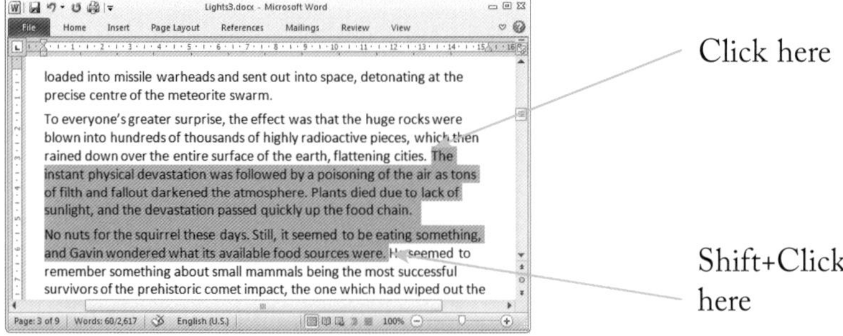
Lights3.docx - Microsoft Word
File
Home
Insert
Page Layout
References
Mailings
Review
View
loaded into missile warheads and sent out into space, detonating at the
precise centre of the meteorite swarm.
To everyone's greater surprise, the effect was that the huge rocks were
blown into hundreds of thousands of highly radioactive pieces, which then
rained down over the entire surface of the earth, flattening cities. The
instant physical devastation was followed by a poisoning of the air as tons
of filth and fallout darkened the atmosphere. Plants died due to lack of
sunlight, and the devastation passed quickly up the food chain.
No nuts for the squirrel these days. Still, it seemed to be eating something,
and Gavin wondered what its available food sources were. He seemed to
remember something about small mammals being the most successful
survivors of the prehistoric comet impact, the one which had wiped out the
Page: 3 of 9
Words: 60/2,617
English (U.S.)
100%
Click here
Shift+Click here

Discontinuous Text Selection

1. Select some text, using any of the previous techniques
2. Now hold down the Control key, click and drag across some text that is separate from your original selection
3. Repeat this process to add more areas to your selection

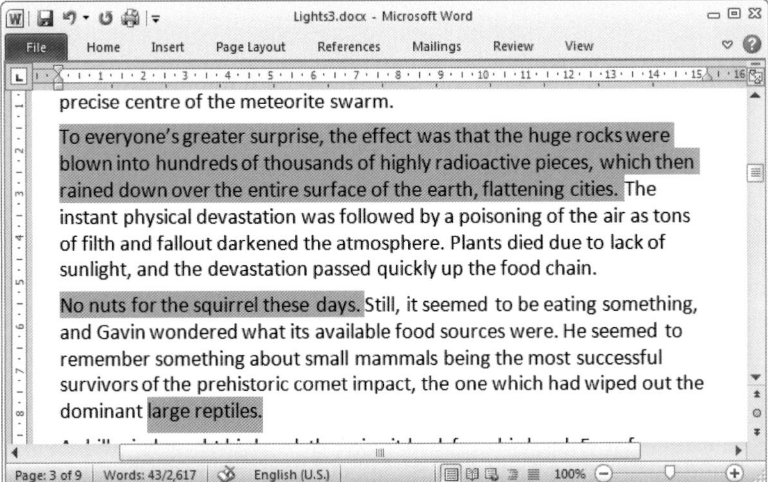
Lights3.docx - Microsoft Word
File
Home
Insert
Page Layout
References
Mailings
Review
View
precise centre of the meteorite swarm.
To everyone's greater surprise, the effect was that the huge rocks were blown into hundreds of thousands of highly radioactive pieces, which then rained down over the entire surface of the earth, flattening cities. The instant physical devastation was followed by a poisoning of the air as tons of filth and fallout darkened the atmosphere. Plants died due to lack of sunlight, and the devastation passed quickly up the food chain.
No nuts for the squirrel these days. Still, it seemed to be eating something, and Gavin wondered what its available food sources were. He seemed to remember something about small mammals being the most successful survivors of the prehistoric comet impact, the one which had wiped out the dominant large reptiles.
Page: 3 of 9
Words: 43/2,617
English (U.S.)
100%

Beware

Anything you type, even a single character, will replace all selected text. For example, if you have three paragraphs selected and you accidentally press the spacebar, then all that text will be replaced with the space. If this happens simply use the Undo button in the Quick Access Toolbar or type Ctrl + Z.

Selection with the Alt Key

If you click and drag while holding the Alt key down, you can select all text in a rectangular area. This is less useful than it might at first appear.

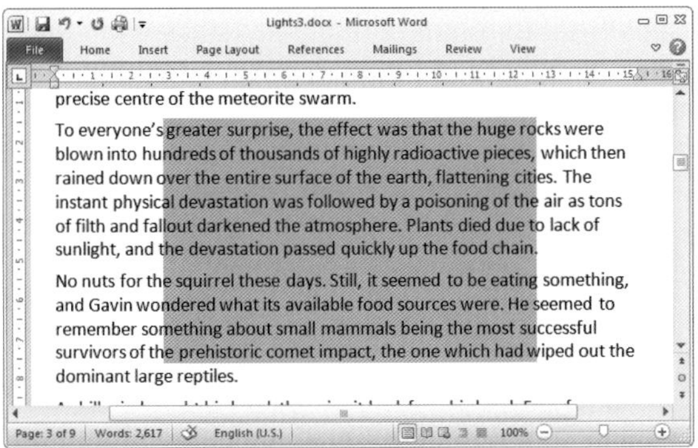
Lights3.docx - Microsoft Word
File
Home
Insert
Page Layout
References
Mailings
Review
View
precise centre of the meteorite swarm.
To everyone's greater surprise, the effect was that the huge rocks were blown into hundreds of thousands of highly radioactive pieces, which then rained down over the entire surface of the earth, flattening cities. The instant physical devastation was followed by a poisoning of the air as tons of filth and fallout darkened the atmosphere. Plants died due to lack of sunlight, and the devastation passed quickly up the food chain.
No nuts for the squirrel these days. Still, it seemed to be eating something, and Gavin wondered what its available food sources were. He seemed to remember something about small mammals being the most successful survivors of the prehistoric comet impact, the one which had wiped out the dominant large reptiles.
Page: 3 of 9
Words: 2,617
English (U.S.)
100%

Working With Files

Chapter Ten, "Backstage View", will look at file manipulation in detail, so, for now, we'll just concentrate on the simplest way to store and retrieve your work.

Starting a New Document

When you start up Word, you'll automatically be shown a new, blank document. If you're ready to create another new document, select the File Tab and click New

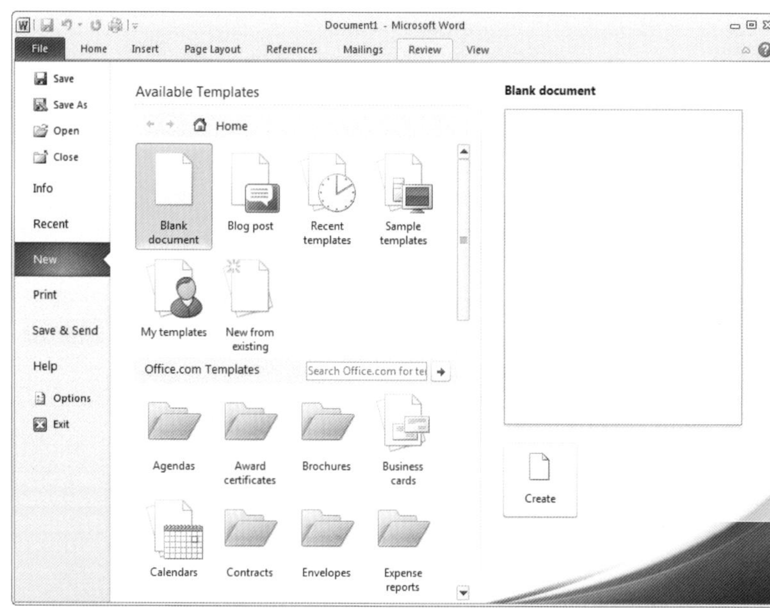

Don't forget

If you're unfamiliar with the way files are stored in Windows, or how to navigate through its structure of disks and folders, then it's worth spending some time learning. There are a number of In Easy Steps books which can help you here. Check which version of Windows you're using (e.g. XP, Vista, Windows 7) and then consult www.ineasysteps.com.

Saving Your Work

If you attempt to close down Word without saving, you'll see the following message. Click Save if you want to save your work before quitting

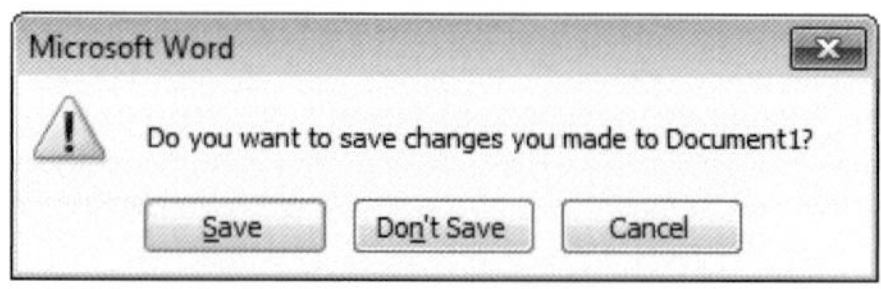

2 Another way to save your work is to click on the Save icon in the Quick Access Toolbar. If you had saved the document before, Word simply saves using the same name and file location as before. If this is the first time saving the document, you'll see the following dialog box:

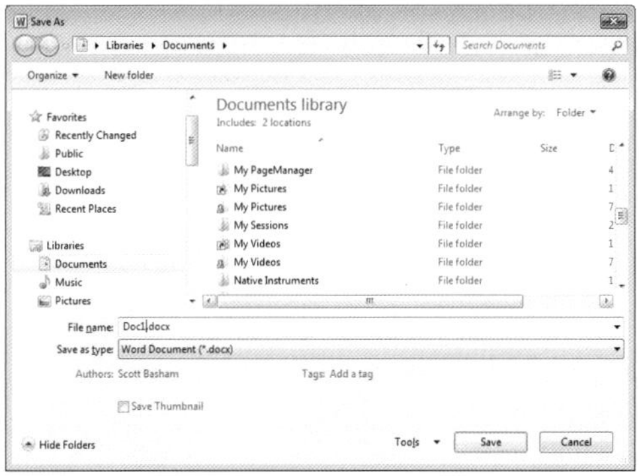

3 Change the file name to something meaningful, check that the displayed disk and folder are where you want to store the file, then click Save

Opening a Saved Document

1 Select the File Tab, then click Open

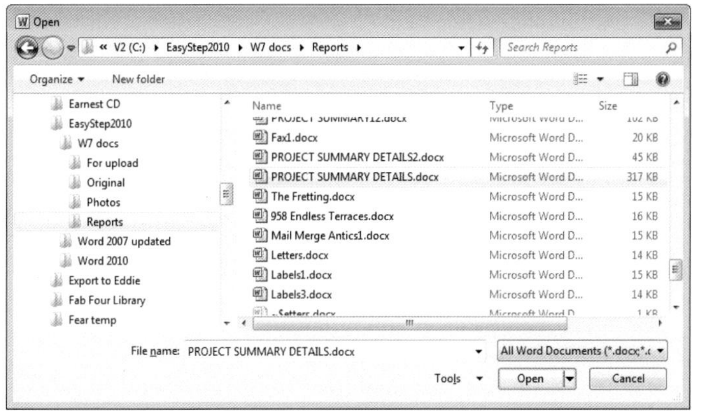

2 Choose the disk and folder using the standard Windows controls, then click Open

Hot tip

If your document has already been saved, but you want to save a new copy rather than overwrite the previous version, go to the File Tab and select Save As instead of Save

If you haven't yet started up Word, then you can speed things up by locating your document then double-clicking on its icon. This will start up Word and open the document automatically.

Click and Type

Provided you are in Word's Print Layout, or Web Layout view, you can easily add text anywhere on the page.

1. First make sure that Print Layout view is selected, from the Page View icons in the Status bar at the bottom of the screen

Print Layout view

2. Move over a blank area. The pointer icon will indicate whether new text will be aligned left, right or centered. The example below shows the icon for centered text. Double-click to establish a new Insertion Point

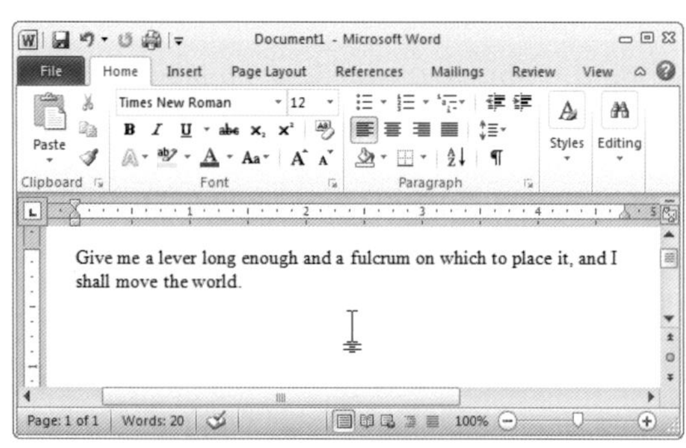

3. Type in some new text. Word will create any new blank lines necessary to allow the text to be positioned correctly. It also applies the correct form of alignment

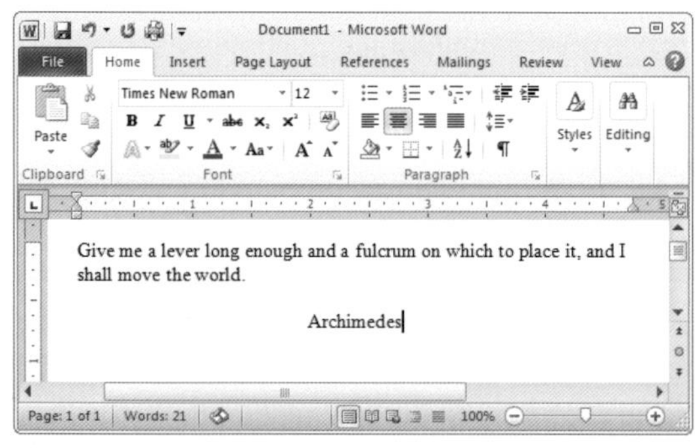

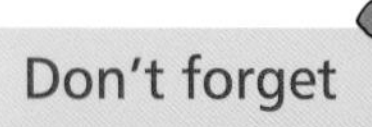

Don't forget

If Click and Type doesn't appear to work, click on the File Tab and choose Options. Select Advanced and make sure that the option "Enable click and type" is activated.

Hot tip

You'll learn more about left, right and centered text in the next chapter.

Basic Navigation

When your text is too large for the document window, you'll need to use one of the following navigation methods:

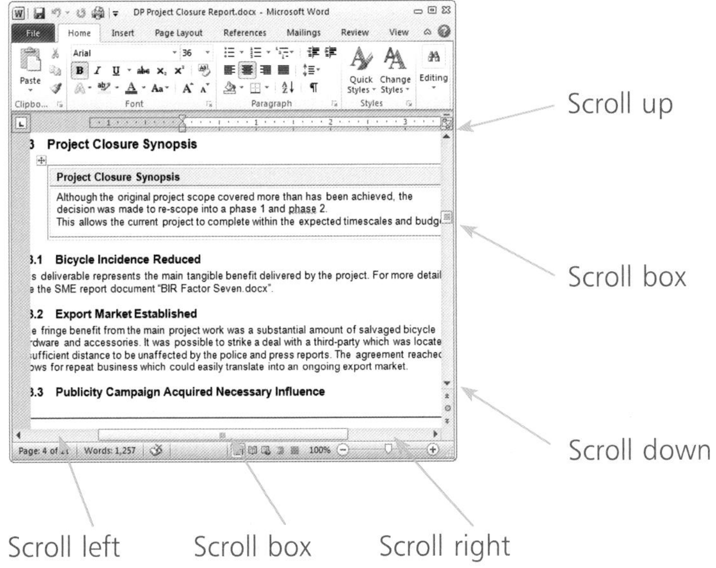

Hot tip

The scroll boxes' positions let you know where you are in a document. When the vertical scroll box is at the top of the scroll bar, you are looking at the top (the beginning) of the document.

Quick Ways to Scroll

1. Drag the scroll box directly to a new position
2. Click in the scroll bar to either side of the scroll box. The document will immediately scroll in that direction, one screen at a time
3. As you move your insertion point with the arrow (cursor) keys, Word will scroll so that it can always be seen
4. If your mouse has a wheel, this can usually be used to scroll vertically through your document
5. The PgUp (Page Up) and PgDn (Page Down) keys will move you up and down one screen at a time

Hot tip 

As you scroll down, the scroll box moves like an elevator down a shaft. The size of the box indicates how much of the document you can see (if the box occupies one third of the scroll bar, then you're viewing a third of the document).

...cont'd

Zooming

This allows you to control the level of magnification on screen. The zoom controls are in the bottom right corner.

Remember to consider the size of Word's main window – in most cases it should be maximized. Note, however, that in this book we often use smaller windows so that we can concentrate on a particular part of the screen or set of controls.

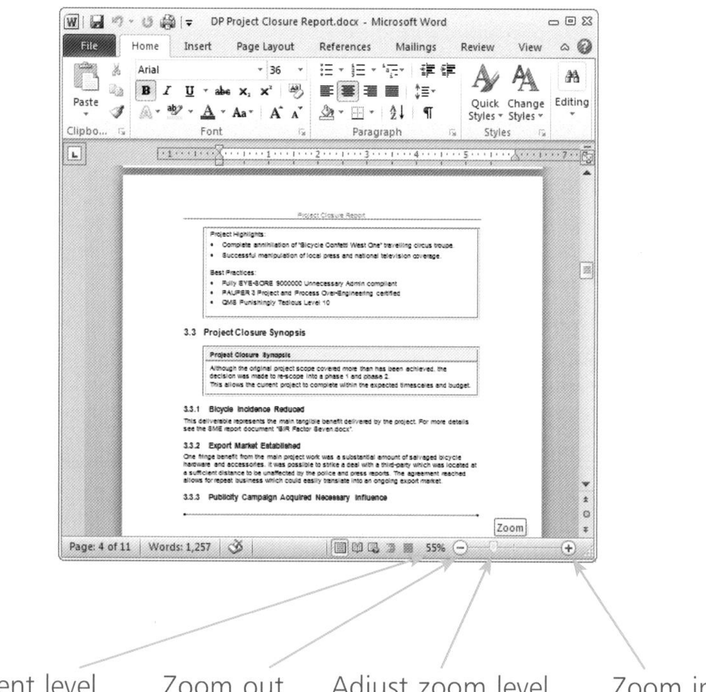

The Zoom Dialog Box

1. Click on the "Current magnification" icon to open the Zoom dialog box

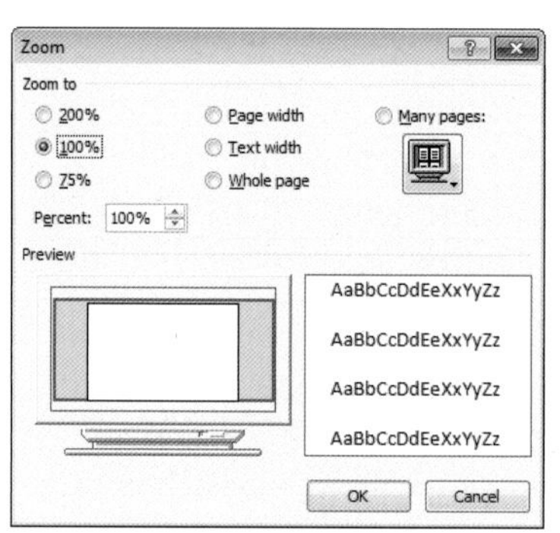

2. Choose one of the options, or enter a percentage value directly. In this example, "Text width" is a good option if you dislike horizontal scrolling

3. Click OK to apply the zoom level

2 The Home Tab

Now that you know your way around Word, we'll look at the first, and the most useful, of the Command Tabs. After reading this chapter, you'll know most things about editing and formatting text.

Font Controls

The Home Tab contains the controls you'll use most often in Word, so it's selected by default whenever you open or create a document.

As you can see, it's organized into five areas: Clipboard, Font, Paragraph, Styles, and Editing controls. We'll start by looking at the Font Controls, as the others will make more sense once you've seen how to change the appearance of text.

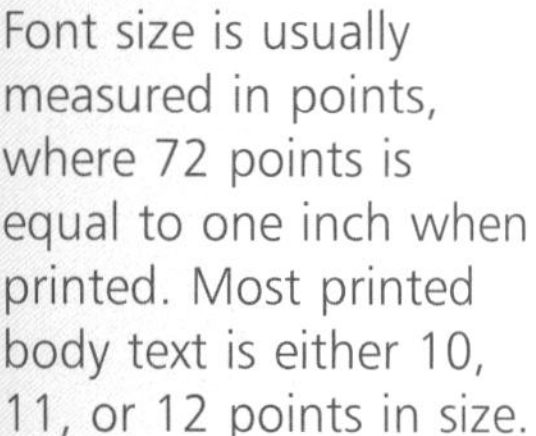

Hot tip

Font size is usually measured in points, where 72 points is equal to one inch when printed. Most printed body text is either 10, 11, or 12 points in size.

Choosing the Font with the Mini Toolbar

The term fonts and typeface come from traditional typography, and they describe the visual design of letters and other symbols. Most people will be familiar with popular typefaces, such as Arial or Times New Roman. Strictly speaking, a font is an instance of a typeface at a certain size and variant, such as normal, light, bold or italic. These days the term font is often used in place of typeface, so, in Word, we might select a font of "Calibri", then choose a size of 12 and finally apply an effect of Bold.

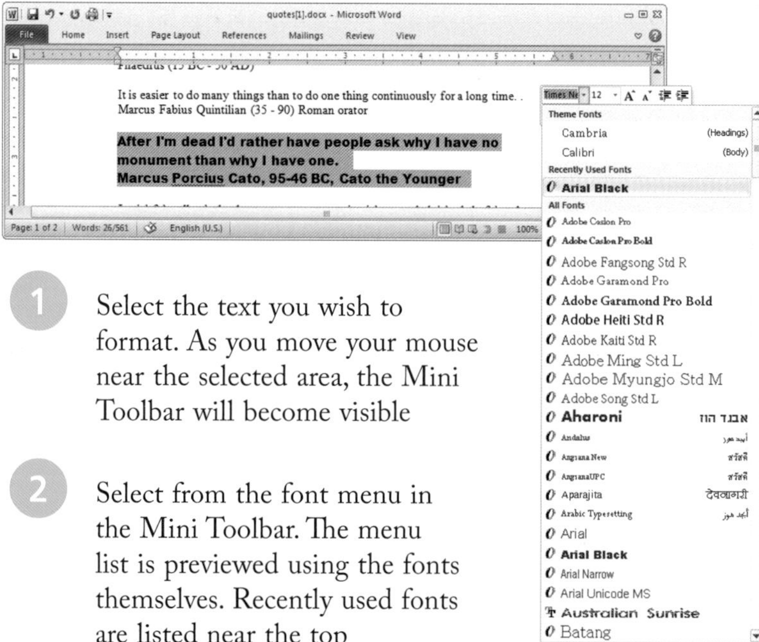

1. Select the text you wish to format. As you move your mouse near the selected area, the Mini Toolbar will become visible

2. Select from the font menu in the Mini Toolbar. The menu list is previewed using the fonts themselves. Recently used fonts are listed near the top

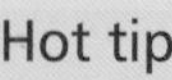

Hot tip

If the Mini Toolbar fails to appear when you hover over some text with your mouse, try right-clicking. A pop-up context menu will appear, with the Mini Toolbar immediately above.

Formatting with the Home Tab

The Font section of the Home Tab gives you access to more ways of controlling the appearance of characters.

1. Select some text. Change font, size, and other attributes, by selecting from the Font section in the Home Tab

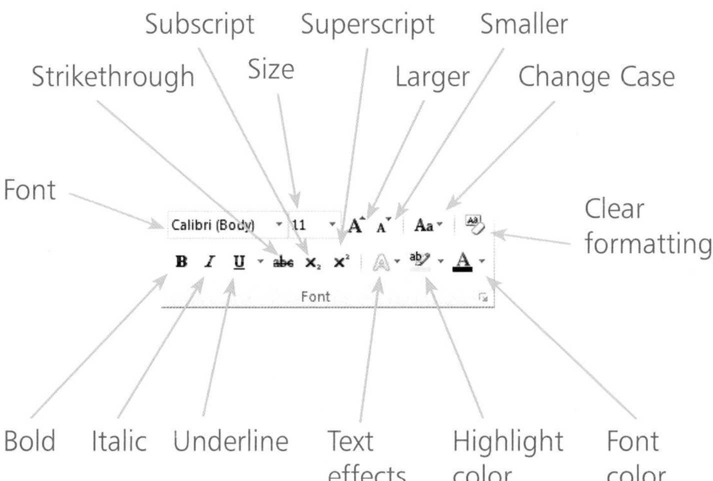

Hot tip

The keyboard shortcuts for Bold, Italic, and Underline are Ctrl+B, Ctrl+I, and Ctrl+U respectively.

2. Whenever you select text, the Font area will show you its current settings (if there are mixed settings within the text you've selected, then the value will be shown as blank)

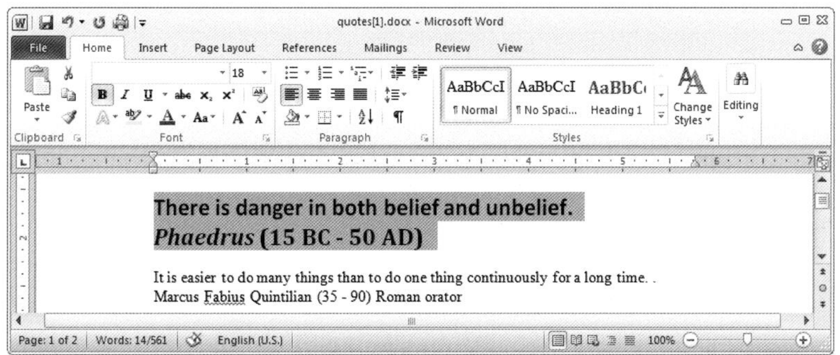

If the settings show as blank, then try selecting a smaller portion of text.

3. In this example, all the selected text is 18 point in size, and in bold. However, since it uses more than one font, the area which usually displays the font name is blank

...cont'd

The Font Dialog

You can call up the Font dialog box to get full character-level control over the appearance of your text.

1. Select some text. Click on the dialog icon, in the lower right corner of the Font area of the Home Tab, or press Ctrl+D

Open font dialog

2. You now have access to additional effects, such as double strikethrough and a variety of underline styles. The Preview box near the bottom gives you an indication of how the text would appear if you clicked OK

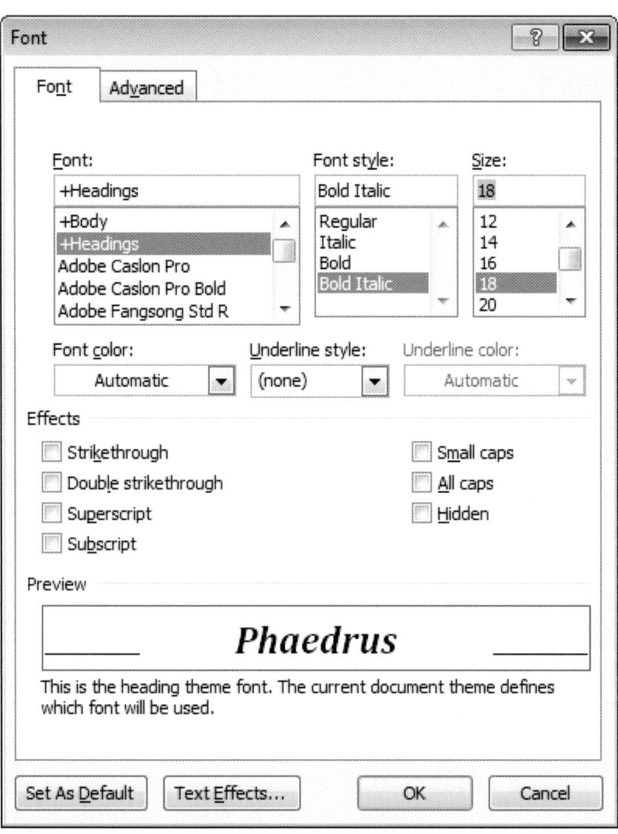

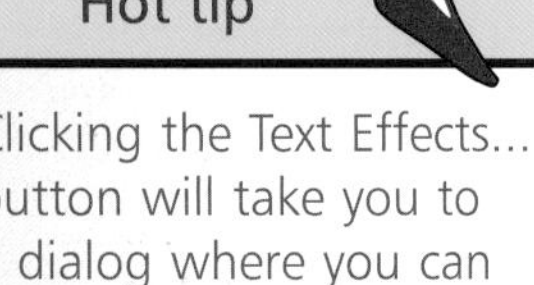

Clicking the Text Effects... button will take you to a dialog where you can apply a wide range of visual effects to your text. These include: fills, outlines, shadow, reflections and 3D formats. You can apply some (but not all) of these directly from an icon in the Home Tab on the Ribbon, as you will see on the next page.

Click on the Advanced tab to control the precise positioning and scaling of the selected characters

Kerning

Kerning is a process used to adjust the space between certain combinations of characters. For example, when the letters "T" and "o" occur next to each other, normal spacing appears too wide. If you activate kerning, then they will be brought closer together to create the illusion of normal spacing. Since kerning can slow down screen redrawing, you might only want to activate it for larger font sizes (where spacing is more noticeable).

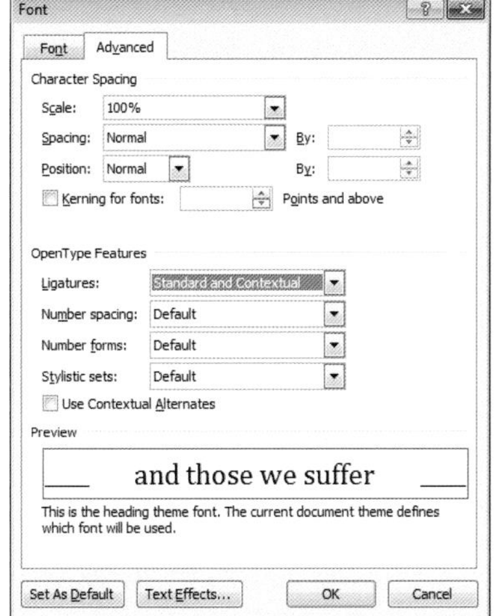

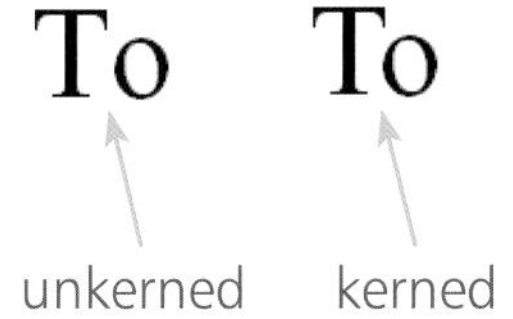

Ligatures

Word 2010 introduces the ability to access a range of OpenType features. OpenType allows Font designers to make use of different features, such as special small caps, ligatures, number forms and spacing. Ligatures are combinations of characters designed as a single entity. In this example, you can see that applying ligatures affects the two consecutive "f" characters, which are displayed as a specially designed single character.

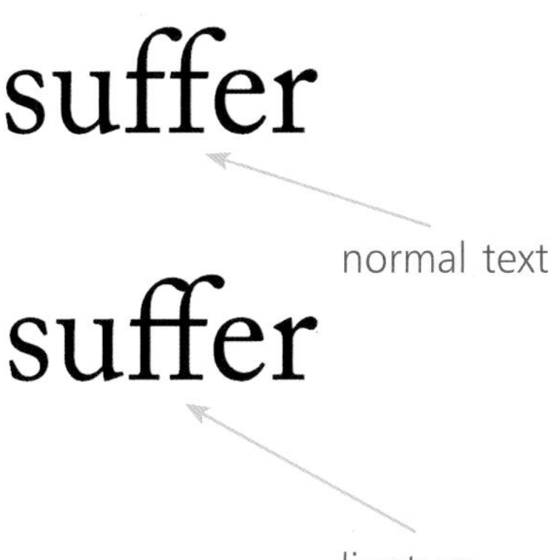

Beware

Scaling allows you to stretch or compress text horizontally. While this can sometimes work well for large titles, it is not recommended for use on main text, as the results are often unreadable. If you need narrower or wider text, then try using a different font that is already the desired shape.

Don't forget

You might not notice any changes to the appearance of your text when you activate ligatures, as this setting will only make a difference if you are using a font which has been specially created with ligature information.

...cont'd

Text Effects

Word 2010 gives you a wide range of effects for adding to your text, and, by using the Toolbar, you'll get an instant preview.

1. Select some text. Click on the Text Effects button within the Font Tools to see a menu of popular effects. As you hover over an item, your text will temporarily preview the effect. Either move to a different effect or, if you are happy with your selection, click once on the effect to apply it permanently

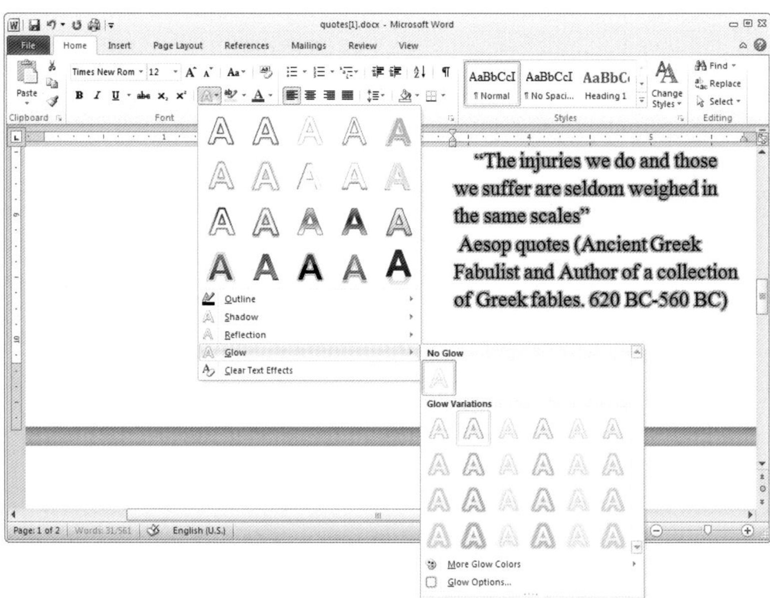

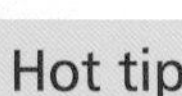

Hot tip

The Text Highlight Color and the Font Color buttons also give you an instant preview of how the text will look as you hover over each color in their pop-up menus.

2. You can use the submenus to access more options within the individual effects of outline, shadow, reflection and glow. Note that you can apply several effects at once, although just one from each category. For example, an outer shadow, a green glow and a medium reflection can all be applied to a single piece of text (see below)

Paragraph Controls

The Mini Toolbar gives you the ability to switch centering on and off, adjust the left indent, or create a bulleted list. For most paragraph-level attributes, however, you'll use the Paragraph section of the Home Tab.

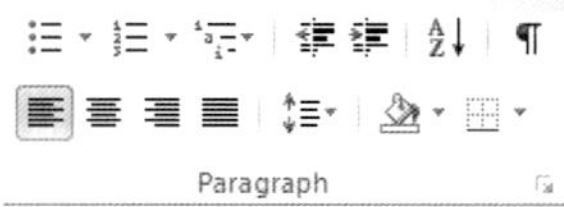

Paragraph

Alignment

1. If you want to change just one paragraph, then simply click anywhere within it. If you want to change multiple paragraphs, then select them using any of the techniques we looked at earlier

2. Click on one of the alignment icons to choose left, centered, right or justified alignment. There is an example of each type illustrated below

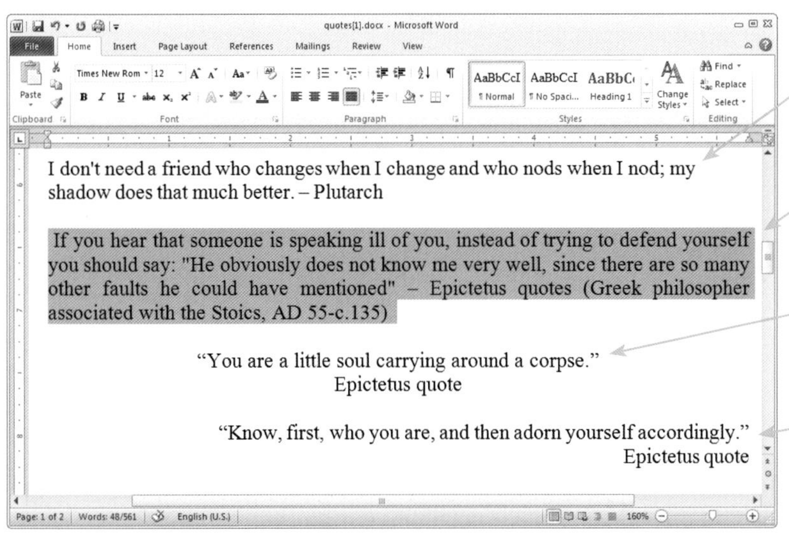

quotes[1].docx - Microsoft Word
File
Home
Insert
Page Layout
References
Mailings
Review
View
Times New Rom
12
Paste
Clipboard
Font
Paragraph
AaBbCcI
¶ Normal
AaBbCcI
¶ No Spaci...
AaBbCc
Heading 1
Change Styles
Styles
Find
Replace
Select
Editing
I don't need a friend who changes when I change and who nods when I nod; my shadow does that much better. – Plutarch
If you hear that someone is speaking ill of you, instead of trying to defend yourself you should say: "He obviously does not know me very well, since there are so many other faults he could have mentioned" – Epictetus quotes (Greek philosopher associated with the Stoics, AD 55-c.135)
"You are a little soul carrying around a corpse."
Epictetus quote
"Know, first, who you are, and then adorn yourself accordingly."
Epictetus quote
Page: 1 of 2
Words: 48/561
English (U.S.)
160%

left(normal)

justified

centered

right

3. To see more paragraph controls, click the small open dialog icon in the lower right corner of this section. The dialog which appears has two tabbed pages: "Indents and Spacing" and "Line and Page Breaks". These give you accurate control over attributes, such as line spacing, indentation and hyphenation

Don't forget

Remember that a heading is regarded as a single-line paragraph by Word.

Hot tip

Justified text is aligned to both the left and the right margins, so that both have a straight edge (apart from the final line in a paragraph). To achieve this, the spacing between words is automatically adjusted.

...cont'd

Bulleted Lists

1. Enter the text for your list, pressing the Return key after each item. Select this text

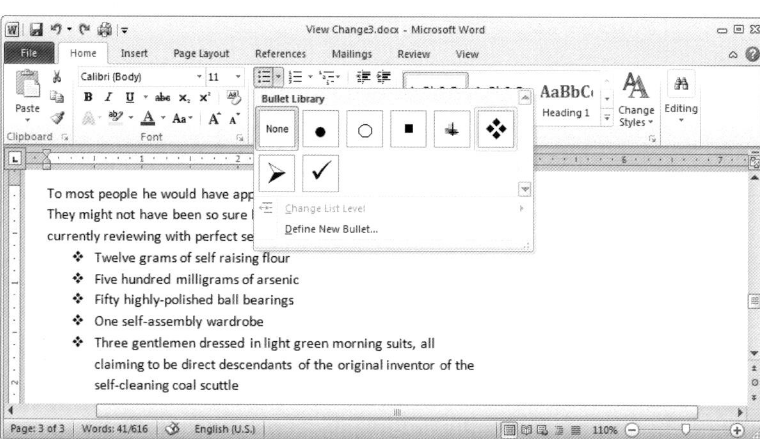

2. Open the Bullets pop-up menu in the Paragraph area of the Home Tab

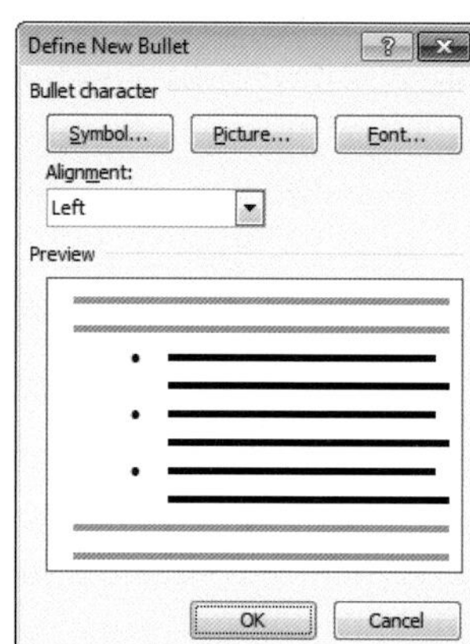

3. Choose the desired type of bullet. If you don't like any of those displayed, then choose Define New Bullet. From this dialog you can select any symbol or picture

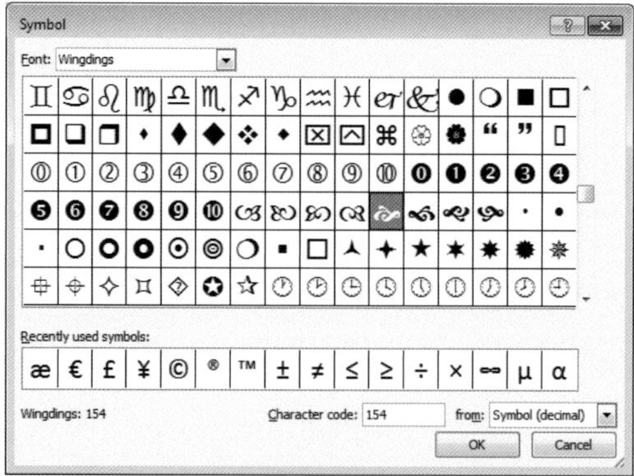

Hot tip

A quick way to create a bulleted list is to type an asterisk at the beginning of the first line. Word will automatically change this to a bullet, formatting this and all subsequent lines for you. When you have finished, leave the next line blank and just press Return. Word will then switch off the bulleted effect.

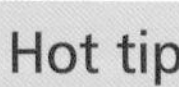

Hot tip

From the Define New Bullet dialog, you can choose any image or character from a font for your bullet. Many fonts, such as Wingdings and Dingbats, are pictorial – this makes them a good source for bullets.

Numbered Lists

1. If you enter, on a new line, text beginning with a "1." then Word will automatically create a numbered list. When you press Return, the next numbered line will be created for you automatically

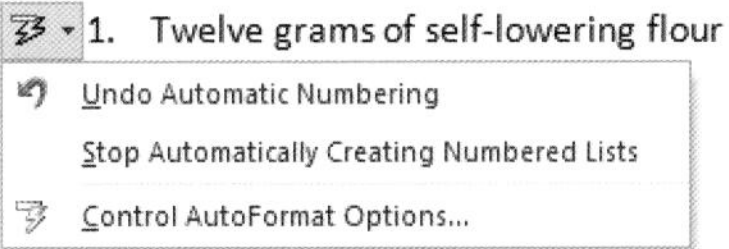

2. This behavior may not always be what you want. If it is not, then click on the AutoCorrect icon that appears by your text. You can then undo the automatic numbering, just for this example, or disable the feature for future lists

3. Another way to create a numbered list is to enter your text with no numbers, then select it in the normal way and open the Numbering pop-up menu in the Paragraph section of the Home Tab. As you hover over the different format options, you'll see a preview of how your text will appear

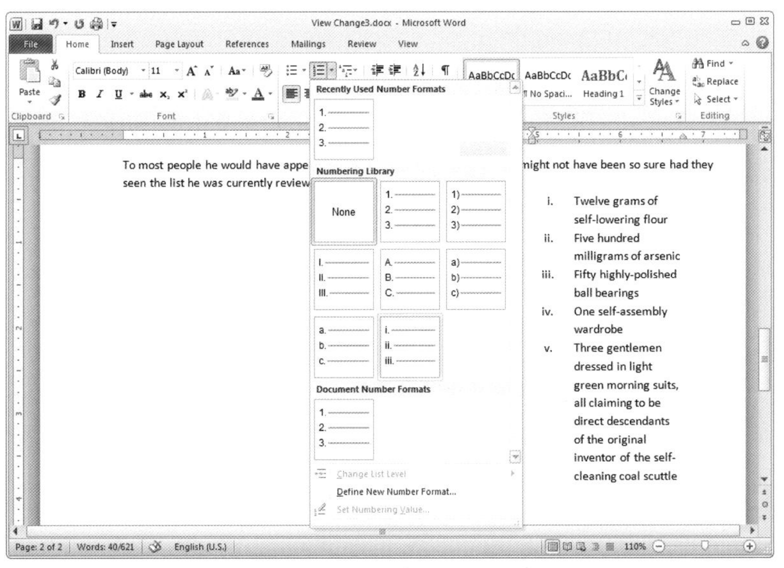

Hot tip

If you choose Control AutoFormat Options... you will call up a dialog with settings for this, plus many other automatic features

Hot tip

From the Numbering pop-up menu, choose Define New Number Format... to fully customize the style, format and alignment.

Define New Number Format
Number format
Number style: 1st, 2nd, 3rd ...
Font...
Number format: 1st.
Alignment: Right
Preview
1st.
2nd.
3rd.
OK
Cancel

...cont'd

Sorting Lists

1. Select your list, then click the Sort button within the Paragraph Tools

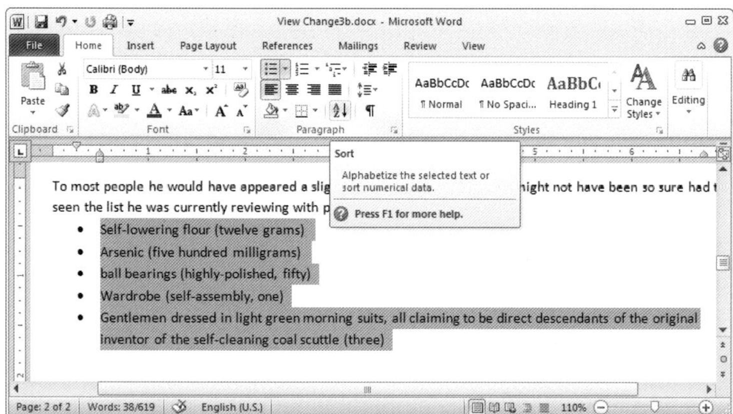

2. The following dialog appears. Choose the appropriate sort type (in this case, text), then click OK

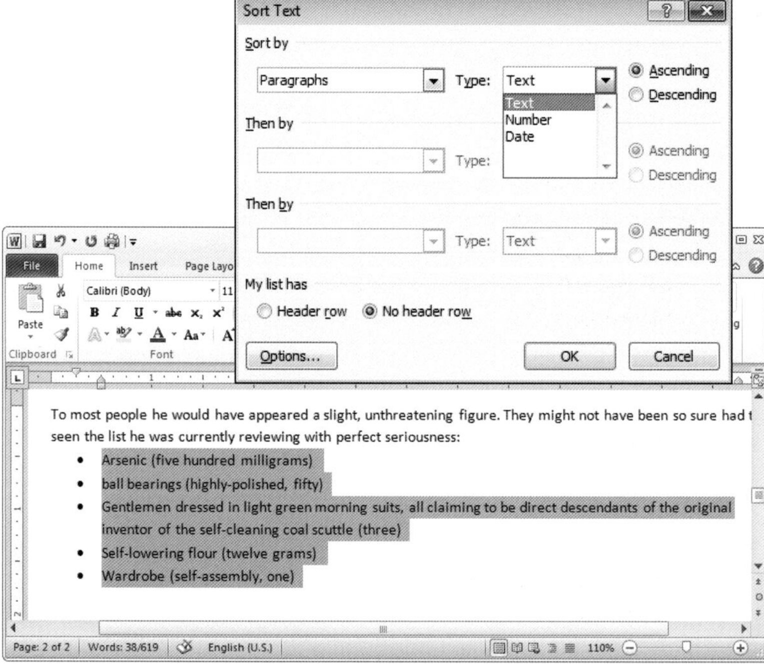

Hot tip

You can also sort multilevel lists (see the next page for creating this type of list). The Sort Text dialog allows you to specify a sort order for up to three levels.

Multilevel Lists

1. Create the text for your list. Press the Tab key at the beginning of a line, once for each level of indent

2. Open the Multilevel pop-up menu in the Paragraph section and select the desired style

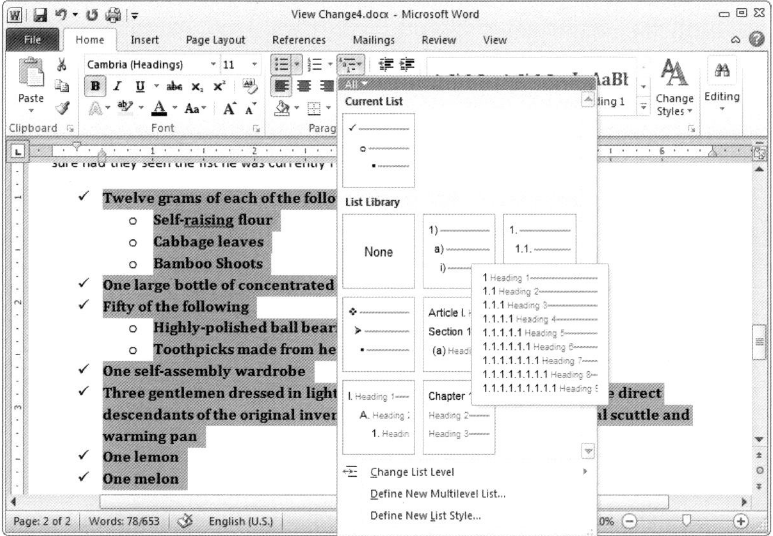

3. If you want to choose your own custom settings, then select Define New Multilevel List...

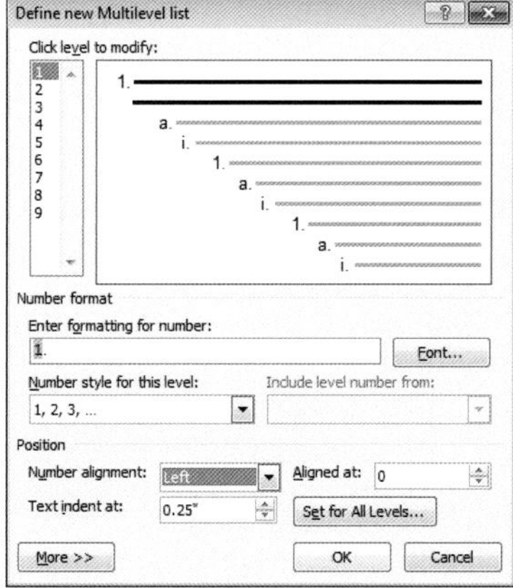

4. By clicking the Font... button, you can control the appearance of the number at each level of the list, separately from the main text

Quick Styles

Styles help you to apply a consistent set of formatting attributes to main text, headings, and other elements of your document. Once you start using styles, you'll be able to control your document's presentation with a minimum of tedious manual editing. Word comes with a set of styles for you to use straight away (in an area of the Home Tab called the Styles Gallery), but it's also easy to create your own. There are two main types of style:

Don't forget

A paragraph of text can only have a maximum of one paragraph style applied to it at any one time. If you select a single word and apply a paragraph style to it, then the whole of the surrounding paragraph will be affected.

Paragraph Styles

These can contain information about virtually any text attribute, e.g. font, size, alignment, spacing, and color. They are called paragraph styles because they are applied at the paragraph level. In the Styles area, paragraph styles are marked with a ¶ symbol.

Applying a Paragraph Style

1. Choose the paragraph of text you want to format by clicking anywhere within it. If you want to format multiple paragraphs, then select these using any of the techniques covered in the previous chapter

2. If you hover over a style from the Styles Gallery in the Toolbar, you'll see a preview of your text using the style. Choose one of the styles marked with a ¶ symbol. To see the full list of available styles, use the scrollbars or the ⯆ symbol in the bottom right of the styles tools

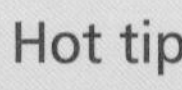

Hot tip

There is a third type, known as a Linked Style. This can contain both character and paragraph level attributes. See page 46, "Linked Styles", for more about this.

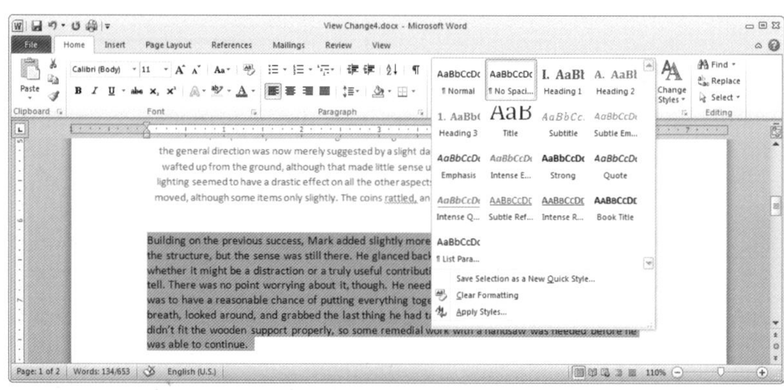

3. Click once on the style to apply it to your text

Character Styles

These can contain information about character-level attributes only, e.g. font and size, but not alignment (which is a paragraph-level attribute). They can be applied to any amount of text, even individual characters or words. Character styles have no ¶ symbol.

Beware

It is very easy to accidentally override all your carefully-chosen text settings, simply by clicking on a style in the toolbar. If this happens, choose Undo from the Quick Access Toolbar.

Applying a Character Style

1. Select the text you want to change

2. Look for a style which doesn't have a ¶ symbol and hover over it with the mouse. Your text will temporarily preview the selected style until you move the mouse elsewhere

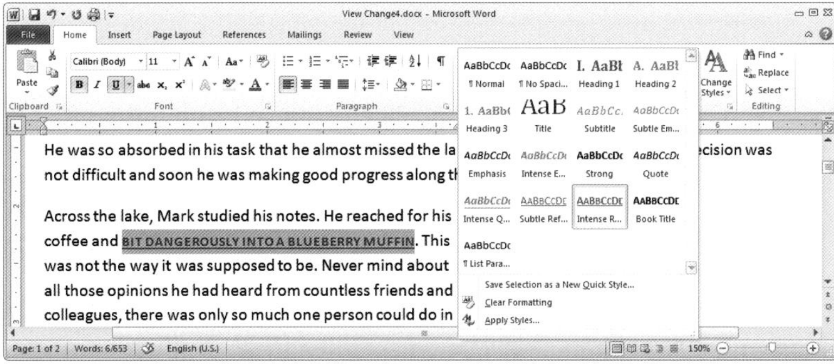

3. Click directly on a style to apply it permanently to the selected text

Removing the Style From Text

1. Select the text in question

2. Click the ⯆ symbol in the bottom right of the styles tools to see the full list of styles, plus a menu below these

3. Choose Clear Formatting. This will reset the text to a style called Normal, which uses "plain text" settings. It's possible to redefine Normal to anything you like, as you will see later on in this chapter

...cont'd

Creating a Style

1. The easiest way to create a new style is to select some text that already has all, or most, of the attributes you want to use

2. Open the Style Gallery by clicking the ▾ icon in the lower right corner of styles area

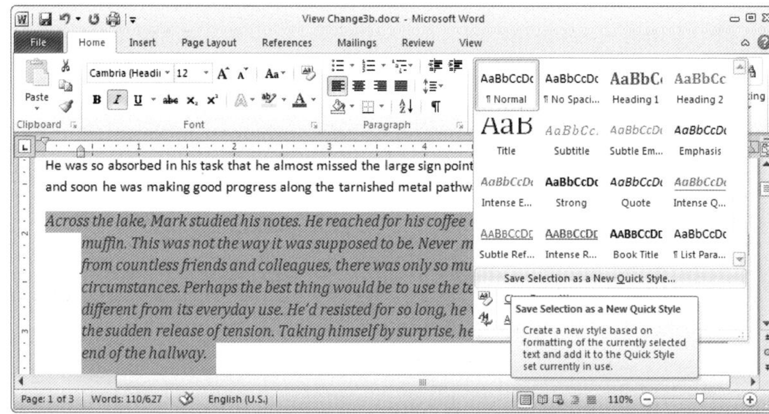

3. Choose "Save Selection as a New Quick Style"

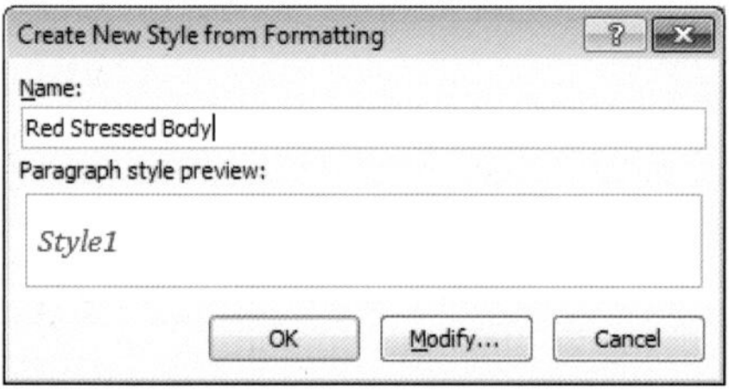

4. Note that the dialog also shows you a preview of the style you're about to create. If this does not look correct, then click the Cancel button and examine the text you selected. If necessary, alter its formatting or select a different sample of text

5. If you're already happy with the style's attributes, then click OK, otherwise select Modify... to edit the settings

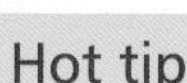

You can apply a Style to text using the keyboard shortcut Ctrl+Shift+S. An Apply Styles window will appear – type the first few letters of the Style's name. If the desired style appears, then click the Apply button; if not, then select from the list.

Modifying a Style using the Dialog Box

1. Right-click the style in the Toolbar and select Modify...

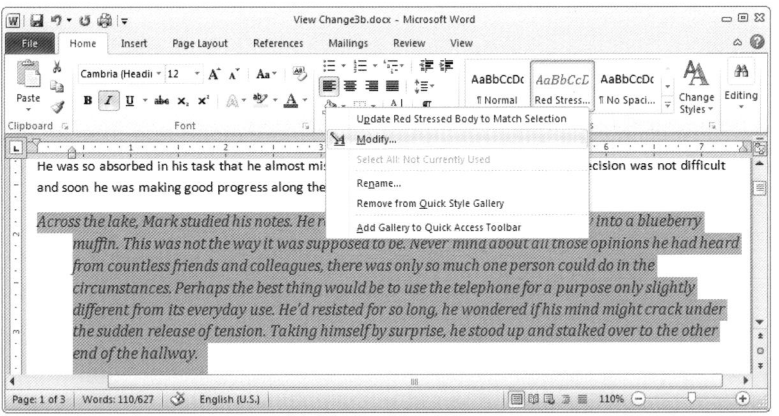

2. The following dialog appears. From here you can rename the style or alter attributes, such as font, size or effects, including bold and italics

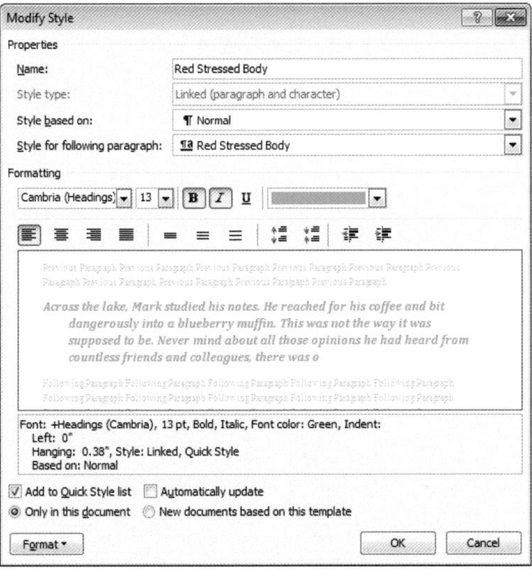

Many other useful settings can be made from this dialog. If you click the Format button you can access dialogs for Font, Paragraph, Tabs, and several other categories.

3. When you're happy with your settings, click OK. Any text in your document this style was applied to will be automatically updated

Another way to modify a Style is to type Ctrl+Shift+S. The Apply Styles window will appear – type the first few letters of the Style's name. If the desired style appears, then click the Modify... button; if not, then select from the list and click Modify...

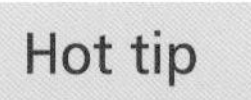

You can also make styles available across different documents. For more on this, see Chapter Ten "Backstage View" and Chapter Eleven, "Advanced Features".

The Change Styles Button

If you've been using Word's built-in styles, or if you've created your own using the same names, then you can switch the style set to redesign your document completely.

1 Click the Change Styles button in the Styles section of the Home Tab to access its pop-up menu

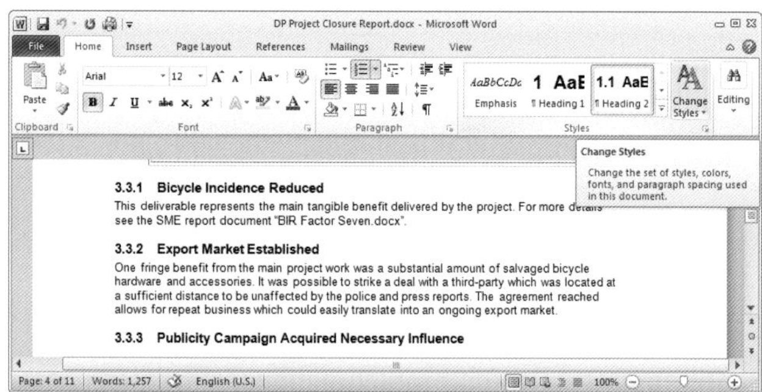

2 Select one of the options from the Style Set submenu

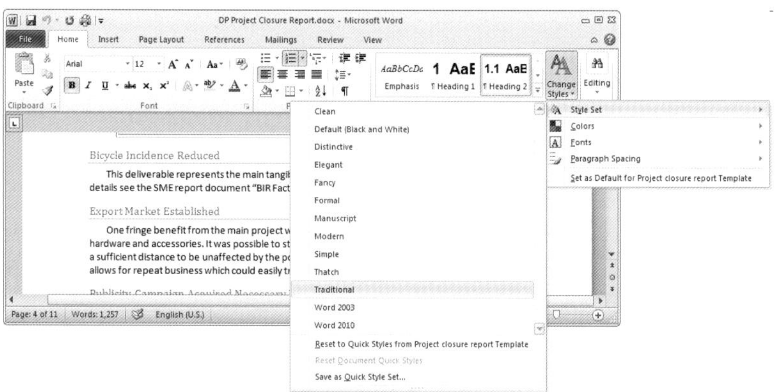

3 Each style in the style set will replace the style of the same name in your current document. Any text which used these styles will be automatically reformatted. This allows you to give even long documents a new but consistent design, with the minimum of fuss

Don't forget

As your documents grow, you will want to check that your formatting and overall design is consistent and easy to change, so make sure you use styles rather than formatting directly on the page.

Modifying a Style using Document Text

One problem with modifying styles via the dialog box is that you don't see the results of your changes until you return to the main document. Here's another way of editing a style that doesn't suffer from this drawback:

1. Select some text that already uses the style you want to modify
2. Make formatting changes directly to this, using the techniques you've learned so far. In this example, the font, size and spacing has been altered

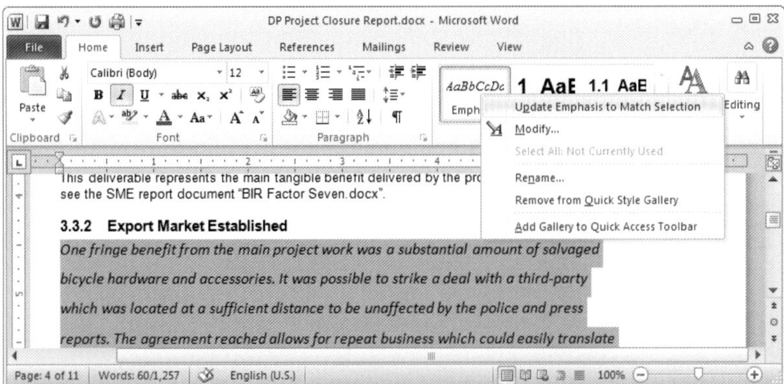
DP Project Closure Report.docx - Microsoft Word
File
Home
Insert
Page Layout
References
Mailings
Review
View
Calibri (Body)
12
Paste
Clipboard
Font
Paragraph
Editing
Update Emphasis to Match Selection
Modify...
Select All: Not Currently Used
Rename...
Remove from Quick Style Gallery
Add Gallery to Quick Access Toolbar
This deliverable represents the main tangible benefit delivered by the pro
see the SME report document "BIR Factor Seven.docx".
3.3.2 Export Market Established
One fringe benefit from the main project work was a substantial amount of salvaged
bicycle hardware and accessories. It was possible to strike a deal with a third-party
which was located at a sufficient distance to be unaffected by the police and press
reports. The agreement reached allows for repeat business which could easily translate
Page: 4 of 11
Words: 60/1,257
English (U.S.)
100%

3. Right-click on the style name in the Styles section of the Home Tab, and choose the "Update ... to Match Selection" option
4. The style's definition will be modified. All other document text that uses this style will be changed automatically
5. Repeat this process for any other styles you'd like to modify. Scroll through your document to check that the formatting is to your liking

Beware

When following these steps, make sure you click the right mouse button rather than the left. Left-clicking will reset the selected text to the original style definition. If you do this accidentally, then use the Undo button, or Ctrl+Z, and try again.

The Styles Window

You can create more advanced types of style from the Styles window.

1. Open the Styles window by clicking on the icon in the bottom right corner of the Styles area

2. You'll see a list of recommended styles

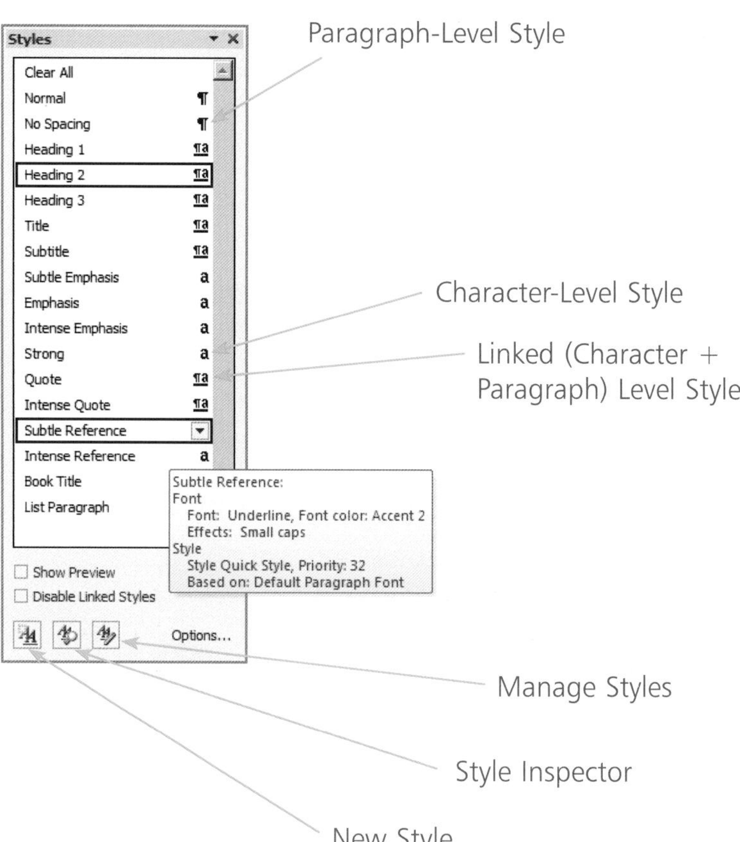

3. If you allow your mouse to hover over a particular style name, a summary box will appear. This lists the essential attributes of that style

4. Click on Options... to select which styles should be shown in the Styles window. You can also control how they are displayed and sorted

If you activate the Show Preview option, located at the bottom of the Styles window, then the style names will appear, using their own attributes.

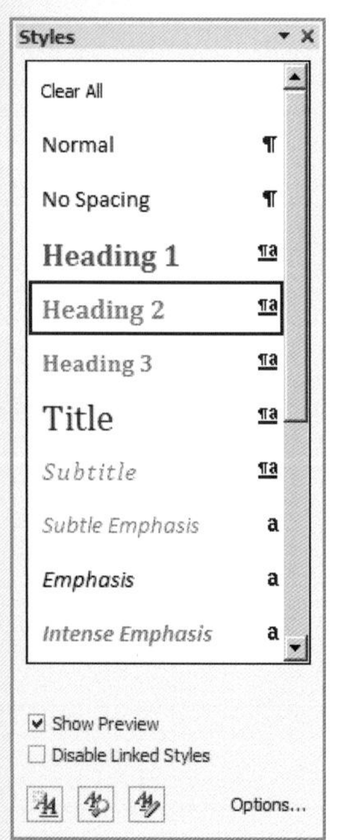

Paragraph-Level Styles

Creating a New Paragraph-Level Style

1. Make sure the Styles window is open. If it isn't, click on the icon in the bottom right corner of the Styles area

2. Click the New Style button near the bottom

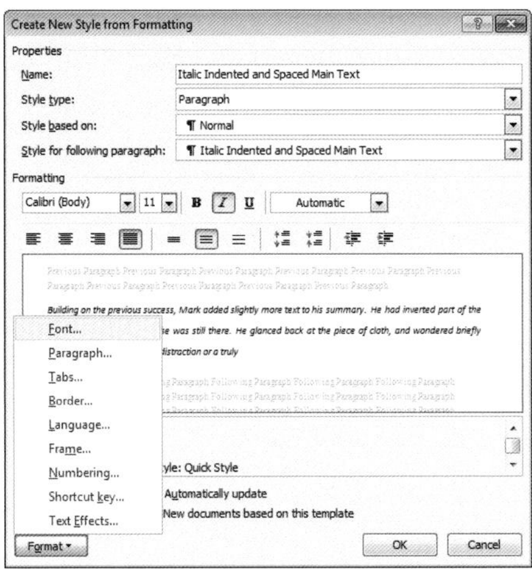
Create New Style from Formatting
Properties
Name:
Italic Indented and Spaced Main Text
Style type:
Paragraph
Style based on:
¶ Normal
Style for following paragraph:
¶ Italic Indented and Spaced Main Text
Formatting
Calibri (Body)
11
Automatic
Building on the previous success, Mark added slightly more text to his summary. He had inverted part of the
Font...
Paragraph...
Tabs...
Border...
Language...
Frame...
Numbering...
Shortcut key...
Text Effects...
Format
Automatically update
New documents based on this template
OK
Cancel

3. Enter a style name, and choose a Style Type of Paragraph

4. Select the other formatting options as appropriate. When you click OK, your new style becomes available in the Styles area. Note the ¶ symbol next to its name

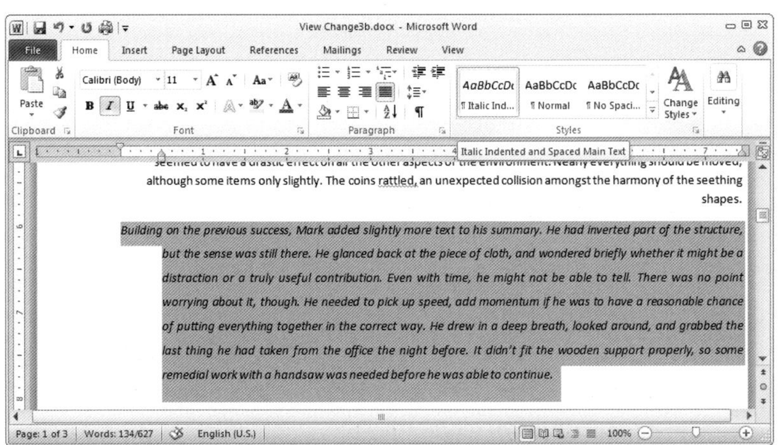
View Change3b.docx - Microsoft Word
File
Home
Insert
Page Layout
References
Mailings
Review
View
Paste
Clipboard
Calibri (Body)
11
Font
Paragraph
AaBbCcDc
¶ Italic Ind...
¶ Normal
¶ No Spaci...
Change Styles
Editing
Styles
Italic Indented and Spaced Main Text
although some items only slightly. The coins rattled, an unexpected collision amongst the harmony of the seething shapes.
Building on the previous success, Mark added slightly more text to his summary. He had inverted part of the structure, but the sense was still there. He glanced back at the piece of cloth, and wondered briefly whether it might be a distraction or a truly useful contribution. Even with time, he might not be able to tell. There was no point worrying about it, though. He needed to pick up speed, add momentum if he was to have a reasonable chance of putting everything together in the correct way. He drew in a deep breath, looked around, and grabbed the last thing he had taken from the office the night before. It didn't fit the wooden support properly, so some remedial work with a handsaw was needed before he was able to continue.
Page: 1 of 3
Words: 134/627
English (U.S.)
100%

Don't forget

Paragraph styles are always applied to entire paragraphs.

Linked Styles

A linked style can be used at either the paragraph or character level, depending on the amount of text selected when it's applied.

Creating a New Linked Style

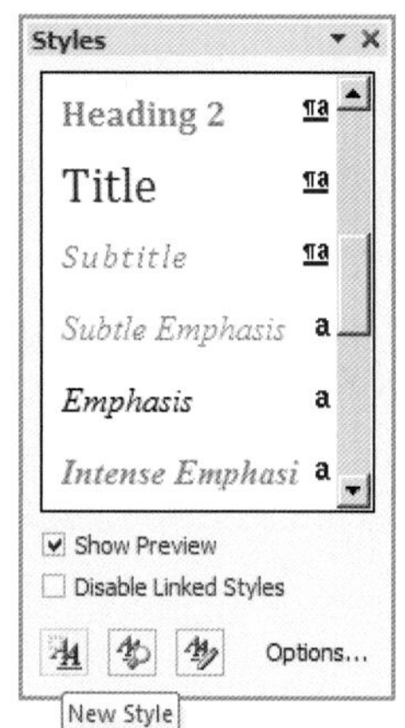

1. Open the Styles window by clicking on the icon in the bottom right corner of the Styles area. Click New Style

2. Give your style a name. For "Style type" select "Linked (paragraph and character)"

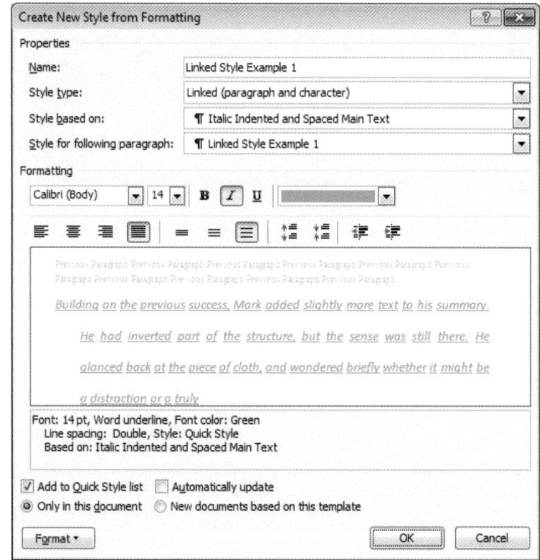

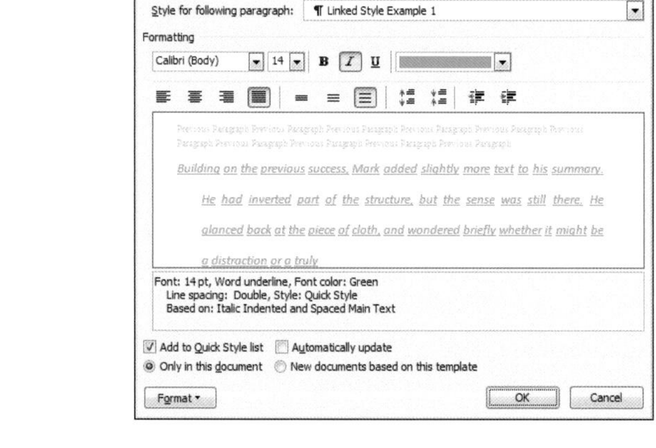

Beware

Try not to use too many effects if you have large amounts of small text, as they can make it unreadable.

3. Select the other formatting options as appropriate. In this example, we've chosen green, italic text, with individual words underlined. You can set the word underline feature by clicking Format and choosing Font...

4. Click OK when you're done. Your new style is now available. In the Styles window, its name is followed by a ¶a symbol to indicate it's a linked style

5. Select a whole paragraph of text (the quickest way to do this is to triple-click anywhere inside the paragraph), locate your new style in the Home Tab, and apply it

6. Now select an individual word in a different paragraph, and apply the style

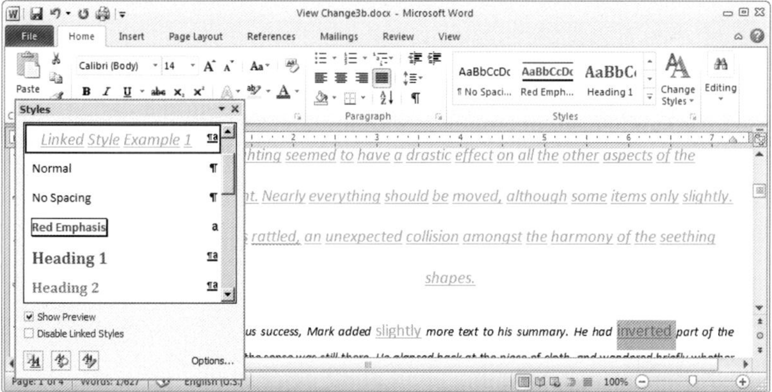

7. To modify a style, click on the ▾ symbol next to the style's name in the Style Window and select Modify... Note that the style type setting is now greyed out. Once a style has been created, its type cannot be changed

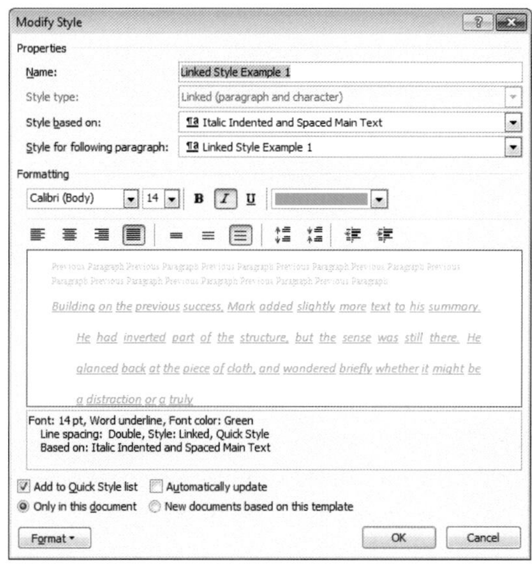

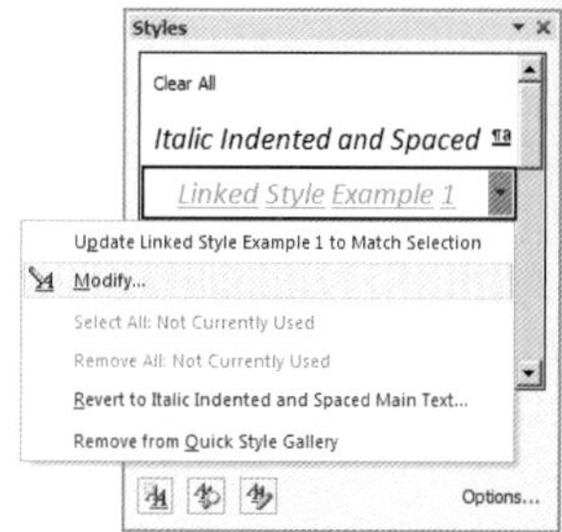

Hot tip

Although you can't change a style type once it is created, you can always create a style based on another – to do this, simply select the style in the Style Window, then click the New Style button.

Mixing Styles in a Paragraph

Character-level and paragraph-level styles can be used in the same paragraph. In this case, the character-level style's attributes take precedence. The following example is a good illustration of this.

1. Select an entire paragraph and apply a paragraph-level style to it. In this example, a style called "Green stressed body" was used. It is Arial, 10 point, green, italic, centered text

2. Now select a small group of words within the paragraph, and apply a character-level style. Here we've used a style called "Blue underline char style", which is 12 point, underlined, and blue. The style definition has no font name built in, so the font remains the same as that for "Green stressed body"

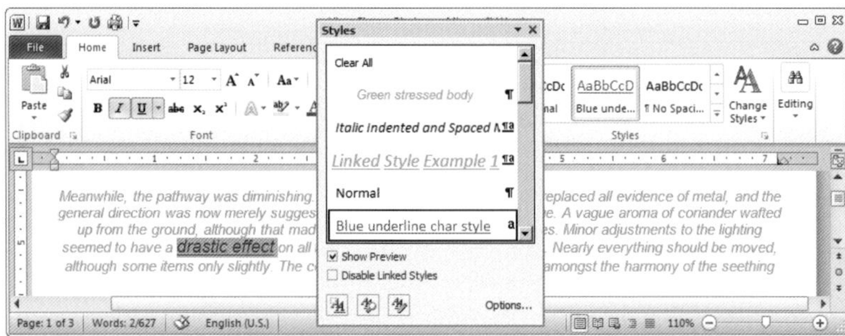

3. Note that the character-level style's attributes override those of the paragraph-level style

4. Now, with the same group of words selected, adjust the size to make it larger

5. Now open the Styles window and click on the Style Inspector icon:

This shows you exactly how the text was formatted.

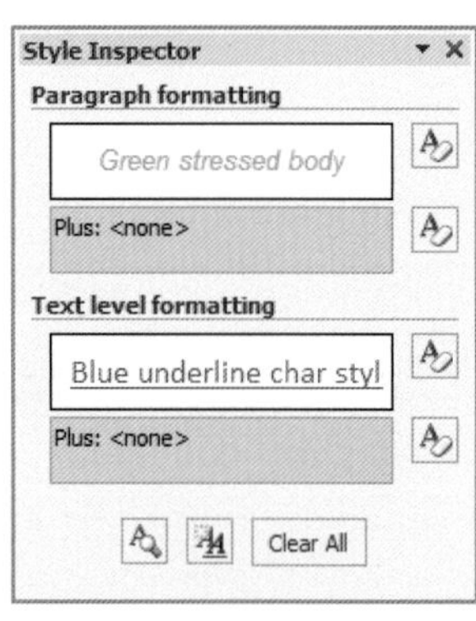

The selected words in this example still follow the attributes of the paragraph style, except where they have been overridden by the character-level style. So, if you edited "Green stressed body" so that its font was Times New Roman, this would affect all the text. If, however, you made "Green stressed body" a darker green color, the text seen highlighted here would still be blue.

The Ruler

Text that is laid out neatly, with accurate horizontal positioning, greatly helps give your documents a professional look. Effective use of white space, including tabulation, is the key to this.

Making the Ruler Visible

1. Move to the very top of the editing area, and then move upwards, so that you have just touched the lower border of the Tab controls area. The ruler will appear temporarily

Left indent for the first line of each paragraph

Left indent for subsequent lines

Drag here to move both left indents at once

Right indent

2. Experiment by moving the left and right indent markers on the Ruler and observing what happens on the page. It helps if you have several lines of text selected

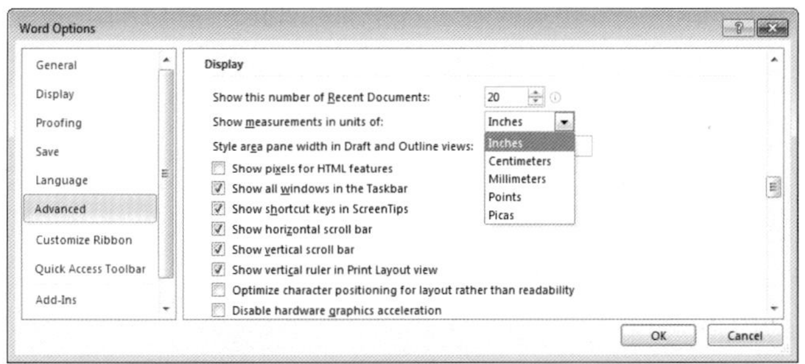

Hot tip

You can keep the Ruler visible permanently if you click the icon at the right-hand edge, just below the Tab controls area. Click the icon a second time to make the ruler disappear again.

Hot tip

You can change the measurements system from the File Tab, by choosing Options and then Advanced. In the Display section, go to the option "Show measurements in units of:" and choose a different value. Points and Picas are sometimes useful, as they match font sizes.

Tabulation

Tab stops are paragraph-level attributes that define what happens when the Tab key is pressed when entering text. If you select a paragraph and examine the Ruler, you'll see any tab stops that have been defined. If no tab stops have been defined for this paragraph, then the default tabs apply. These are marked in the Ruler as small vertical lines, spaced out at regular intervals, in its lower section.

Overriding Default Tabulation

When you click the Show/Hide ¶ button, paragraph marks also appear visibly as the ¶ character.

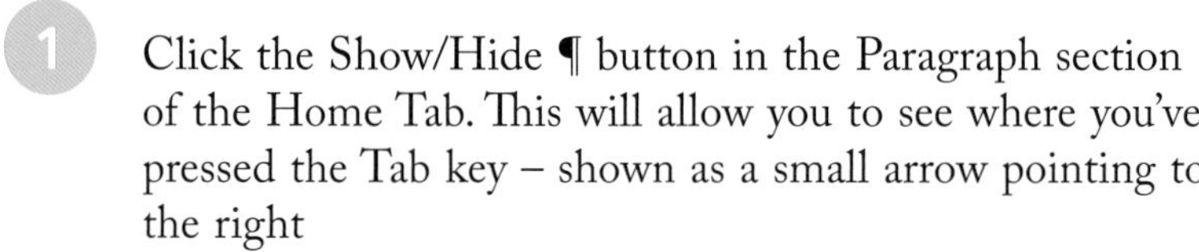

1. Click the Show/Hide ¶ button in the Paragraph section of the Home Tab. This will allow you to see where you've pressed the Tab key – shown as a small arrow pointing to the right

2. Type in some text similar to the example below. Note that each text element is separated from the next by a Tab character. Don't worry about how far across the screen the Tab takes you: this will be altered soon. Make sure you only press Tab once between one element and the next

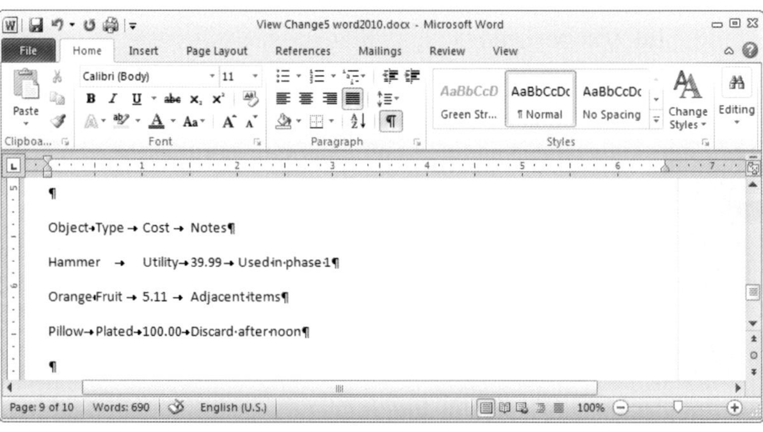

3. Also make sure that you press Return once at the end of each line. This will show up as a ¶ character, as in the illustration above

4. Now select all your newly-entered text

5 Make sure that the [L] icon is visible at the left side of the Ruler. This means that, when you create a tab stop, it will use left alignment. If it looks different, then click on it until it changes to the correct symbol

6 Click in the Ruler around the 1 inch mark to create a new left tab. Drag it left or right to adjust its position

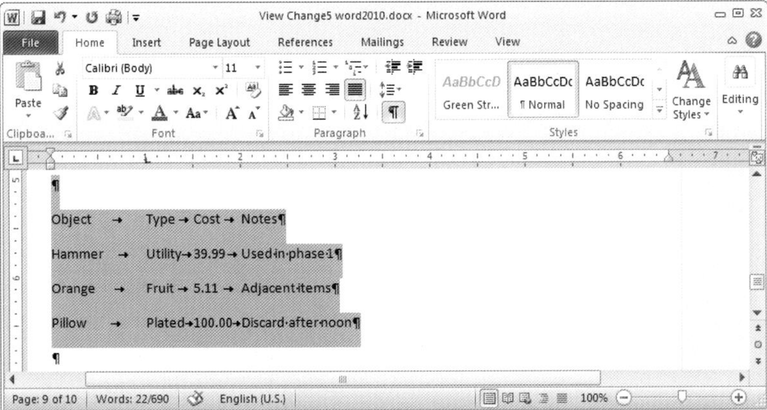

7 The text should move, so that the text following the first tab lines up vertically along its left edge. Making sure that your text is still selected, create some more tab stops

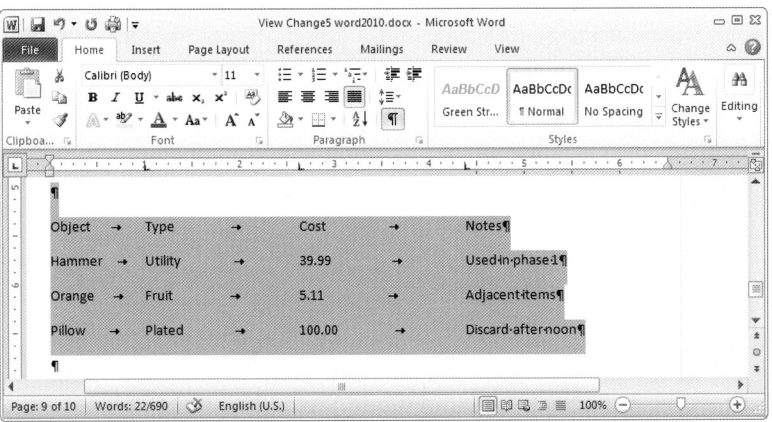

As you create and move tab stops, note that the text automatically moves to follow your new design

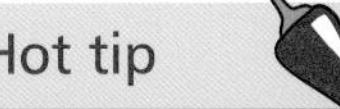

To see the distances between tab stops and the left and right indents hold down the Alt key as you drag any of the Ruler icons horizontally.

...cont'd

Different Types of Tabs

1. Keeping your text selected, delete the right-most tab by dragging it downwards from the ruler, until it disappears

2. Now click on the symbol, until it changes into a

3. Click in the Ruler fairly near the right edge of the page. A new right-aligned tab is created – this time the text is moved so that it lines up vertically along its right edge

When you click on the symbol, the icons cycle between left, center, right and decimal-aligned tabs. After these, there is the bar (vertical line) icon, followed by first-line indent and hanging indent icons.

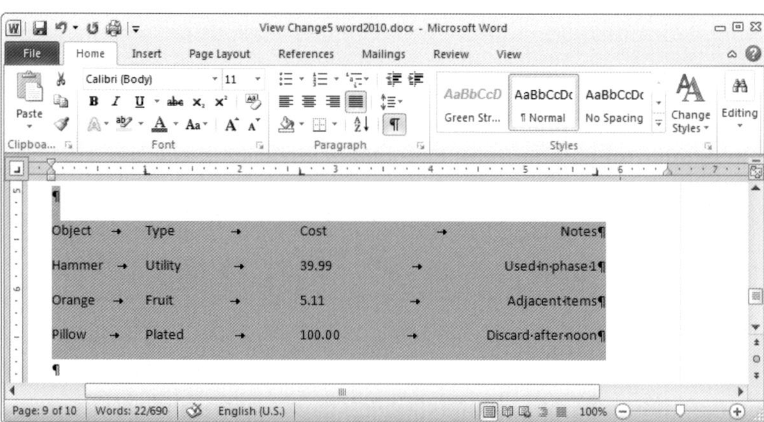

4. If the text fails to line correctly, then adjust the tab positions by dragging them left or right. You can call up the Tabs dialog by double-clicking directly on any tab:

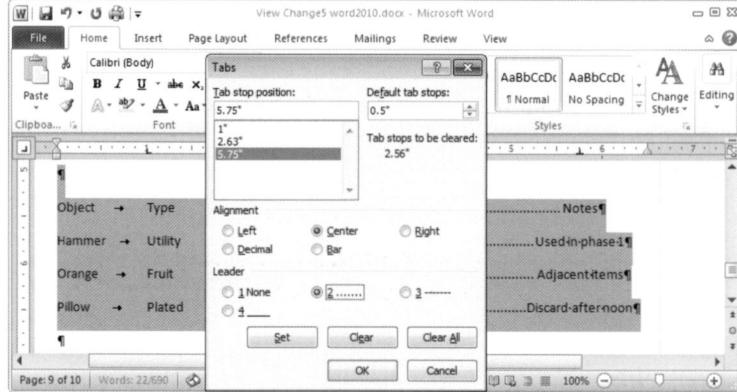

5. Select a tab from the list on the left. You can now change its type, add a leader (as in the example below, which leads into the third tab with a series of dots), set new tabs, or clear tabs

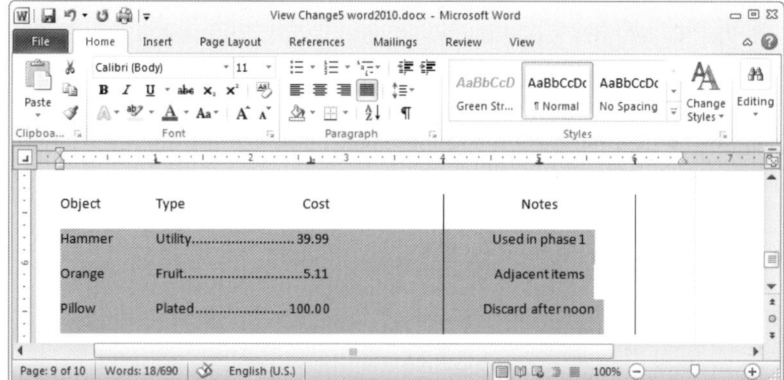

Tabulation can be built into a style definition, so it can be used consistently throughout a document.

6. In this example, bar tabs were created at 4 inches and 6 inches. These create vertical lines

7. Sometimes the first line, since it contains headings, needs a slightly different form of alignment, compared with the main text. In this example, the first line was selected on its own so that the word "Cost" could have a centered tab, rather than the decimal tab with the leader of dots. Then the remaining lines were selected, so that the formatting of the main text could continue

8. When you're done, click the Show/Hide ¶ button in the Paragraph section of the Home Tab. This makes the hidden characters invisible again, so that you get a better idea of the appearance of the final result

Removing all Tabs

1. Make sure all the relevant text is selected, then double-click on a tab to summon the Tabs dialog

2. Click Clear All, then OK

Clipboard Tools

The Clipboard is a temporary storage area that can hold text, or even other items, such as graphic images. It can be used to help you move or copy text you have selected.

Cut and Paste

1. Select the text to be moved. Right-click on the selected text, and then choose Cut

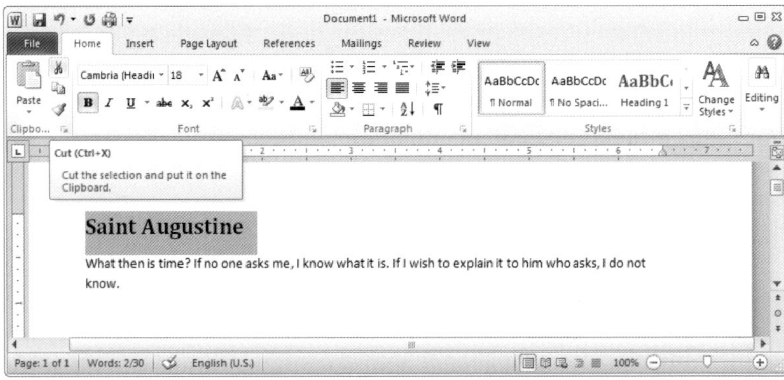

2. The text is removed and placed on the Clipboard. Now place your insertion point at the desired destination and right-click. A pop-up menu appears, which includes three paste options

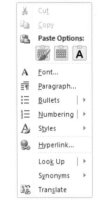

Cut
Copy
Paste Options:
A
Font...
Paragraph...
Bullets
Numbering
Styles
Hyperlink...
Look Up
Synonyms
Translate

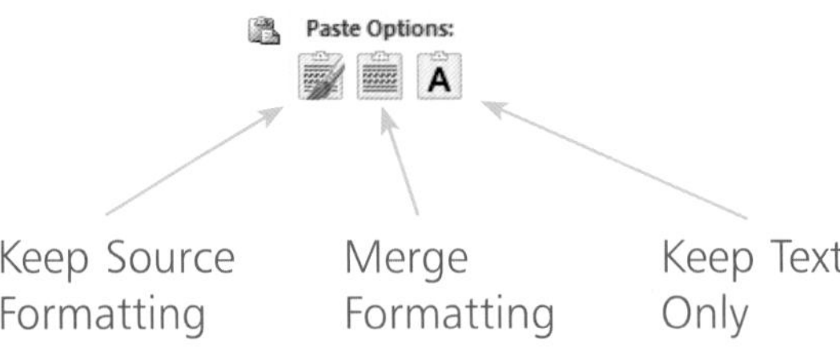

3. Note that the source text was 18 point Cambria bold. If you want to use the text with these attributes, then click on the Keep Source Formatting option. If you want to use the attributes already defined at the destination, click on Keep Text Only. In the following example, we right-clicked in an area of 11 point Calibri normal text and chose Keep Text Only

The Clipboard Tools give you instant access to Cut, Copy, and Paste, in the form of icons

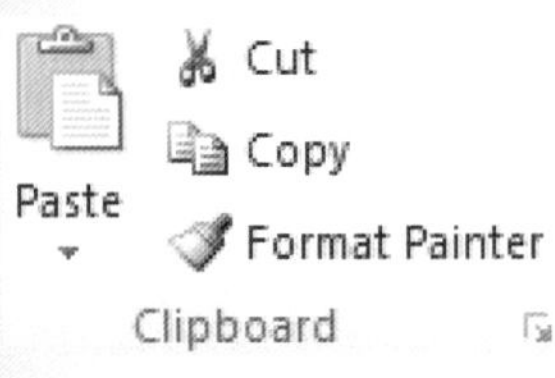

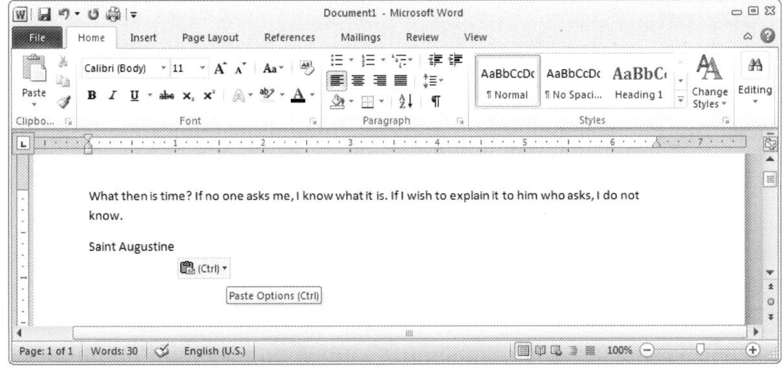
Document1 - Microsoft Word
File
Home
Insert
Page Layout
References
Mailings
Review
View
What then is time? If no one asks me, I know what it is. If I wish to explain it to him who asks, I do not know.
Saint Augustine
(Ctrl)
Paste Options (Ctrl)
Page: 1 of 1
Words: 30
English (U.S.)
100%

Even after you've pasted text, you can still change your mind about the paste formatting options.

Altering Paste Options After Pasting

1. After you've pasted text, you'll see the Paste Options icon nearby. Either click the icon or press the Ctrl key to review the available Paste Options

2. In the example below, we chose the second option: Merge Formatting. The font and size are that of the destination, but the bold effect has been taken from the source

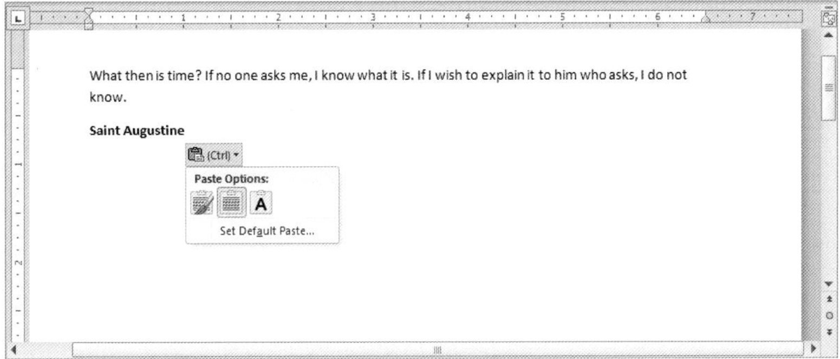
What then is time? If no one asks me, I know what it is. If I wish to explain it to him who asks, I do not know.
Saint Augustine
(Ctrl)
Paste Options:
Set Default Paste...

The Paste Options are available to you until you start typing, at which point, the icon disappears. If you change your mind after this, then you'll need to either undo the last few steps and try again, or manually alter the text attributes.

Hot tip

You can also cut and paste using the keyboard shortcuts Ctrl+X and Ctrl+V respectively.

...cont'd

Copy and Paste

1. Select the text you want to copy, right-click and choose Copy from the pop-up menu

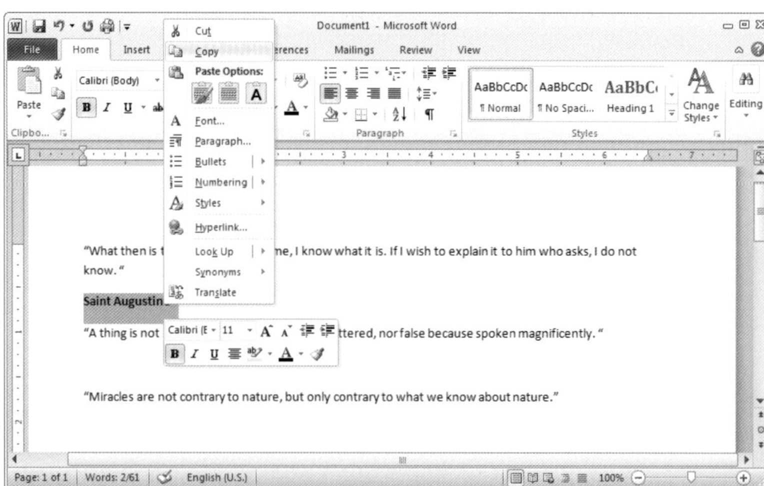

2. Place the insertion point at the destination for the copied text, right-click and choose the appropriate Paste option

3. Pasting text doesn't actually remove it from the Clipboard, so you can paste the same text many times

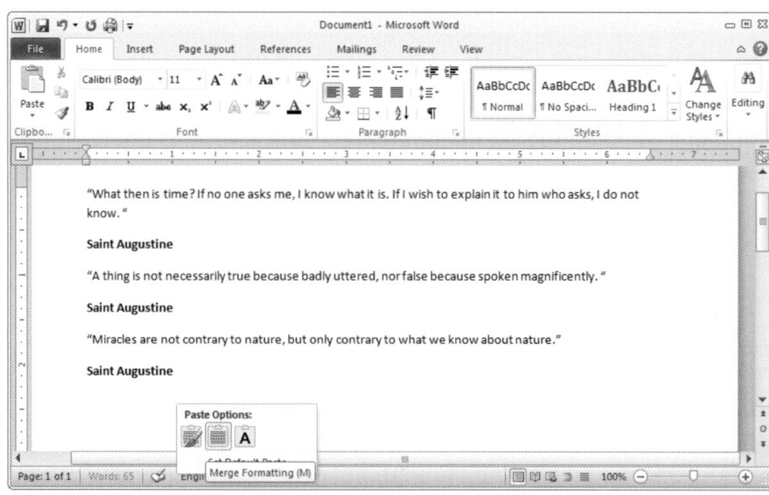

Don't forget

You can also click on the Copy and Paste icons in the Clipboard Tools. A third way to copy and paste is to use the keyboard shortcuts Ctrl+C and Ctrl+V respectively.

The Spike

The Spike is similar to the Clipboard in that it's a temporary storage area for text. The main difference is that you can add more and more text onto the Spike with a keyboard shortcut.

1. Select some text and type Ctrl+F3. The text disappears. It has been impaled on the Spike

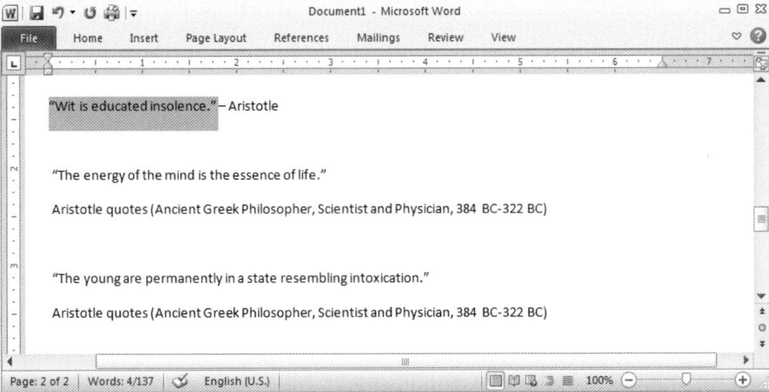
Document1 - Microsoft Word
File
Home
Insert
Page Layout
References
Mailings
Review
View
"Wit is educated insolence." – Aristotle
"The energy of the mind is the essence of life."
Aristotle quotes (Ancient Greek Philosopher, Scientist and Physician, 384 BC-322 BC)
"The young are permanently in a state resembling intoxication."
Aristotle quotes (Ancient Greek Philosopher, Scientist and Physician, 384 BC-322 BC)
Page: 2 of 2
Words: 4/137
English (U.S.)
100%

2. Repeat the process with a second piece of text

3. If you want to add even more text to the Spike, then repeat the previous step as many times as you want

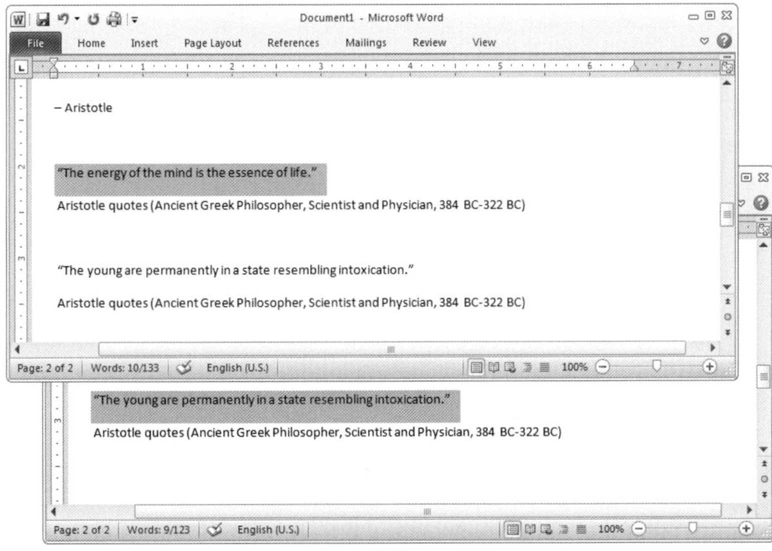
Document1 - Microsoft Word
File
Home
Insert
Page Layout
References
Mailings
Review
View
– Aristotle
"The energy of the mind is the essence of life."
Aristotle quotes (Ancient Greek Philosopher, Scientist and Physician, 384 BC-322 BC)
"The young are permanently in a state resembling intoxication."
Aristotle quotes (Ancient Greek Philosopher, Scientist and Physician, 384 BC-322 BC)
Page: 2 of 2
Words: 10/133
English (U.S.)
100%
"The young are permanently in a state resembling intoxication."
Aristotle quotes (Ancient Greek Philosopher, Scientist and Physician, 384 BC-322 BC)
Page: 2 of 2
Words: 9/123
English (U.S.)
100%

Hot tip

You can repeat this more times if necessary, if you want to collect more pieces of text onto the Spike. Each time you press Ctrl+F3, any selected text is removed from the page and added to the Spike. Note, however, that you only press Ctrl+Shift+F3 once – as soon as the text is back on the page, it has been removed from the Spike.

4. Finally, position the insertion point at the destination for the text and press Ctrl+Shift+F3. The text is pulled off the Spike and placed back into the document

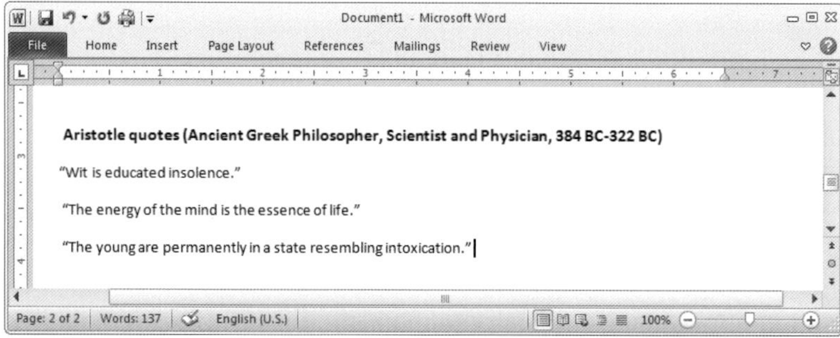

Multiple Clipboard Items

Pasting will normally just give you back the last item that was placed on the Clipboard. However, Word's Clipboard actually has space for up to 24 items.

1. Select some text and choose either Copy or Cut, using one of the techniques shown earlier

2. Repeat this with different pieces of text, so that you have at least three or four items on the Clipboard

3. Click on the icon in the lower right corner of the Clipboard Tools. The full Clipboard appears to the left of the text area

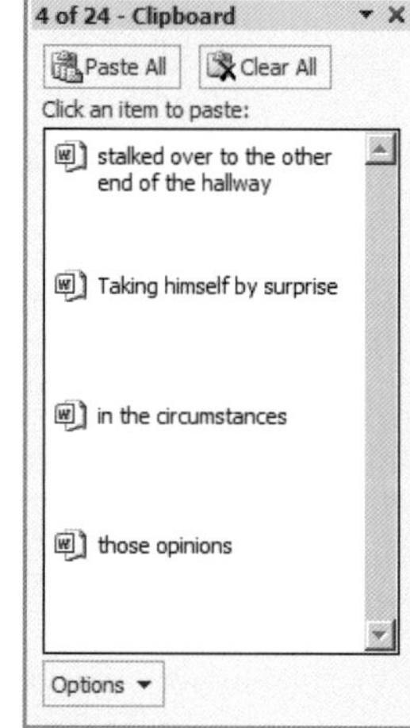

4. Click directly on any item to paste it back into your document. Alternatively, hover over the item and you'll see a small downward-pointing arrow. If you click on this you will see a pop-up menu, with options to either paste or delete the item from the Clipboard

Hot tip

From the Clipboard pane, you can also click on a button to Paste All items in one operation, or click the Clear All button to remove everything from the Clipboard.

The Format Painter

The Format Painter gives you a very easy way to copy attributes from one place to another.

1. Select a sample of text that has the desired attributes

2. Click the Format Painter icon in the Clipboard section of the Home Tab. This "loads" the icon with the attributes of the selected text

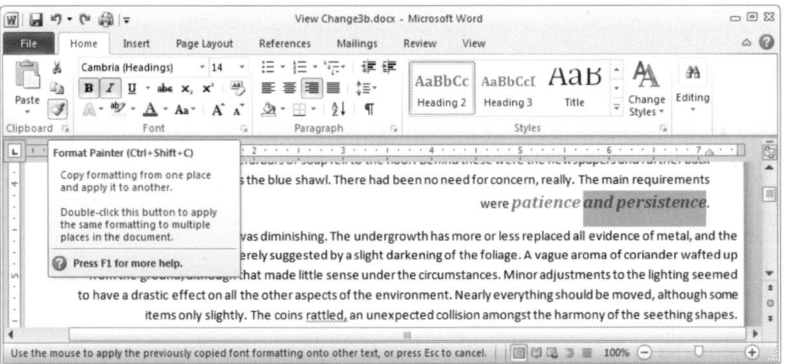

View Change3b.docx - Microsoft Word
File
Home
Insert
Page Layout
References
Mailings
Review
View
Cambria (Headings)
14
Paste
AaBbCc
Heading 2
AaBbCcI
Heading 3
AaB
Title
Change Styles
Editing
Clipboard
Font
Paragraph
Styles
Format Painter (Ctrl+Shift+C)
Copy formatting from one place and apply it to another.
Double-click this button to apply the same formatting to multiple places in the document.
Press F1 for more help.
the blue shawl. There had been no need for concern, really. The main requirements
were patience and persistence.
vas diminishing. The undergrowth has more or less replaced all evidence of metal, and the
erely suggested by a slight darkening of the foliage. A vague aroma of coriander wafted up
that made little sense under the circumstances. Minor adjustments to the lighting seemed
to have a drastic effect on all the other aspects of the environment. Nearly everything should be moved, although some
items only slightly. The coins rattled, an unexpected collision amongst the harmony of the seething shapes.
Use the mouse to apply the previously copied font formatting onto other text, or press Esc to cancel.
100%

3. Note that your mouse pointer has changed to show that you have attributes loaded. Now use it to drag across your target text. The attributes are applied to the text

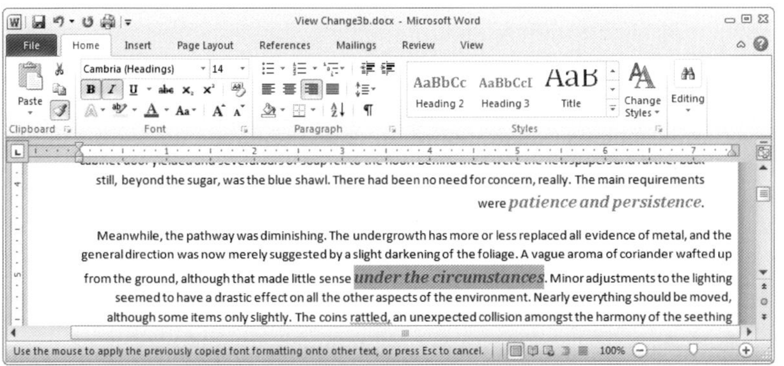

View Change3b.docx - Microsoft Word
File
Home
Insert
Page Layout
References
Mailings
Review
View
Cambria (Headings)
14
Paste
AaBbCc
Heading 2
AaBbCcI
Heading 3
AaB
Title
Change Styles
Editing
Clipboard
Font
Paragraph
Styles
still, beyond the sugar, was the blue shawl. There had been no need for concern, really. The main requirements
were patience and persistence.
Meanwhile, the pathway was diminishing. The undergrowth has more or less replaced all evidence of metal, and the
general direction was now merely suggested by a slight darkening of the foliage. A vague aroma of coriander wafted up
from the ground, although that made little sense under the circumstances. Minor adjustments to the lighting
seemed to have a drastic effect on all the other aspects of the environment. Nearly everything should be moved,
although some items only slightly. The coins rattled, an unexpected collision amongst the harmony of the seething
Use the mouse to apply the previously copied font formatting onto other text, or press Esc to cancel.
100%

This normally just copies character-level attributes. However, if you select an entire paragraph, click the Format Painter, then select an entire destination paragraph, all attributes (including paragraph settings, such as alignment) will be copied.

Hot tip

To copy formatting to more than one destination simply double-click on the Format Painter icon. You can then apply the formatting to as many pieces of text as you wish. When you've finished, either click back on the icon to discharge the loaded attributes or press the Escape key.

Editing Controls

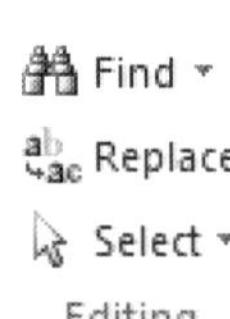

The last set of controls on the right hand side contain Find, Replace, and Select tools. These sometimes work in conjunction with the Navigation and Selection panes, which you'll see later on.

Find

1. Press Ctrl+F or click the Find button in the Toolbar. If you click on its pop-up menu, rather than the main part of the icon, you'll see two options, one of which is Find

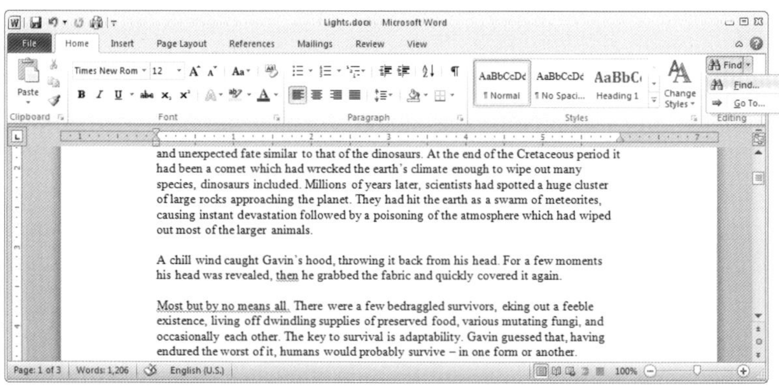

2. The Navigation Pane appears along the left side of the screen. Enter your search text

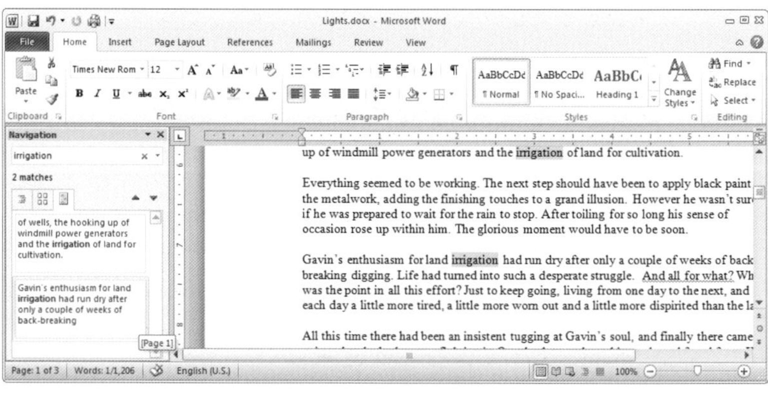

3. Word will immediately highlight all matches in the document, and also list them in the Navigation Pane. If you scroll through these and click on an item, the main page will automatically move to that particular instance

Hot tip

If you click the pop-up menu icon (the small black triangle) next to the search text, you can ask Word to find other elements, such as graphics, tables or equations. See Chapter Eleven, "Advanced Features", for more details.

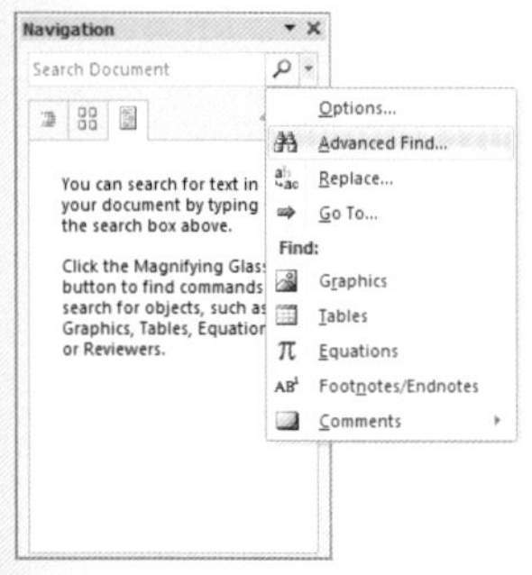

Find using the Dialog Box

Although the Navigation Pane is useful for instant searches, you may want to use the Find dialog box to access more flexible and powerful options.

1. To access the dialog box, open the pop-up menu next to the search area of the Navigation Pane and choose Find...
2. Click the More >> button to see the full set of options

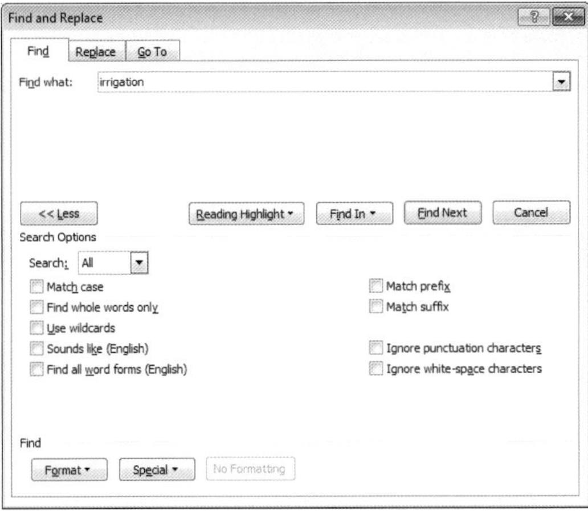

3. Enter the search text in the "Find what" box
4. Note the option to Match case – keeping this switched off means that searches are not case sensitive
5. By clicking the Format button, you can base your search on text attributes, such as font or size. If you set some attributes and also enter text in the "Find what" box, then Word will look for that particular text, but only if its attributes match what you've selected
6. To go ahead and run the search, click the Find In button and choose Main Document. If you happened to have selected some text within your document, it's also possible to just search the selection

...cont'd

Search and Replace

Word can be instructed to search through your document, or selected text, and automatically substitute text, text attributes, or even a combination of the two.

Hot tip

You can also summon the Replace dialog box by using the pop-up menu in the Navigation Pane, if available.

1. To access the Find and Replace dialog, you can either click directly on the Replace icon in the Toolbar, or use the keyboard shortcut Ctrl+H

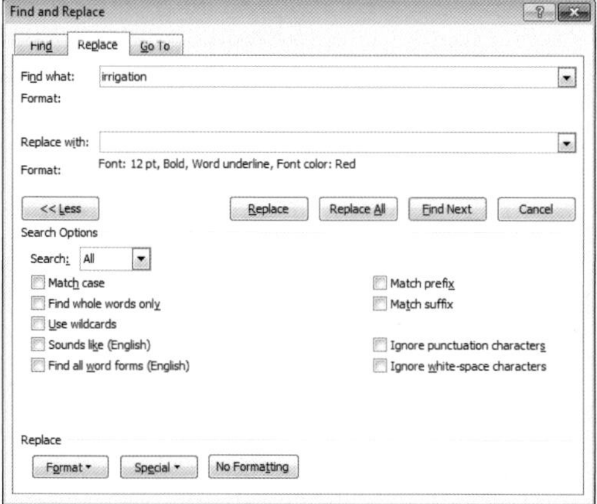

2. Enter the search text in the "Find what" area. While the cursor is still in this field, you can also, optionally, click the Format button to specify search attributes

3. If you want to replace existing text with new text, then enter it in the "Replace with" area. In this example, we have decided to change the formatting rather than the text. Remember to make sure the cursor is inside the "Replace with" box before you click the Format button

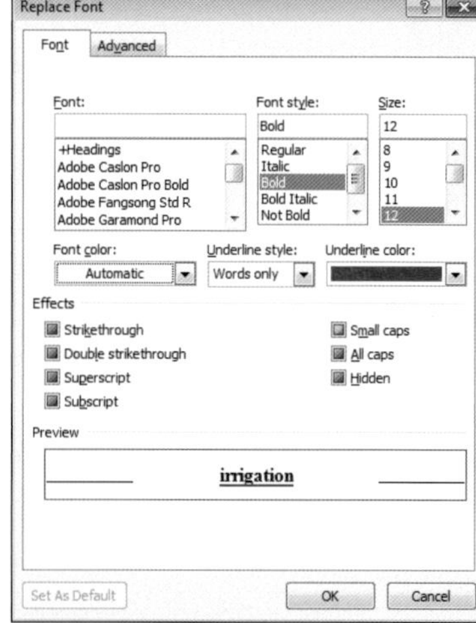

4 You can now either use the Find Next and Replace buttons to check each substitution one at a time, or, if you're confident to do it all at once, click Replace All.

Microsoft Word
Word has completed its search of the document and has made 2 replacements.
OK
Help

5 A confirmation message informs you how many changes were made. If the number of replacements worries you at all, then it is a good idea to use the Undo button (or Ctrl+Z) and then step the changes one at a time, with the Find Next and Replace buttons

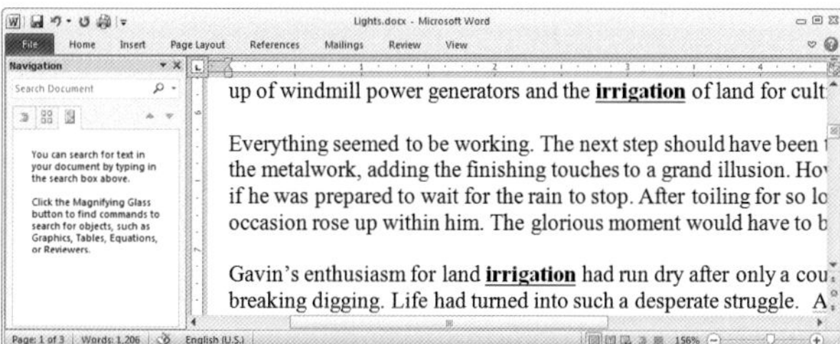
Lights.docx - Microsoft Word
File
Home
Insert
Page Layout
References
Mailings
Review
View
Navigation
Search Document
You can search for text in your document by typing in the search box above.
Click the Magnifying Glass button to find commands to search for objects, such as Graphics, Tables, Equations, or Reviewers.
up of windmill power generators and the irrigation of land for cult
Everything seemed to be working. The next step should have been t
the metalwork, adding the finishing touches to a grand illusion. Ho
if he was prepared to wait for the rain to stop. After toiling for so lo
occasion rose up within him. The glorious moment would have to b
Gavin's enthusiasm for land irrigation had run dry after only a cou
breaking digging. Life had turned into such a desperate struggle. A
Page: 1 of 3
Words: 1,206
English (U.S.)
156%

6 In the above example, all instances of the word "irrigation" were made bold and underlined in red

Beware

The Replace function can make drastic changes to your document, particularly if you use the Replace All button.

Go To

The pop-up menu on the Find button in the Toolbar has a Go To option, which summons this dialog. It lets you jump easily to another location in the document, using a range of target options.

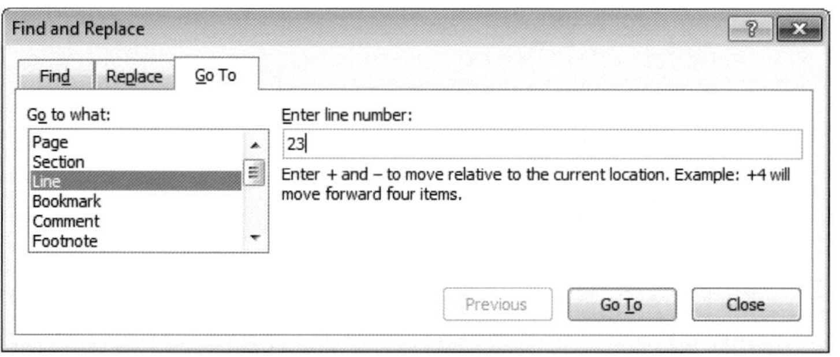
Find and Replace
Find
Replace
Go To
Go to what:
Page
Section
Line
Bookmark
Comment
Footnote
Enter line number:
23
Enter + and – to move relative to the current location. Example: +4 will move forward four items.
Previous
Go To
Close

Hot tip

You can also access the Go To feature by using the pop-up menu in the Navigation Pane, or with the keyboard shortcut Ctrl+G.

...cont'd

Using Special Characters

The Find and Replace dialog box also allows you to work with special characters, such as paragraph markers or wildcards. It can even match words which sound similar to the search text.

Type Ctrl+F to open the dialog and enter your search text. Click Special to see a list of special search characters

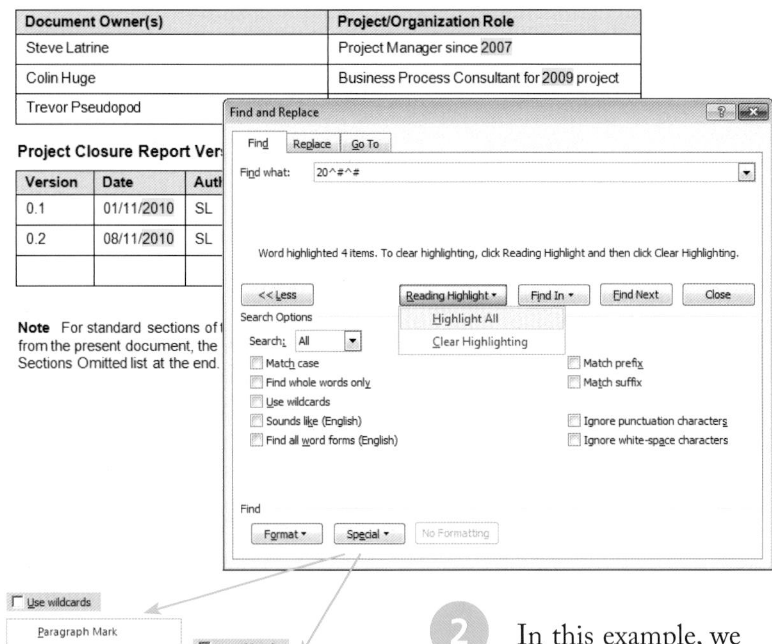

Use wildcards (unchecked):
Paragraph Mark
Tab Character
Any Character
Any Digit
Any Letter
Caret Character
§ Section Character
¶ Paragraph Character
Column Break
Em Dash
En Dash
Endnote Mark
Field
Footnote Mark
Graphic
Manual Line Break
Manual Page Break
Nonbreaking Hyphen
Nonbreaking Space
Optional Hyphen
Section Break
White Space

Use wildcards (checked):
Any Character ?
Character in Range [-]
Beginning of Word <
End of Word >
Expression ()
Not [!]
Num Occurrences {,}
Previous 1 or More @
0 or More Characters *
Tab Character
Caret Character
Column Break
Em Dash
En Dash
Graphic
Manual Line Break
Page / Section Break
Nonbreaking Hyphen
Nonbreaking Space
Optional Hyphen

If you activate the "Use wildcards" checkbox, then the Special pop-up menu contains some different options, which can help make your searches very powerful. The illustration on the right shows both versions of the menu.

2 In this example, we selected "Any Digit" twice to insert the special code "^#" into the "Find what" box. The pattern "20^#^#" tells Word to look for the literal text "20", followed immediately by any two digits. As you can see in the yellow highlight, it has found "2007", "2009", and two instances of "2010"

3 The Insert Tab

This chapter covers adding pages, bookmarks, hyperlinks, headers and footers, as well as equations, symbols, and some interesting text effects.

The Pages Tools

The Pages area, on the left hand side of the Insert Command Tab, has three controls for working with pages.

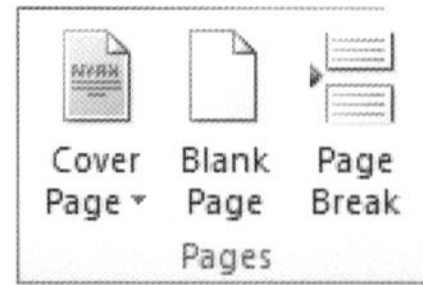
Cover Page
Blank Page
Page Break
Pages

Adding a Blank Page

Normally you don't need to do anything to add pages to your document – as you add text and other objects Word automatically makes room for them, by creating new pages as necessary. Sometimes, however, you may want to force Word to create a new blank page in a specific part of your document.

1. Click the Blank Page icon to add a new blank page

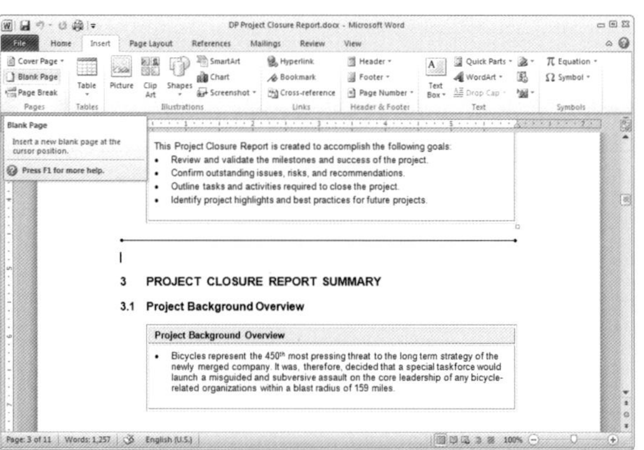
DP Project Closure Report.docx - Microsoft Word
Blank Page
Insert a new blank page at the cursor position.
Press F1 for more help.
This Project Closure Report is created to accomplish the following goals:
Review and validate the milestones and success of the project.
Confirm outstanding issues, risks, and recommendations.
Outline tasks and activities required to close the project.
Identify project highlights and best practices for future projects.
3 PROJECT CLOSURE REPORT SUMMARY
3.1 Project Background Overview
Project Background Overview
Page: 3 of 11 | Words: 1,257 | English (U.S.)

2. Any text before your Insertion Point will remain on its own before the new blank page. Any text after the Insertion Point will be moved after the new blank page

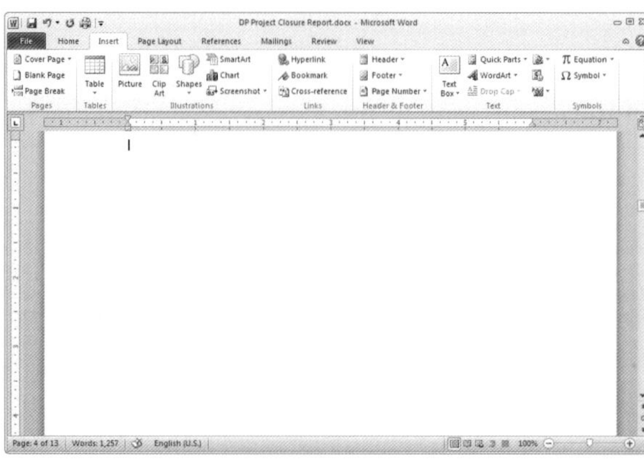
DP Project Closure Report.docx - Microsoft Word
Page: 4 of 13 | Words: 1,257 | English (U.S.)

Adding a Page Break

1. Click the Page Break icon. Everything after the current cursor position will move to the next page

2. If the ¶ tool in the Home Tab is active, you'll be able to see the Page Break as a visible marker

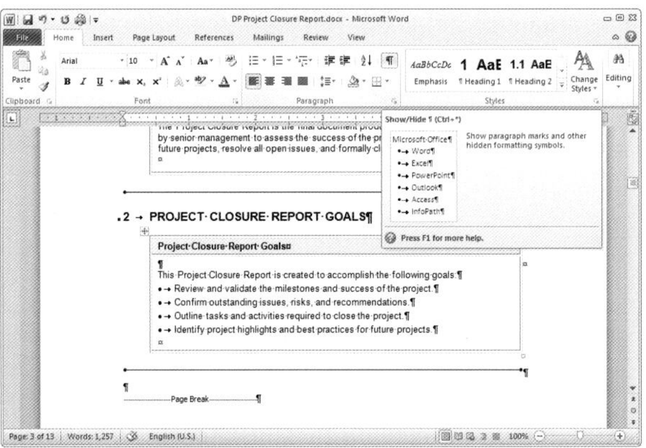

DP Project Closure Report.docx - Microsoft Word
File
Home
Insert
Page Layout
References
Mailings
Review
View
Show/Hide ¶ (Ctrl+*)
Show paragraph marks and other hidden formatting symbols.
Press F1 for more help.
.2 → PROJECT·CLOSURE·REPORT·GOALS¶
Project·Closure·Report·Goals¤
This·Project·Closure·Report·is·created·to·accomplish·the·following·goals:¶
Review·and·validate·the·milestones·and·success·of·the·project.¶
Confirm·outstanding·issues,·risks,·and·recommendations.¶
Outline·tasks·and·activities·required·to·close·the·project.¶
Identify·project·highlights·and·best·practices·for·future·projects.¶
Page Break
Page: 3 of 13
Words: 1,257
English (U.S.)

Hot tip

When you're entering text, you can type Ctrl+Return to insert a Page Break

Adding a Cover Page

1. Click the Cover Page icon, and select from the Gallery of styles available. The new page is inserted at the start

2. Select the placeholder text and type in your own. Since you are replacing text, the original formatting is kept

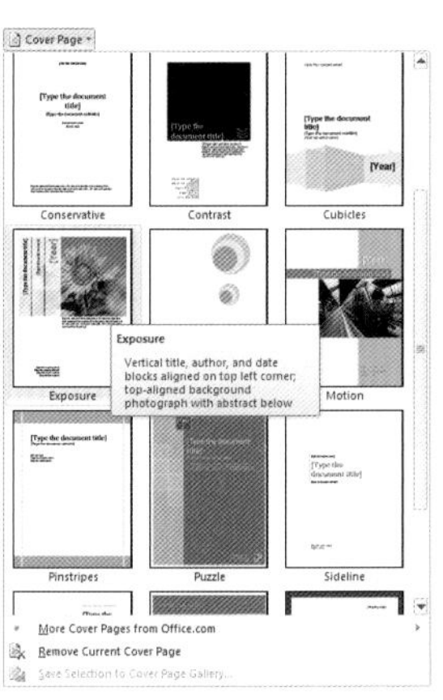

Cover Page
Conservative
Contrast
Cubicles
Exposure
Vertical title, author, and date blocks aligned on top left corner; top-aligned background photograph with abstract below
Motion
Pinstripes
Puzzle
Sideline
More Cover Pages from Office.com
Remove Current Cover Page

DP Project Closure Report.docx - Microsoft Word
[Type the document title]
Scott Basham
[Year]
[Type the abstract of the document here. The abstract is typically a short summary of the contents of the document. Type the abstract of the document here. The abstract is typically a short summary of the contents of the document.]

Hot tip

Like any other character, the Page Break can be selected and deleted, if necessary

Tables and Illustrations

These tools give you a way of adding graphical elements to your document. As soon as you start working with tables or pictorial items, a new tab with relevant controls appears – these will be covered in detail in the next chapter, "Special Tabs".

Beware

Always check the Status Bar to see which display mode you're using. If it's set to Draft or Outline, then you will not see any graphical elements at all (you will see the text contained within tables, but not the tables themselves). For graphical work, you should choose Print Layout.

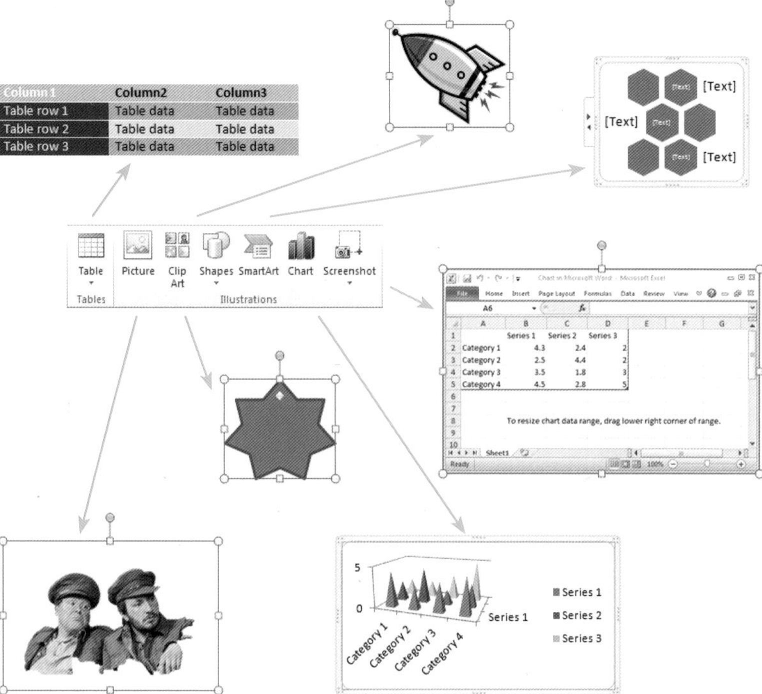

Note that some of the predesigned cover pages seen earlier contain graphic elements. If you use one of these, it's possible to edit and format its pictorial components as if you added them yourself.

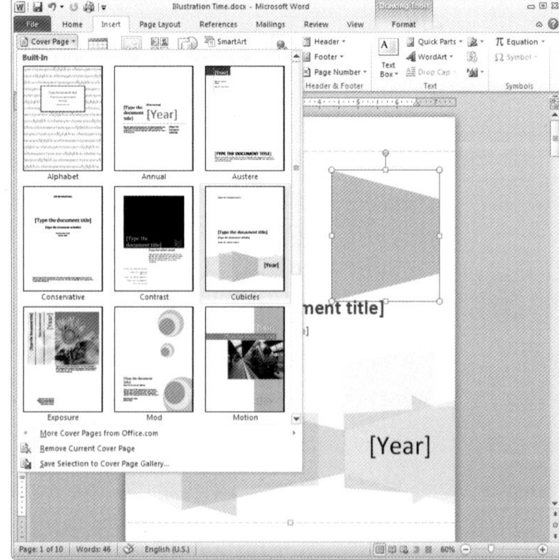

The Links Tools

This section of the Insert Command Tab lets you add Hyperlinks, Bookmarks, and Cross-references.

Bookmarks

Defining Bookmarks at key places in your document makes it easy to navigate to them, or even to create hyperlinks from other areas.

Creating a Bookmark

1. Navigate to the appropriate position in your document. Click on the Bookmark icon in the Links area

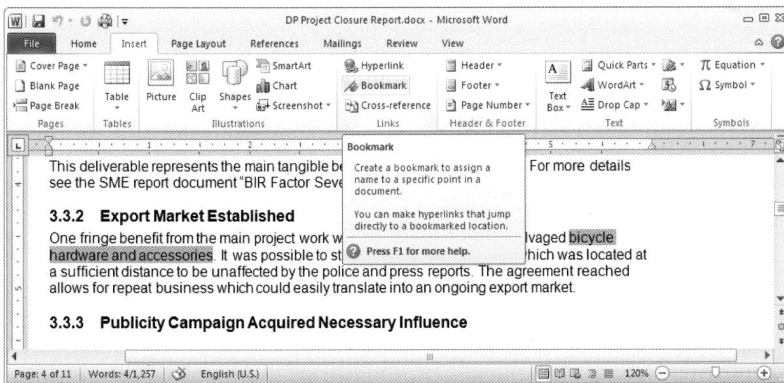

2. The Bookmark dialog appears. Enter a name for your bookmark and click on the Add button. Note that spaces are not allowed in the name

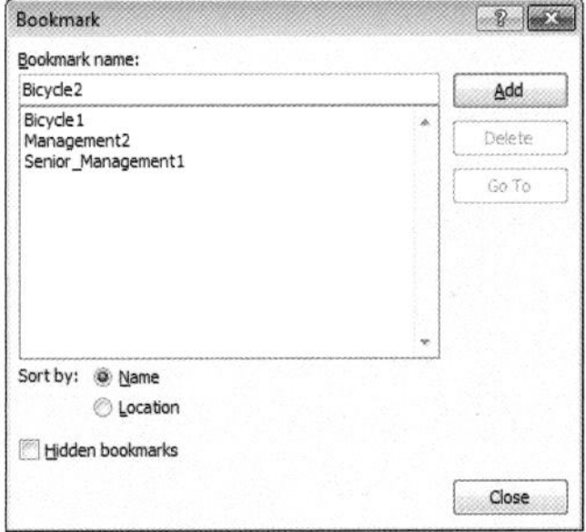

3. You can now use the Go To dialog to move instantly to a bookmark

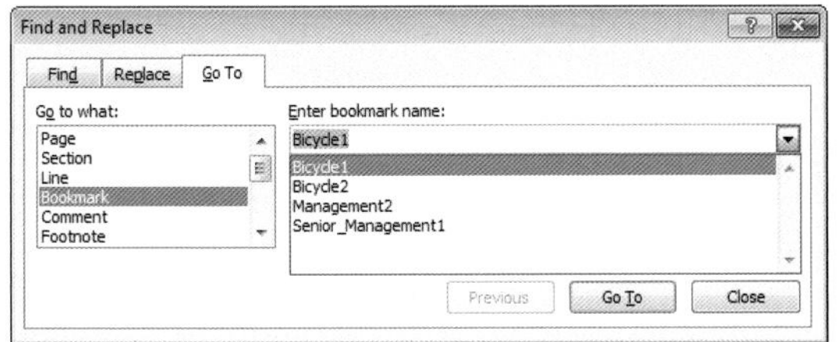

This quickest way to get to the Go To dialog is to type Ctrl+G.

...cont'd

Hyperlinks

A hyperlink is usually presented as a colored underlined text. Clicking on a hyperlink will normally transport you somewhere else – perhaps to a web page, a different document, or to a different position within the current document.

Creating a Hyperlink to a Document on Disk

1. Place your Insertion Point wherever you want the hyperlink to be added

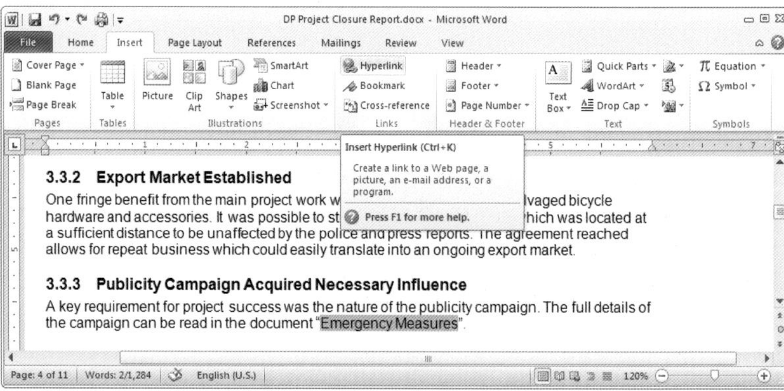

2. In the Links area of the Insert Tab, click Hyperlink – or press Ctrl+K

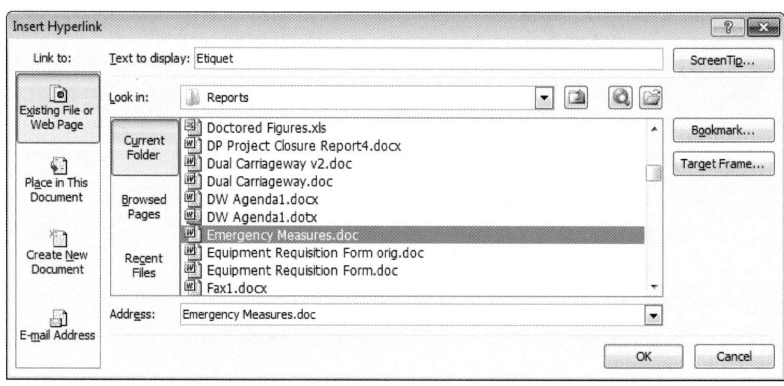

3. For "Link to" choose "Existing File or Web Page" and locate the desired document. Select this and click OK

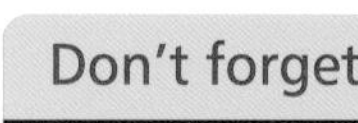

Don't forget

This hyperlinking feature works in much the same way across all Microsoft Office applications.

The hyperlink is inserted into your document. To follow it to its destination, hold down the Ctrl key and click the link.

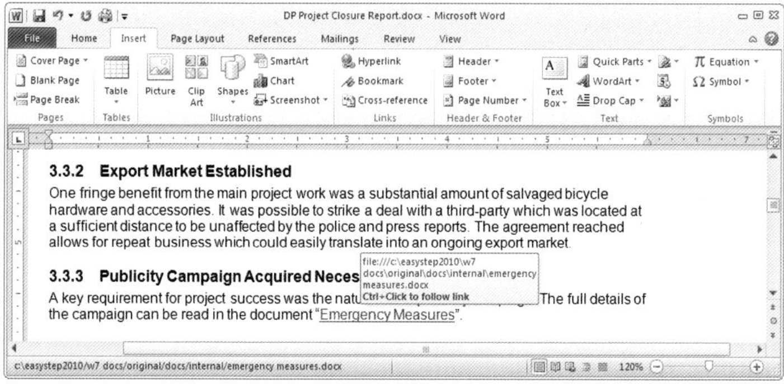
DP Project Closure Report.docx - Microsoft Word
3.3.2 Export Market Established
One fringe benefit from the main project work was a substantial amount of salvaged bicycle hardware and accessories. It was possible to strike a deal with a third-party which was located at a sufficient distance to be unaffected by the police and press reports. The agreement reached allows for repeat business which could easily translate into an ongoing export market.
3.3.3 Publicity Campaign Acquired Neces
file:///c:\easystep2010\w7 docs\original\docs\internal\emergency measures.docx
Ctrl+Click to follow link
A key requirement for project success was the natu
The full details of the campaign can be read in the document "Emergency Measures".
c:\easystep2010/w7 docs/original/docs/internal/emergency measures.docx

Cross References

Sometimes you'll want your text to refer to another location, e.g. "see page 89 for more information". If you actually type in the number "89", then you'll need to go back many times to check if the reference has changed, perhaps because you've added more pages or edited some text. You can avoid this problem by creating automatic cross references in Word.

Hot tip

You can cross-refer to a range of possible targets, including Headings, Bookmarks, and Tables.

1. Place your Insertion Point wherever you want the cross reference to appear, then click the Cross Reference tool

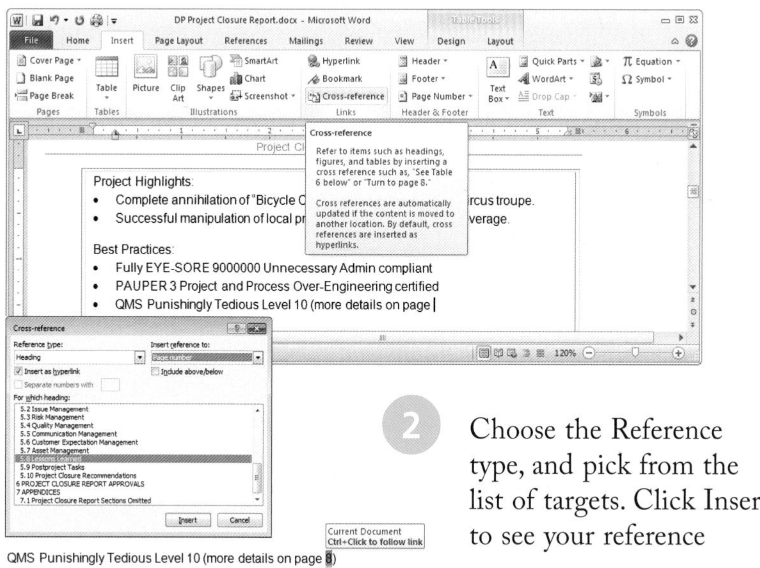
DP Project Closure Report.docx - Microsoft Word
Cross-reference
Refer to items such as headings, figures, and tables by inserting a cross reference such as, "See Table 6 below" or "Turn to page 8."
Cross references are automatically updated if the content is moved to another location. By default, cross references are inserted as hyperlinks.
Project Highlights:
Complete annihilation of "Bicycle C
Successful manipulation of local pr
Best Practices:
Fully EYE-SORE 9000000 Unnecessary Admin compliant
PAUPER 3 Project and Process Over-Engineering certified
QMS Punishingly Tedious Level 10 (more details on page
Cross-reference
Reference type:
Heading
Insert reference to:
Page number
Insert as hyperlink
Include above/below
For which heading:
5.2 Issue Management
5.3 Risk Management
5.4 Quality Management
5.5 Communication Management
5.6 Customer Expectation Management
5.7 Asset Management
5.9 Postproject Tasks
5.10 Project Closure Recommendations
6 PROJECT CLOSURE REPORT APPROVALS
7 APPENDICES
7.1 Project Closure Report Sections Omitted
Insert
Cancel
Current Document
Ctrl+Click to follow link
QMS Punishingly Tedious Level 10 (more details on page 8)

2. Choose the Reference type, and pick from the list of targets. Click Insert to see your reference

Hot tip

In the Cross-reference dialog, you can also choose the form of the reference. For example, if your Reference type is a Heading, you might want to use the Heading number, the Heading text itself, or the page number.

Headers and Footers

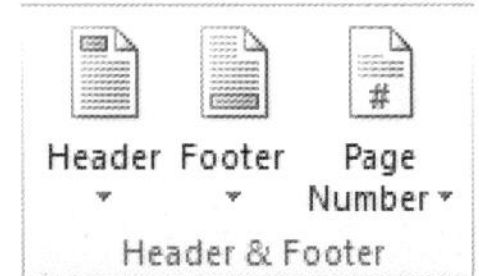

Headers and footers appear at the top and bottom of each page. There are built-in items available, with standard designs for these.

Adding a Header or Footer

1. In the Header & Footer area of the Insert Tab, click Header or Footer as appropriate

2. Select the design you want. The header or footer will be added to your document

Editing a Header or Footer

1. Click Header or Footer and then select Edit Header or Edit footer

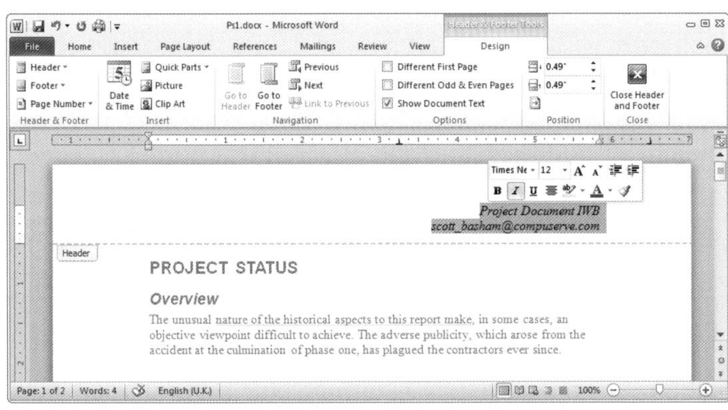

2. You will now be able to edit directly in the Header or Footer area of the page. The Header & Footer Tools Tab appears. From this, you can adjust the position of the header and footer, add graphic items, and decide whether headers and footers should be separately defined for odd and even pages (this is useful if your document will be printed double-sided)

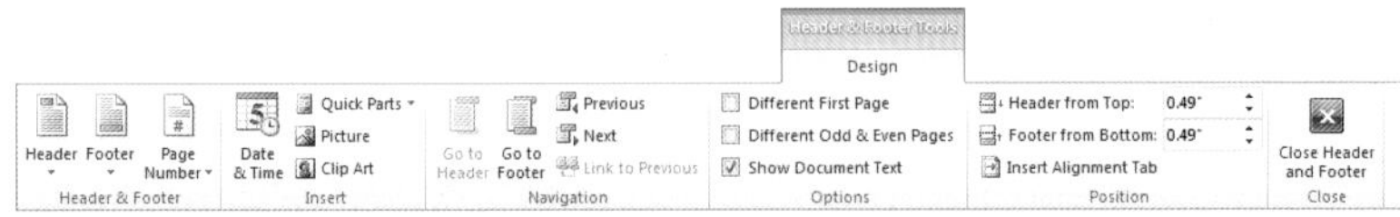

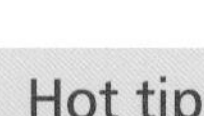

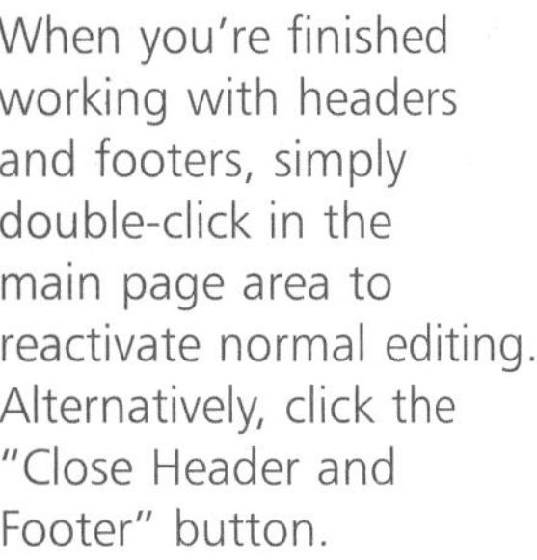

Hot tip

When you're finished working with headers and footers, simply double-click in the main page area to reactivate normal editing. Alternatively, click the "Close Header and Footer" button.

3. There is also a Navigation area in the Tab, which allows you to switch between Header and Footer. If your document is divided into sections, then Headers and Footers can be defined independently for each section

Hot tip

See the next chapter ("The Page Layout Tab") to learn how to divide your document into sections.

Inserting a Date and Time

1. Place your Insertion Point, then click Date & Time

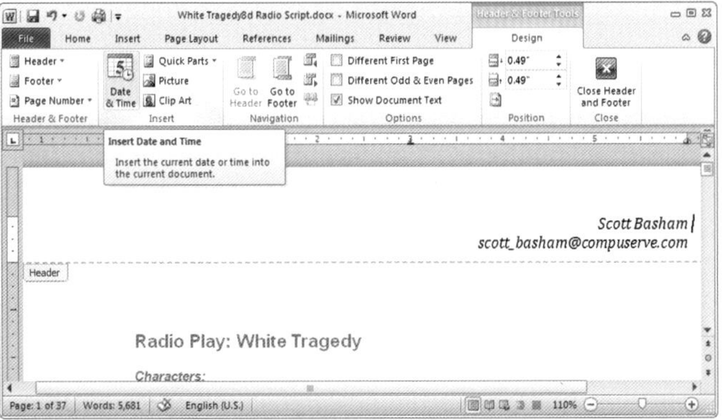

2. Choose from one of the formats listed in the dialog box, and then click OK

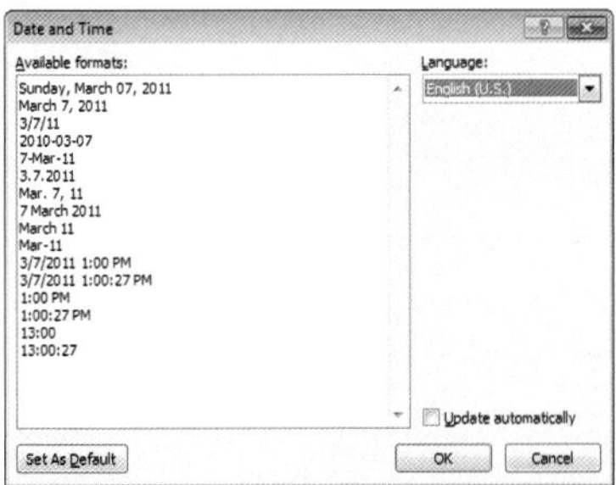

Hot tip

If you select the "Update automatically" option in this dialog, then the date/time value is updated when the document is saved or printed.

3. The current system date and/or time, taken from the computer clock, are inserted into the current position in your document

Scott Basham 3/7/2011
scott_basham@compuserve.com

The Text Tools

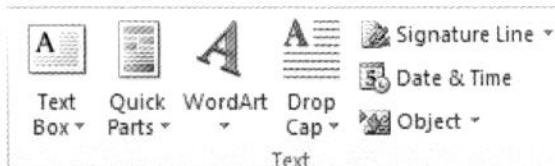

This section of the Insert Command Tab lets you add a variety of text-based objects.

Text Boxes

These give you a lot of freedom in positioning and formatting small amounts of text. Text can also be flowed automatically between boxes, which can help with more advanced page layouts.

Using Text Boxes, Building Blocks and Quick Parts

1 Click the Text Box icon to access the popup menu

Text Boxes, like other shapes, can have text wrap applied to them. This is useful if you have a text-filled page – you can decide how the main text will flow around the edges of the Text Box. See the next chapter, "Special Tabs", for more on Text Wrap.

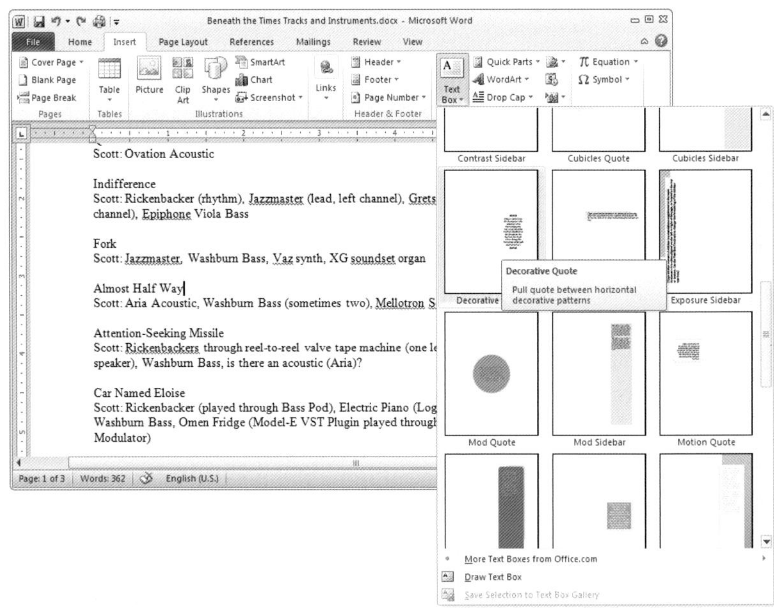

In the Gallery that appears, you see examples of Building Blocks. These are components that can be used in any document. You can define your own Building Blocks, or download more from Office.com. Other types of Building Blocks are Headers, Footers, Page Number styles, Cover Pages, Watermarks and Equations.

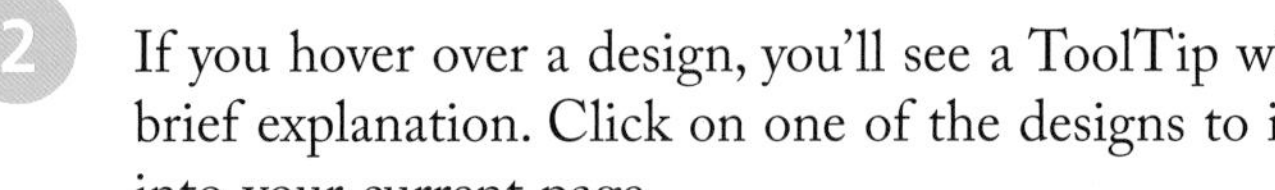

2 If you hover over a design, you'll see a ToolTip with a brief explanation. Click on one of the designs to insert it into your current page

The Text Box appears on the page, in whichever is the default position for this particular design.

3. To resize the Text Box, drag on one of its circular "handles"

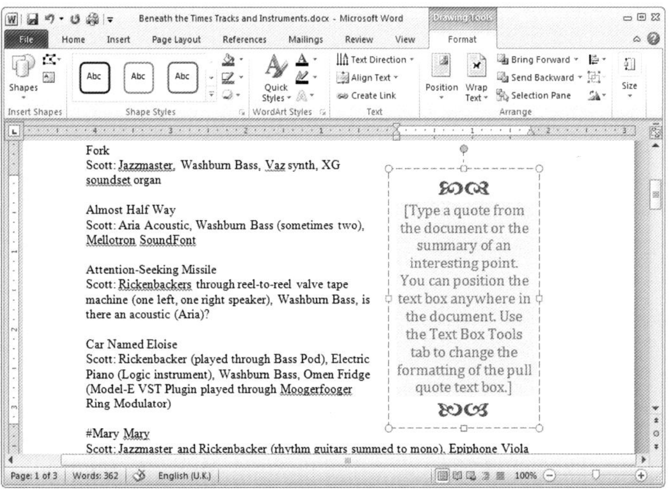
Beneath the Times Tracks and Instruments.docx - Microsoft Word
Drawing Tools
File
Home
Insert
Page Layout
References
Mailings
Review
View
Format
Shapes
Abc
Quick Styles
Text Direction
Align Text
Create Link
Position
Wrap Text
Bring Forward
Send Backward
Selection Pane
Size
Insert Shapes
Shape Styles
WordArt Styles
Text
Arrange
Fork
Scott: Jazzmaster, Washburn Bass, Vaz synth, XG soundset organ
Almost Half Way
Scott: Aria Acoustic, Washburn Bass (sometimes two), Mellotron SoundFont
Attention-Seeking Missile
Scott: Rickenbackers through reel-to-reel valve tape machine (one left, one right speaker), Washburn Bass, is there an acoustic (Aria)?
Car Named Eloise
Scott: Rickenbacker (played through Bass Pod), Electric Piano (Logic instrument), Washburn Bass, Omen Fridge (Model-E VST Plugin played through Moogerfooger Ring Modulator)
#Mary Mary
Scott: Jazzmaster and Rickenbacker (rhythm guitars summed to mono), Epiphone Viola
[Type a quote from the document or the summary of an interesting point. You can position the text box anywhere in the document. Use the Text Box Tools tab to change the formatting of the pull quote text box.]
Page: 1 of 3
Words: 362
English (U.K.)
100%

4. If you want to move the Text Box, then drag somewhere on its edge, but not on any of the circular "handles"

5. The Text Box comes with some sample dummy text. Select this and enter your own

6. You can change the appearance of the text, or the box itself, using the controls in the Command Tab or the Quick Access Toolbar

7. If you've changed the design and would like to reuse it later on, make sure the Insert Tab is active, click on the Quick Parts tool and choose "Save Selection to Quick Part Gallery..." Give your design a name, then click OK

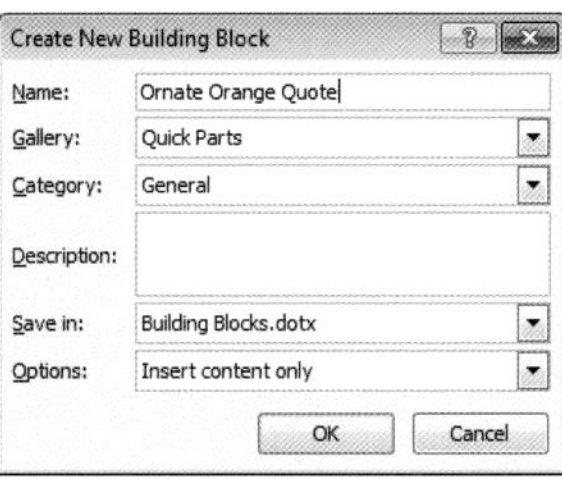
Create New Building Block
Name: Ornate Orange Quote
Gallery: Quick Parts
Category: General
Description:
Save in: Building Blocks.dotx
Options: Insert content only
OK
Cancel

...cont'd

Creating a Text Box Manually

1. Make sure the Insert Tab is active. Click the Text Box icon and choose Draw Text Box

2. Drag a rectangular area to define the box perimeter

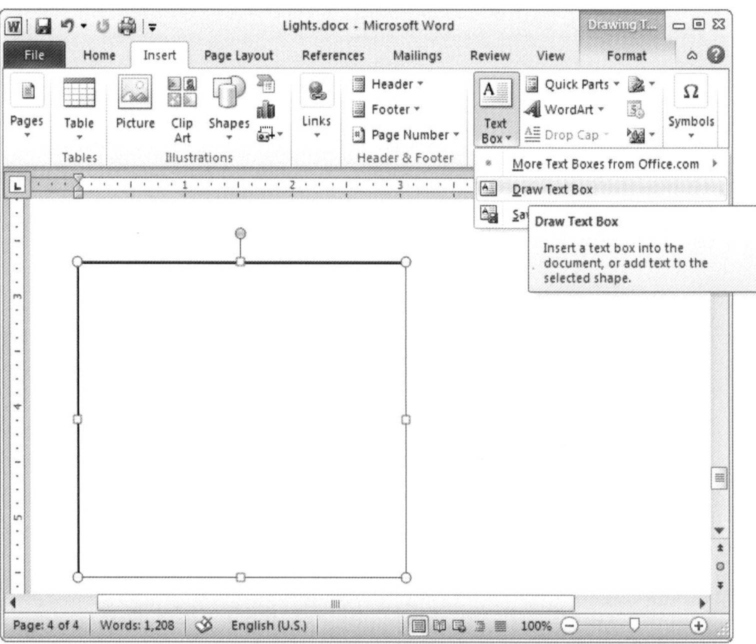

3. Enter the text within the box. You can use all the normal editing and formatting controls, and the techniques you learned in earlier chapters

4. When the text box is selected, the Format Tab will be available. You can use this to control the line and fill style of the box, as well as to change the layering (using "Bring to Front" and "Send to Back"), or to apply effects, such as shadowing or 3D boxes

See Chapter Four, "Special Tabs", for more on the Format Tab.

Sometimes the box may be too small for your text. If this happens, you can either increase the box size, reduce the text size, or create more boxes and link them using text flow. We'll see how to use text flow next.

Flowing Text Between Boxes

1. Locate a Text Box that has too much text to display within its defined area

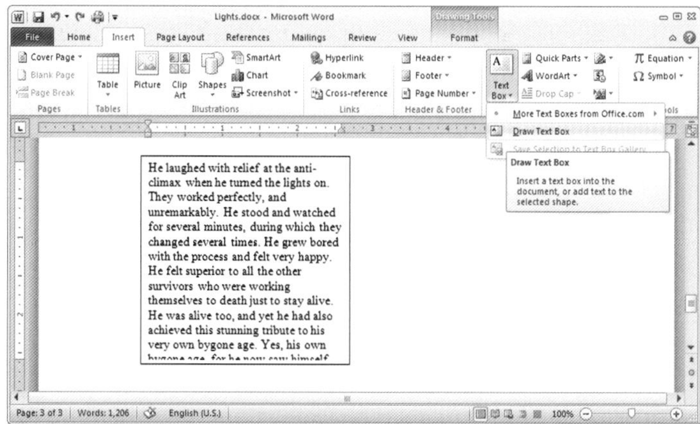

2. Click on the Text Box icon in the Toolbar and, in the popup menu which appears, choose Draw Text Box

3. Click and drag to define the size and position of the second text box

4. Select the first Text Box and make sure the Format Tab is visible. Click the Create Link button

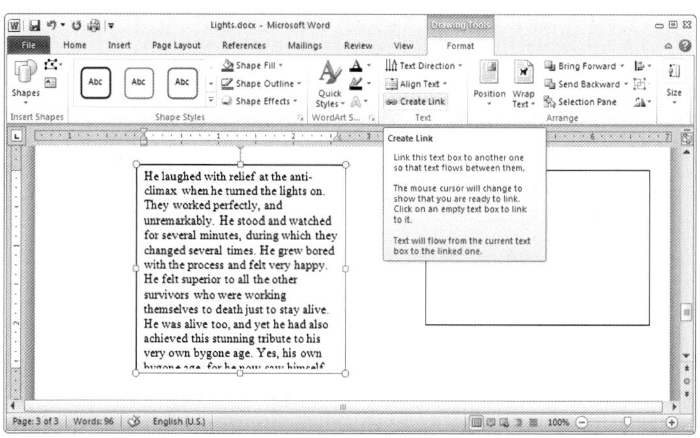

Hot tip

Text flow works, not just on Text Boxes, but on any Shapes that are capable of containing text. See Chapter Four, "Special Tabs", for more on this.

...cont'd

5. Now click anywhere within the second Text Box. The text that didn't fit into the first box will automatically flow into the second

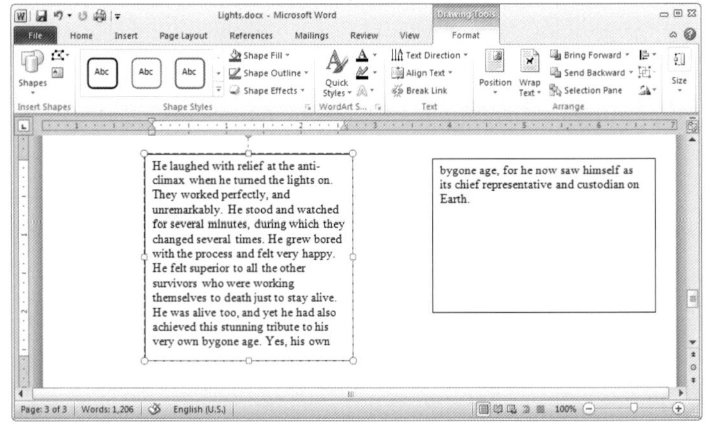
Lights.docx - Microsoft Word
Drawing Tools
File
Home
Insert
Page Layout
References
Mailings
Review
View
Format
Shapes
Insert Shapes
Shape Fill
Shape Outline
Shape Effects
Shape Styles
Quick Styles
WordArt S...
Text Direction
Align Text
Break Link
Text
Position
Wrap Text
Bring Forward
Send Backward
Selection Pane
Arrange
Size
He laughed with relief at the anti-climax when he turned the lights on. They worked perfectly, and unremarkably. He stood and watched for several minutes, during which they changed several times. He grew bored with the process and felt very happy. He felt superior to all the other survivors who were working themselves to death just to stay alive. He was alive too, and yet he had also achieved this stunning tribute to his very own bygone age. Yes, his own
bygone age, for he now saw himself as its chief representative and custodian on Earth.
Page: 3 of 3
Words: 1,206
English (U.S.)
100%

6. If there is still too much text, you can repeat this process to create a longer sequence of Text Boxes, with the same text continuously threaded through them

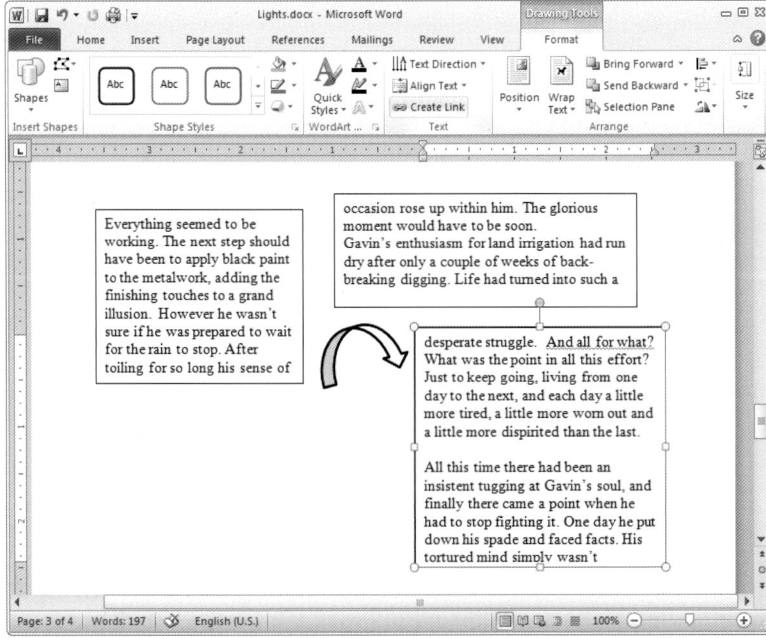
Lights.docx - Microsoft Word
Drawing Tools
File
Home
Insert
Page Layout
References
Mailings
Review
View
Format
Shapes
Insert Shapes
Shape Styles
Quick Styles
WordArt ...
Text Direction
Align Text
Create Link
Text
Position
Wrap Text
Bring Forward
Send Backward
Selection Pane
Arrange
Size
Everything seemed to be working. The next step should have been to apply black paint to the metalwork, adding the finishing touches to a grand illusion. However he wasn't sure if he was prepared to wait for the rain to stop. After toiling for so long his sense of
occasion rose up within him. The glorious moment would have to be soon.
Gavin's enthusiasm for land irrigation had run dry after only a couple of weeks of back-breaking digging. Life had turned into such a
desperate struggle. And all for what? What was the point in all this effort? Just to keep going, living from one day to the next, and each day a little more tired, a little more worn out and a little more dispirited than the last.
All this time there had been an insistent tugging at Gavin's soul, and finally there came a point when he had to stop fighting it. One day he put down his spade and faced facts. His tortured mind simply wasn't
Page: 3 of 4
Words: 197
English (U.S.)
100%

Hot tip

You can reverse this operation by selecting the first Text Box and then clicking on Break Link. All the text will now be moved back into the first box. You will now need to edit the text, change its size, or change the size of the Text Box, to see all the text.

Creating Your Own Building Blocks

You can select any text, or other objects within Word, and make these into new building blocks.

1. Create and format the content that will become your new building block

2. Select your content, then click Quick Parts and select "Save Selection to Quick Parts Gallery"

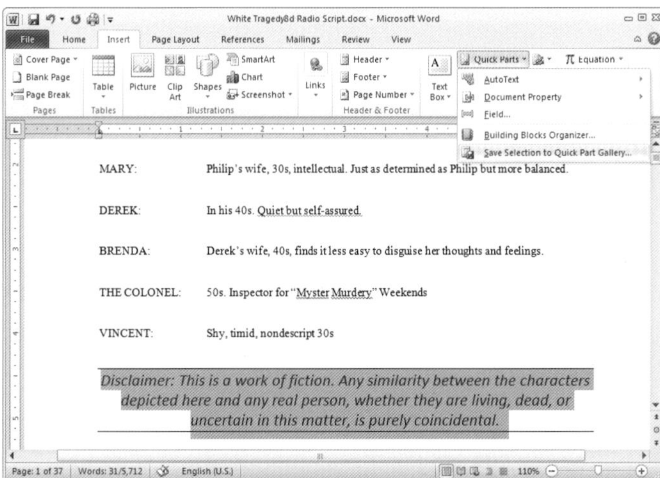

3. The Create New Building Block dialog appears. Enter a name and select a Gallery to use (in most cases this should be the Quick Parts Gallery)

4. Choose a Category and enter a text description

5. Next, choose the Word template that will store the building block. If you select "Building Blocks.dotx" then the building block will be available to all documents

6. The Options available are "Insert content only", "Insert content in its own paragraph", and "Insert content in its own page". Choose the appropriate option and then click OK. Your building block is now installed and ready for you to use

Don't forget

Quick Parts are useful if you need to use standard formatted text across many documents. An example may be a disclaimer that has been agreed with the legal department of your company – it may be company policy to include this in any correspondence with customers.

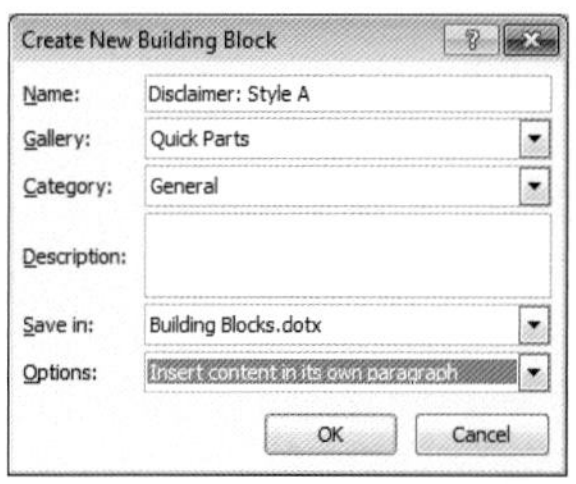

...cont'd

Using Your Own Building Blocks

Once you have created your own building blocks, you can use them in the same way as the others.

1. Navigate to the part of your document where you want to add your building block, and click an Insertion Point

2. Click the Quick Parts button and select your building block from its gallery. It will be added at the current position

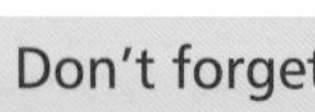

To replace an existing building block, you must precisely enter the same name in the Create New Building Block dialog.

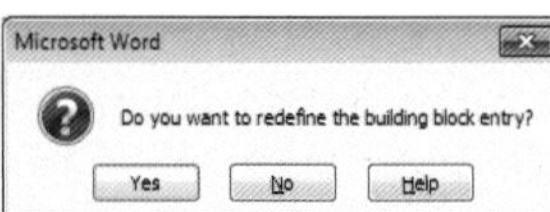

Editing an Existing Building Block

If you have an example of a building block somewhere in your document, then you can edit this and reattach it to the gallery.

1. Make the necessary changes to the content, then select it
2. Click on Quick Parts and choose "Save Selection to Quick Parts Gallery"
3. If you enter the same name and Gallery as before, then the original building block's definition will be overwritten

The Building Blocks Organizer

Building Blocks can be very flexible, and there are many different types. In this chapter we have seen tools, such as Cover Page, Header, Footer, Page Number, Text Box, and the more general Quick Parts. Each of these has its own Gallery, containing a particular type of Building Block. Here we'll see how to manage all these objects in one place.

1. Click on the Quick Parts tool and choose Building Blocks Organizer to see this dialog

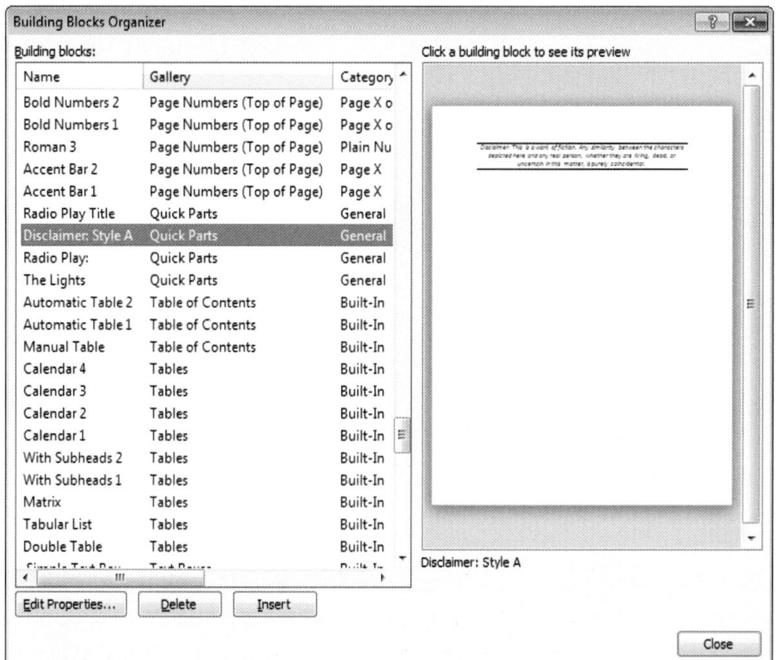

2. If you scroll down through the predesigned elements, you should be able to find Quick Parts objects you created yourself. Click Edit Properties... to change an item's attributes

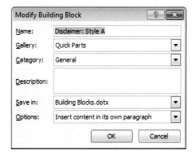

Modify Building Block
Name: Disclaimer: Style A
Gallery: Quick Parts
Category: General
Description:
Save in: Building Blocks.dotx
Options: Insert content in its own paragraph
OK
Cancel

Hot tip

If you previously saved a customized Text Box as a Quick Part, you might want to use this dialog to change its Gallery to Text Boxes. It'll then appear directly in the popup menu, which you see when you click on the Text Box tool.

Advanced Text Effects

WordArt lets you present text using a wide range of visual effects.

Using WordArt

1. Select your text and click WordArt in the Text area of the Insert Tab

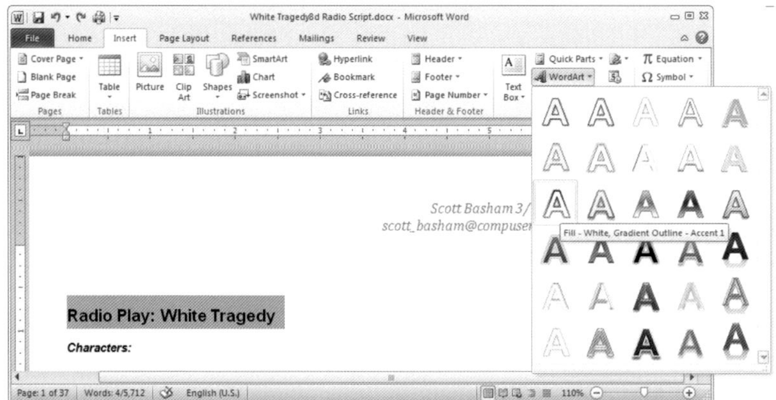

2. Choose an effect from the gallery

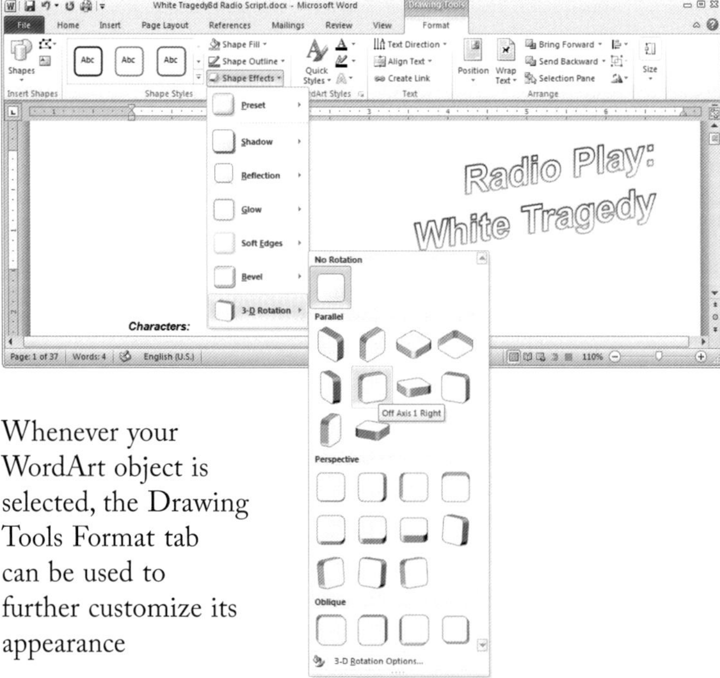

Whenever your WordArt object is selected, the Drawing Tools Format tab can be used to further customize its appearance

Don't forget

Initially, the new WordArt object is independent of the main text, so you can't easily move it by dragging. You can make it part of the main text by right-clicking, choosing Wrap Text, then "In Line with Text".

3 There's a set of WordArt tools in the Drawing Tools/ Format tab. Click on the symbol in WordArt Styles

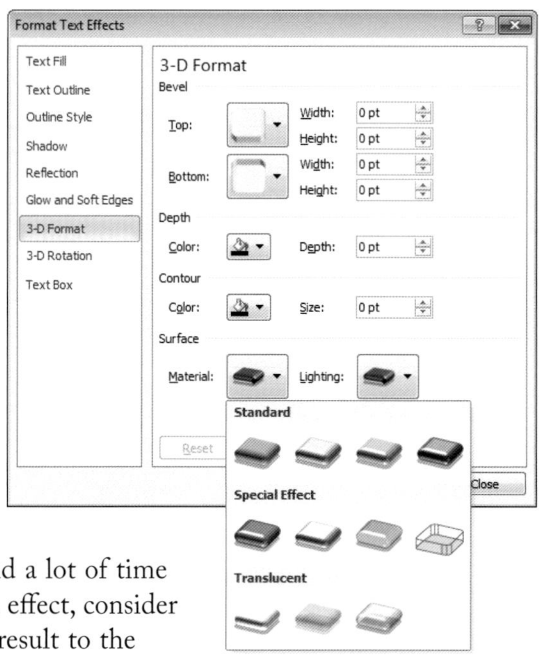

If you spend a lot of time creating an effect, consider saving the result to the Quick Parts Gallery

Drop Cap

1 Click anywhere inside a paragraph, then on the Drop Cap tool to select a Drop Cap style. This will affect the first character in the paragraph

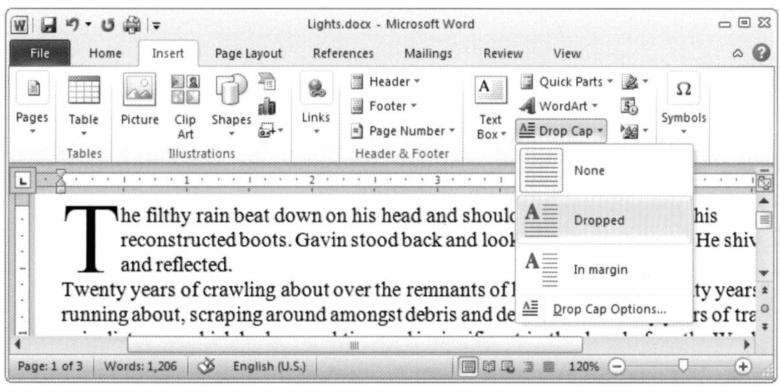

Equations and Symbols

π Ω
Equation Symbol
Symbols

The final set of tools in the Insert Tab lets you add equations and special symbols to your document.

Creating and Editing an Equation

1. Click an Insertion Point in the appropriate place. Click on the Equation icon in the Symbols area of the Insert Tab and choose Insert New Equation

2. You can now select one of the prebuilt equations, or choose Insert New Equation to enter one manually

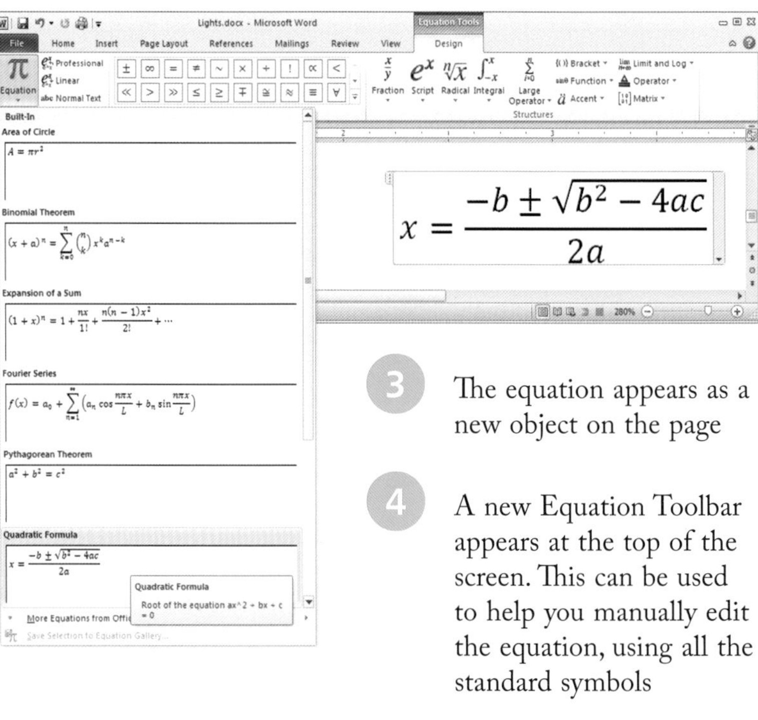

3. The equation appears as a new object on the page

4. A new Equation Toolbar appears at the top of the screen. This can be used to help you manually edit the equation, using all the standard symbols

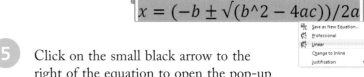

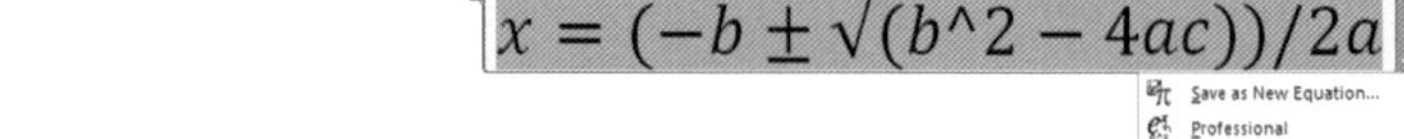

5. Click on the small black arrow to the right of the equation to open the pop-up menu. From here you can change the format to Linear, or even save the equation for later use via the gallery. The illustration below shows the example equation presented as Linear (all on one line)

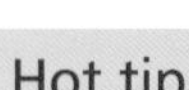

Hot tip

If you can find something similar to what you need, then it's much easier to select an existing preset equation and edit it, rather than entering the whole thing manually.

Inserting a Symbol

1. Click an Insertion Point in the appropriate place. Click on the Symbol icon in the Symbols area of the Insert Tab to open the pop-up menu

2. If the symbol you want is in the display of commonly-used items, simply click to insert it into your document...

3. ...otherwise click on More Symbols to access the following dialog box:

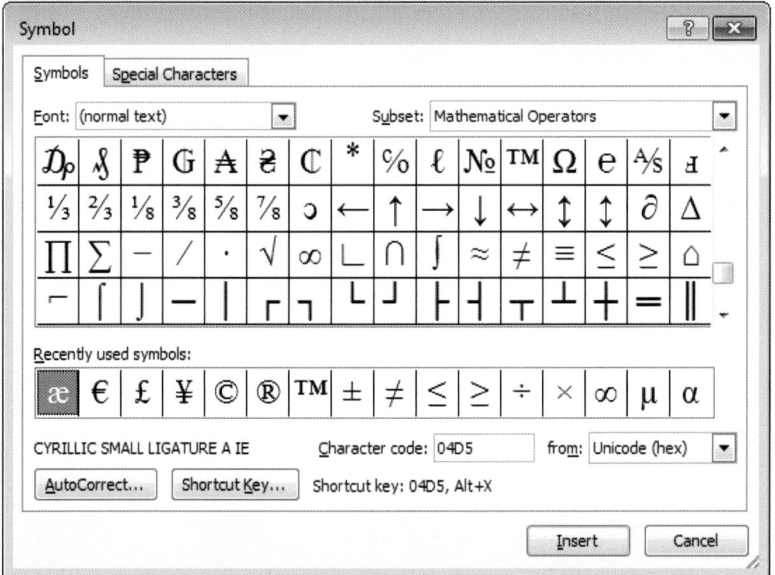

4. When you've located the symbol, select it and click Insert

To assign a keyboard shortcut to a symbol or special character, select it from this dialog and then click Shortcut Key.

...cont'd

Once the symbol has been added, it behaves just like a normal character, so it can be selected and reformatted along with its neighboring text:

Special Characters

These are not very easy to access from the keyboard, but can be very useful. For example, an En Dash is similar to a hyphen, but always the same width as a letter N in the current font/size.

1. When you're ready to enter the special character, click on the Symbol Tool and choose More Symbols

2. The Symbols dialog appears. Activate the Special Characters tab

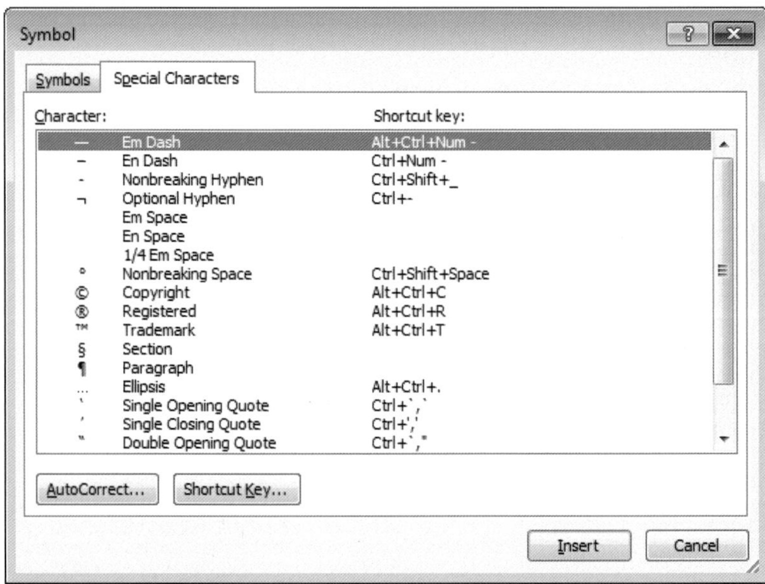

3. Select the desired Symbol and click Insert

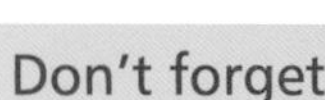

Don't forget

It isn't usually necessary to use these dialogs to enter opening and closing quotation marks, because Word normally translates the "straight" quotes on your keyboard into opening or closing quotes, depending on current context

Hot tip

From this dialog, you can see which symbols already have keyboard shortcuts. For example, you can enter an Em Dash using Alt+Ctrl+Num -

4 Special Tabs

The last chapter covered adding tables, pictures and charts. Whenever you work with these, extra tabs become visible. This chapter helps you to explore and understand their features.

Tables

Tables allow you to organize and manage text in rows and columns. They provide a more visual way of working than you would have with normal text formatted via tab stops.

Inserting a Table

1. Click on the Table icon in the Insert Tab

2. In the grid that appears, click and drag to define an initial table size. Don't worry too much about getting this right first time, it's easy to change a table's dimensions later on

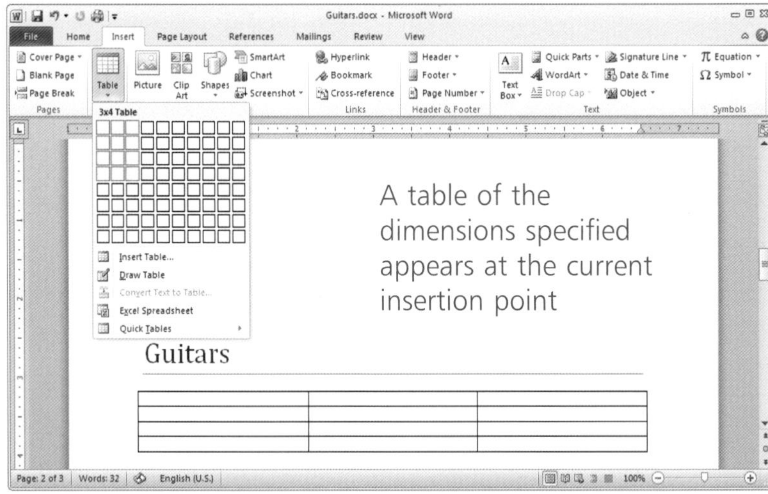

3. Alternatively, if you click the Table icon and then choose Insert Table from the submenu, this dialog box appears. You can then specify the table dimensions numerically. Click OK to go ahead and create the table

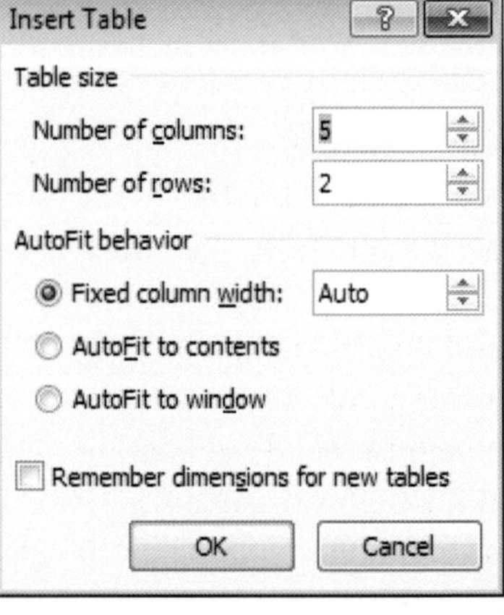

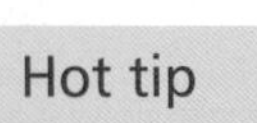

Hot tip

If you already have some text formatted using tab characters, then it's easy to convert this to a table, automatically. To do this, select the text, click the Table icon and choose "Convert Text to Table".

Resizing a Table

1. Click and drag on the boundary between rows or columns to resize them. Your Insertion Point will turn into a double-headed arrow as you do this

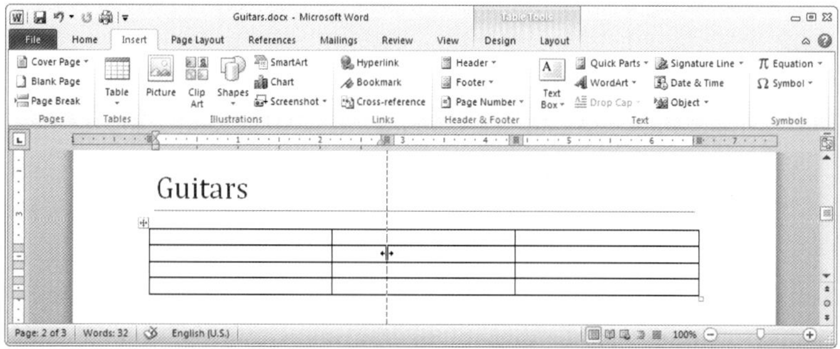

As soon as you have a table, or part of a table, selected, the Command Tab Table Tools will appear. These are organized into two tabs: Design, and Layout.

Drawing a Table

You may prefer to use the table drawing tool to create tables. This gives you more flexibility, particularly when you're trying to create irregularly-shaped tables.

1. Click the Table icon and choose Draw Table

2. Click and drag to draw a rectangle, which defines the overall table size

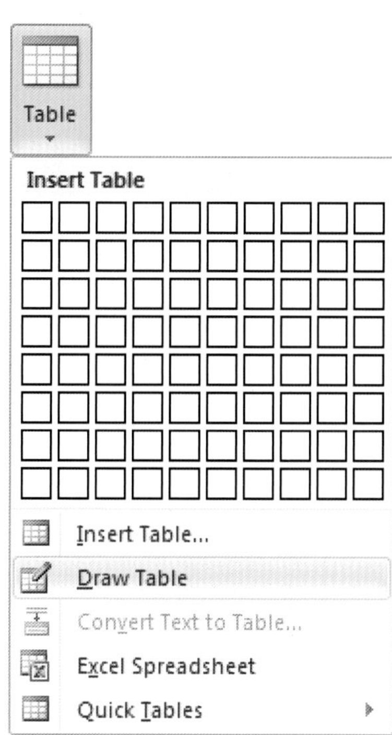

The rectangle you drew represents the table perimeter. Your next task is to draw in the rows and columns. The special Table Tools/Design Tab is automatically activated, and its Draw Table tool is selected, ready for you to start work.

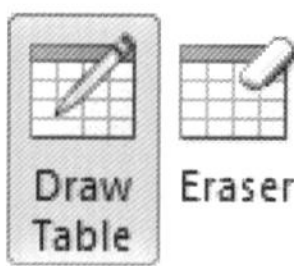

...cont'd

3. Click and drag horizontally across the table to draw in the rows. As you drag, a dotted line appears, giving you a preview of the new line. If you accidentally draw the line in the wrong place, simply use Ctrl + Z to undo and then try again

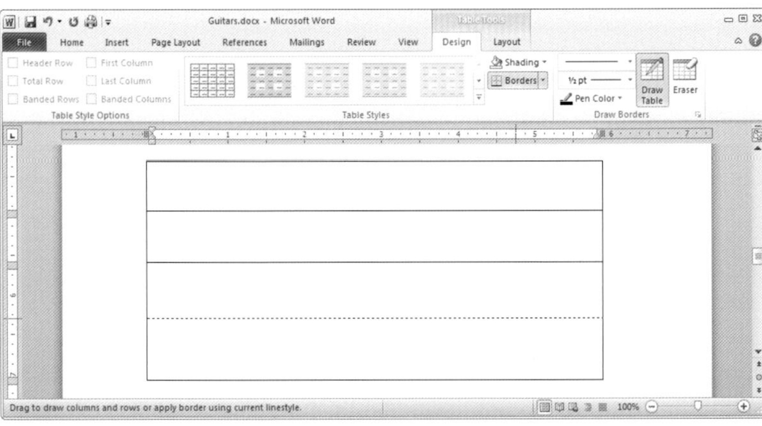

4. Now drag vertically to draw in the column boundaries

5. You can even drag diagonally, to create a new line that will divide cells in two, as in the example below

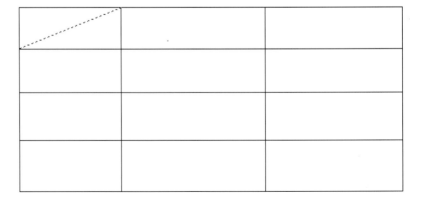

Note that if you drag from inside to an area outside of the table, then the table will be automatically extended. However, if you begin and end dragging completely outside the table, then a new independent table will be created.

All these features are still available to you, even after you add text into the cells of your table. Sometimes it's useful to see how much text you need before you finalize the table's dimensions.

6 Sometimes you will want to remove lines to create an irregular table, where some of the cells are much larger. To do this, select the Eraser tool and then click directly on the part of the line you wish to remove

Hot tip

A single click will normally remove the shortest segment at the current mouse position. If you want to remove larger sections of a line, or even a whole line, then click and drag over the desired area.

7 Once you have erased a fairly large area, switch back to the Draw Table tool. You can now add in more lines to this area

8 In the example below, you can see how flexible this technique is, allowing for a complex patchwork of odd-sized cells to be created

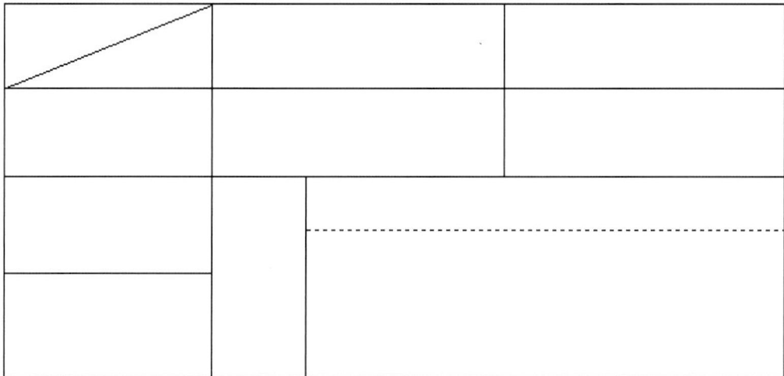

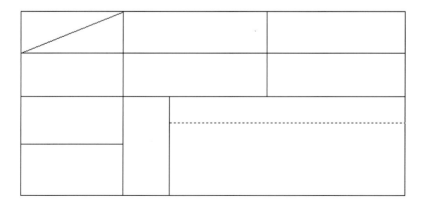

Table cells are normally filled with text, and can have their background shaded and different line styles applied. It's also possible to place graphic items inside a table cell.

...cont'd

Formatting Your Table

You can use all the formatting techniques learned in earlier chapters on your table text. You will often start by dragging across an entire row or column to select it, prior to formatting.

Guitars

Name	Type	Price
Rickenbacker 330	Hollow Body Electric	$1871.00
Epiphone Viola	Bass	$499.99
Squire Telecaster	Solid Electric	$283.65

Hot tip

If you have changed the dimensions of individual rows, or columns, but now want to make your table more regular again, select the relevant area, right-click, and then choose either Distribute Rows Evenly or Distribute Columns Evenly.

Inserting and Deleting Rows or Columns

1. To insert a row, first select an existing row, either just above or just below the place where you want to position the new row

2. Right-click and choose Insert, and then either Insert Rows Above or Insert Rows Below

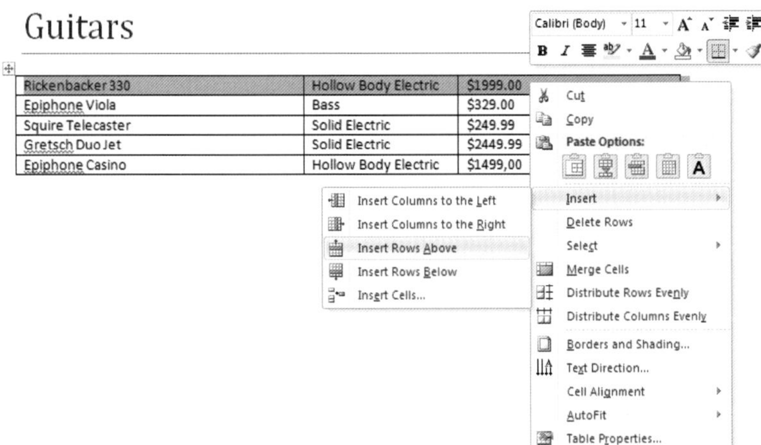

3. The new row will appear in the desired position

4. To insert multiple rows, first click and drag to select the number of rows you wish to add. When you choose Insert Rows Above or Below, this number of rows will be added

Merging Cells

Each cell can contain text that is formatted and aligned independently of other cell text (if desired). Sometimes it's useful to group or merge cells together, so that they behave as a single cell.

1. Select the cells you wish to merge. Note that these must be next to each other

2. Right-click and choose Merge Cells

Guitars

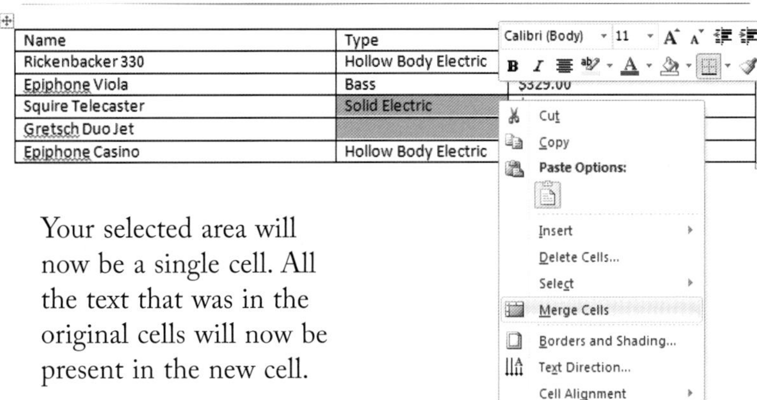

Your selected area will now be a single cell. All the text that was in the original cells will now be present in the new cell.

Guitars

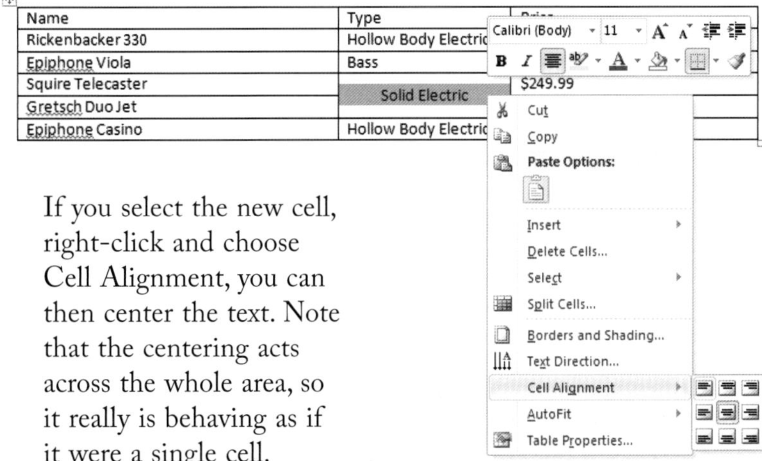

If you select the new cell, right-click and choose Cell Alignment, you can then center the text. Note that the centering acts across the whole area, so it really is behaving as if it were a single cell.

If you accidentally merge the wrong cells, then type Ctrl+Z or click on the Undo button in the Quick Access Toolbar.

...cont'd

Table Properties

1. Make sure your Insertion Point is somewhere inside the table (or select part or all of the table), right-click and then choose Table Properties

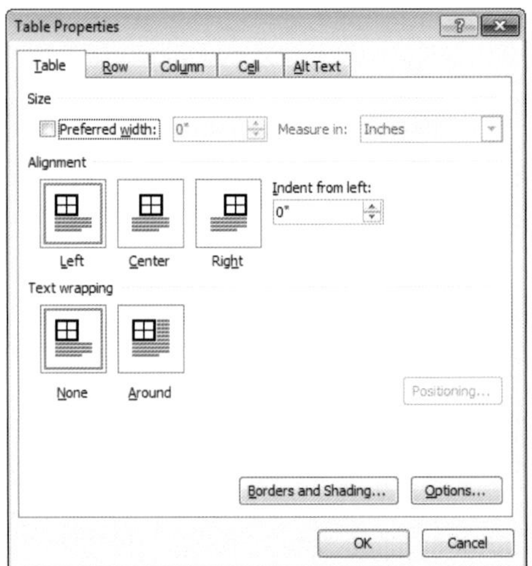

From this dialog, you can define properties for the entire table, or at the row, column, or cell level.

You can also use the "Borders and Shading..." button to set the visual properties for the whole table.

Hot tip

From the Cell page of the Table Properties dialog, you have individual control over the vertical alignment of text within each cell. Horizontal text alignment is controlled via the Paragraph area in the Home Command Tab.

Table Styles

1. Select, or click within your table to make sure the Table Tools Tab is active. As you hover over each style, you will see a preview of your table

2. Click on the style to apply it permanently to your table

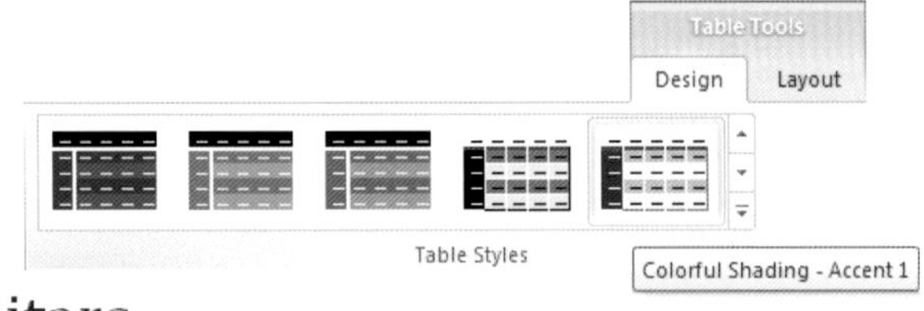

Guitars

Name	Type	Price
Rickenbacker 330	Hollow Body Electric	$1999.00
Epiphone Viola	Bass	$329.00
Squire Telecaster	Solid Electric	$249.99
Gretsch Duo Jet	Solid Electric	$2449.99
Epiphone Casino	Hollow Body Electric	$1499,00

The Table Design Controls

1. Select your table and activate the Table Tools/Design Tab

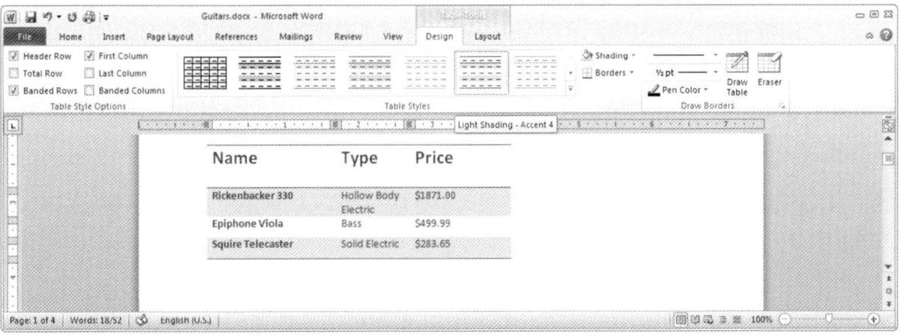

2. As you hover over the Table Styles, you'll see a Tooltip and your table will preview the Style

The Table Layout Controls

If you activate the Layout Controls, you'll see that there are tools for operations on tables, rows, columns, and individual cells.

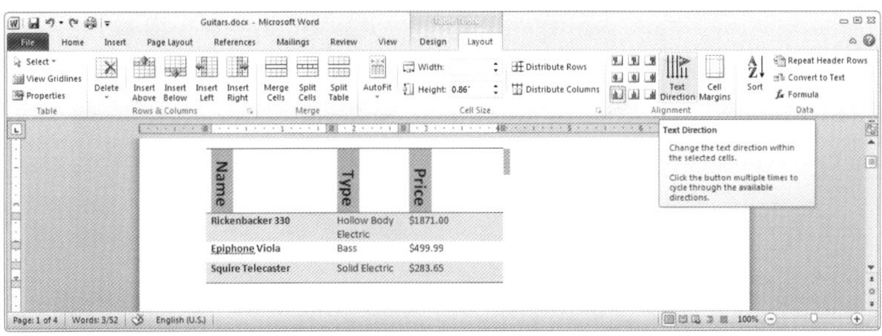

In this example, the Formula button was used to calculate the sum of the values in the cells above the one selected

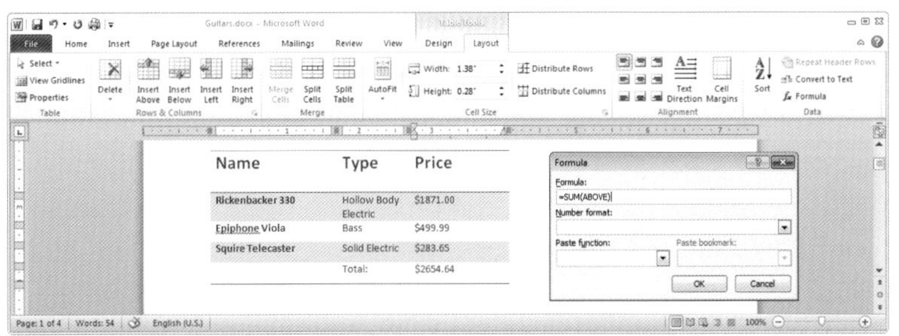

Many of the features in the Table Layout Controls are also present in the pop-up menu, when you right click within a table.

Pictures

The Illustrations area

The Illustrations area of the Insert Tab allows you to add a range of different graphical objects.

Don't forget

Word can import many types of graphic file format, but they fall into two categories. Draw-type graphics are represented as mathematical objects. They can usually be scaled up or down with no loss in quality. Others are bitmapped, i.e. stored as a structure of dots or pixels. Be careful not to enlarge bitmapped images too much, as the pixels get bigger and more noticeable.

Adding a Photo from a File on Disk

In this example, we imported an image created by a digital camera. We'll assume that you have some photo files available on your hard disk, or on other storage medium.

1. Navigate to the appropriate part of your document, then click on Picture, in the Illustrations area of the Insert Tab

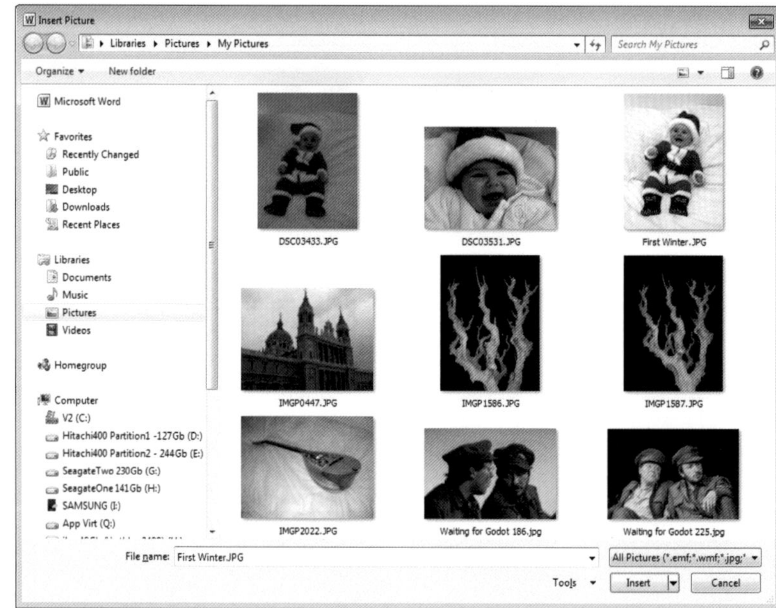

2. Use the standard Windows controls at the top and the left of the dialog to locate your photo files

3. Once you have found the image you want, select it and then click the Insert button

Hot tip

If you move your mouse over one of the images, you'll see some additional file details.

4 The image is brought into the current page. Note that it has eight round "handles", these can be dragged around if you want to manipulate the image

Drag the green handle to rotate the image; any other handle will resize it

Don't forget

Note that the Command Tabs have changed now that we have a picture selected. The Picture Tools Tab is now active – this gives you access to a range of controls for working on your graphic.

5 Sometimes you'll want to cut away unnecessary parts of the picture. Click on the Crop tool and you'll see some heavy black corners and edges. Dragging inwards on these will prepare the image for cropping

Hot tip

In the Crop Tool's popup menu there are also options to "Crop to Shape", and many preset shapes to choose from.

6 When you're happy with your adjustments, click on the Crop tool again and choose Crop, to apply the changes. If you change your mind later simply reselect Crop and drag the black handles outward again

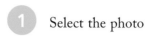

...cont'd

Remove Background

If your photo has a prominent main object which is easily distinguishable from its background, then you can get help from Word to remove the background automatically.

1. Select the photo

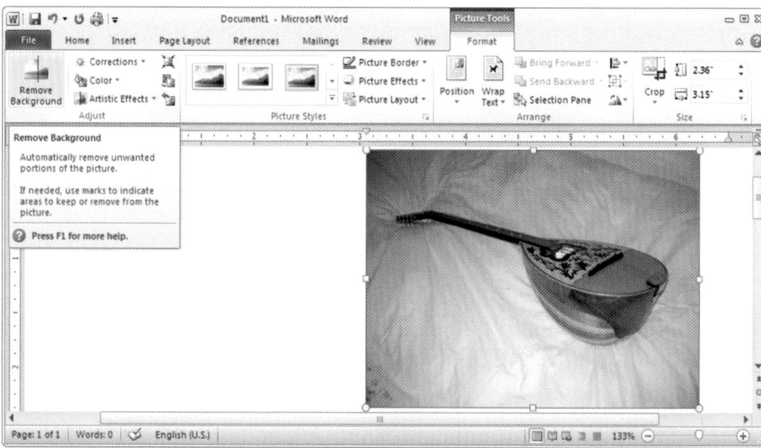

2. Click the Remove Background Tool

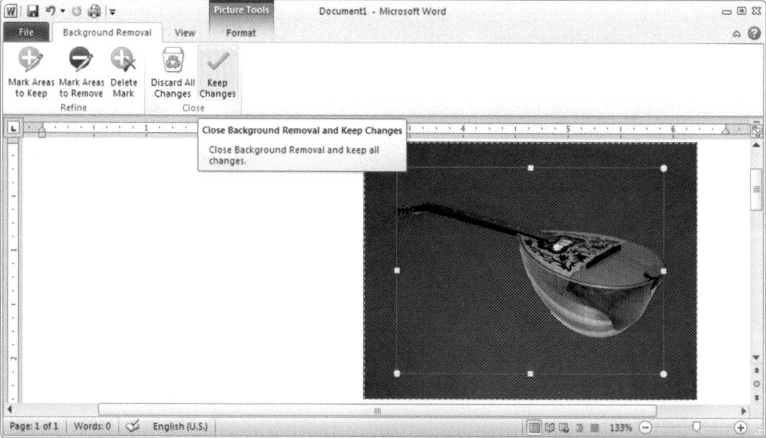

3. The magenta colored area indicates Word's guess at what the background is. If it hasn't got it quite right, then use the "Mark Areas to Keep" and "Mark Areas to Remove" tools to subtract from or add to the magenta area

4. When you're satisfied that the correct area is defined, click the Keep Changes icon, and the background will be then removed

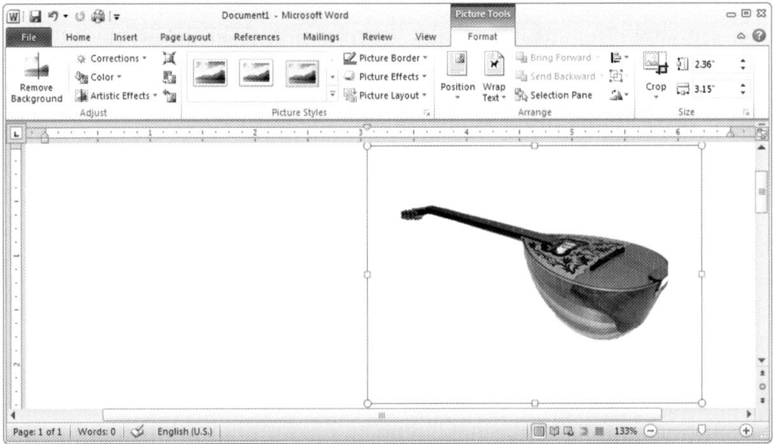

Don't forget

Most of the Tools described here are in the Picture Tools/Format tab. If you select a picture, the tab, although available, may not be currently active. In this case, simply click on the tab title (depicted below) to activate it.

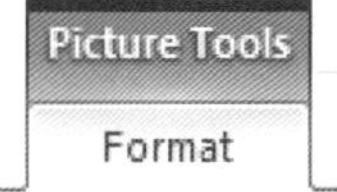

Photo Corrections

Although Word isn't a full-blown photo manipulation package, it does have a respectable range of effects and tools for both creative and corrective work

1. Select the photo and click the Corrections tool

2. The popup menu contains options for sharpening/ softening and for adjusting brightness and contrast. If you hover over an option, you'll see a preview of the effect

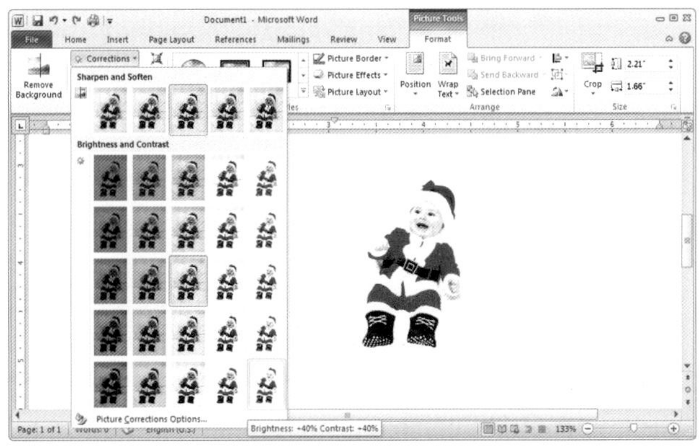

The Adjust Tools

There are some useful tools in the Adjust area of the Picture Tools/Format tab, although three don't have captions

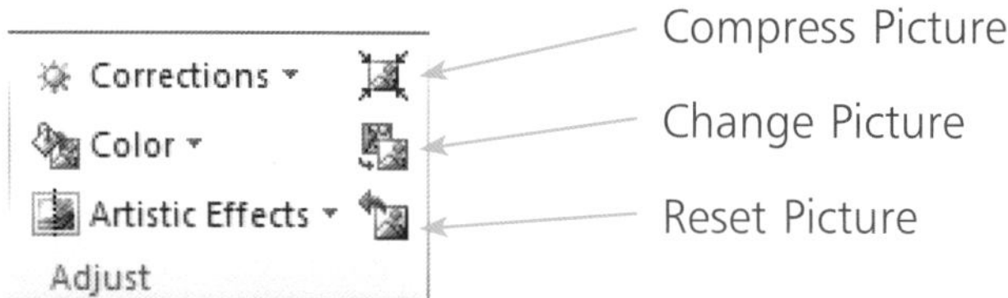

Compress Picture gives you the opportunity to reduce the file size taken up by your image (and also reduce upload and download time, if copying across the web or via email). You can do this by permanently removing cropped out areas, or by changing the detail level (resolution).

Change Picture lets you substitute in a new picture file, whilst preserving the attributes, such as size and crop information.

Reset Picture removes all the formatting, effectively returning the image to how it was when first imported.

Picture Styles

The Picture Styles area lets you easily apply a wide range of visually-interesting effects, such as shadow, glow, reflection, rotation, or a combination of these, in a preset style.

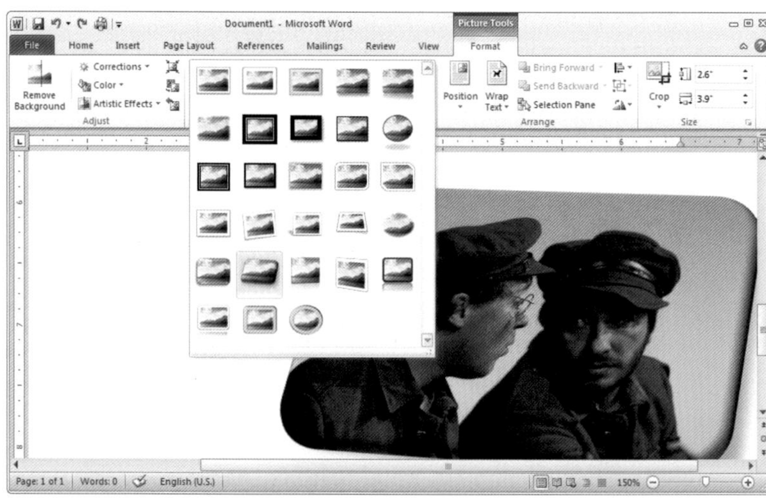

Adding a Draw-Type Picture From a File on Disk

In this example, we'll import and manipulate a draw-type object.

1. Navigate to the appropriate part of your document, then click on Picture, in the Illustrations area of the Insert Tab

2. Once you've found a suitable draw-type graphic, select it and then click the Insert button

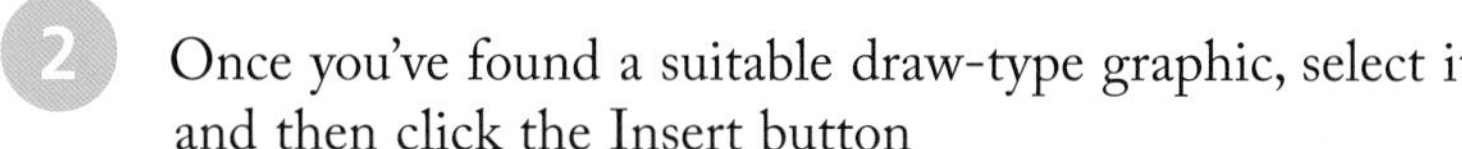

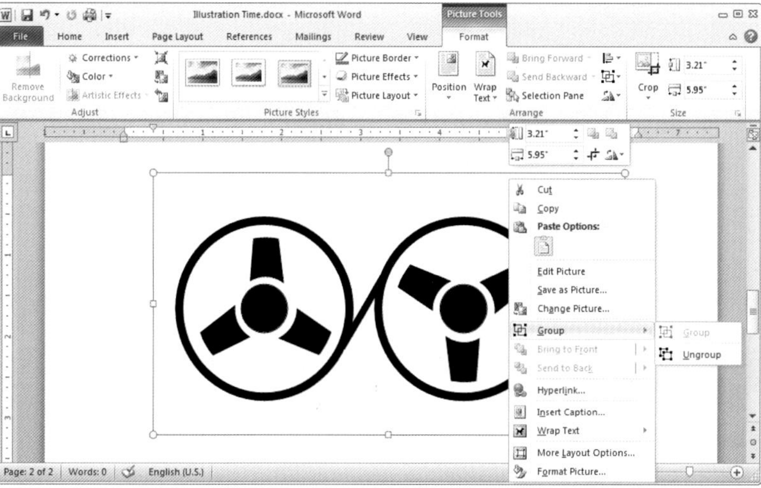

3. If the graphic consists of a number of shapes, then it's usually possible to edit its individual components. To do this, right-click and choose Edit Picture

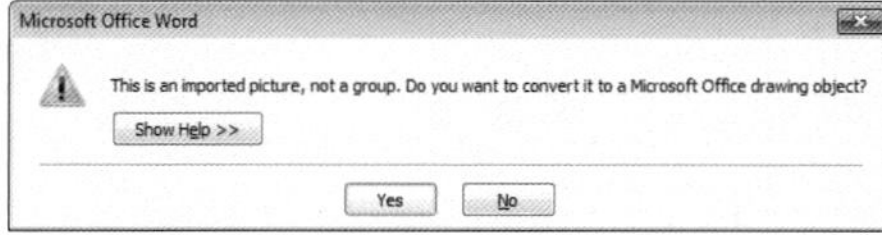

4. If you see the dialog box pictured above, click Yes

5. This will often be sufficient for you to start editing individual elements. Experiment by clicking on different areas of the graphic, to see what you can select. Once an element is selected, it can usually be moved, resized, rotated, or formatted, using color or line styles

Draw-type graphics can generally be edited with no appreciable loss in quality, as they are stored as a set of mathematical objects.

...cont'd

6. Sometimes a draw-type graphic consists of items that are grouped together. If it does, you can break it down further by right-clicking, choosing Grouping and then Ungroup

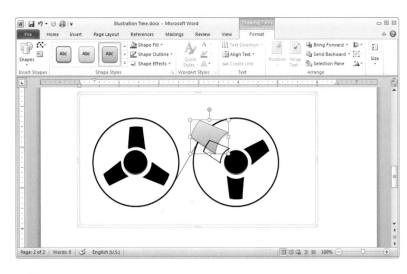

Beware

Paint-type graphics cannot be manipulated in this way. They are represented as a grid of rectangular pixels (picture cells), rather than mathematical objects. This means they cannot be broken down into simpler objects.

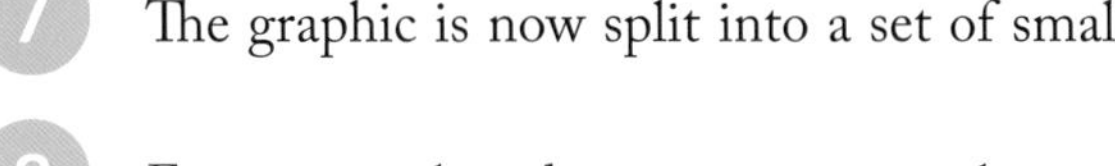

7. The graphic is now split into a set of smaller objects

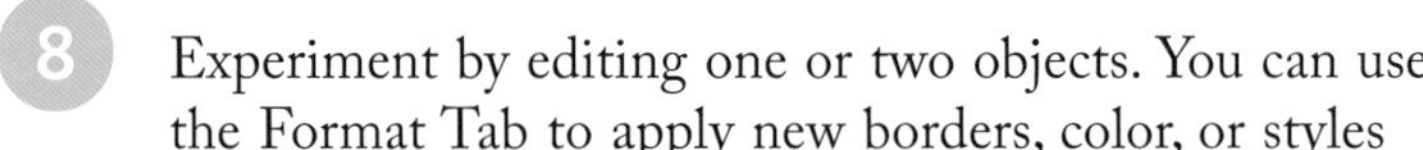

8. Experiment by editing one or two objects. You can use the Format Tab to apply new borders, color, or styles

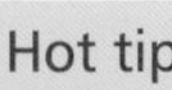

Hot tip

The easiest way to select all the objects within the general graphics frame is to click on one (to establish selection within the frame), then type Ctrl + A for Select All.

9. When you have finished, you might want to select all the small objects, then right-click, choose Grouping and then Regroup. The graphic will behave as a single item once more

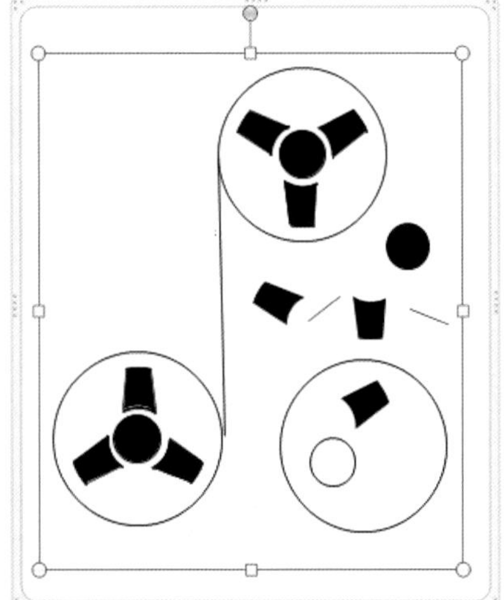

Clip Art

Clip
Art

Clip art refers to collections of standard images available for use in your document. These are usually organized in some way, so you can easily search for a particular symbol or image.

1. Click the Clip Art icon in the Illustrations area of the Insert Tab. A set of Clip Art controls appear at the right-hand edge of the screen

2. Enter some text in the "Search for" area, open the menu next to "Search in" and choose where to search. If the checkbox "Include Office.com content" is selected, then make sure you're connected to the Internet

3. There may be a delay while Word searches the online content (depending on your connection speed). You will then see the matching results in the Clip Art pane

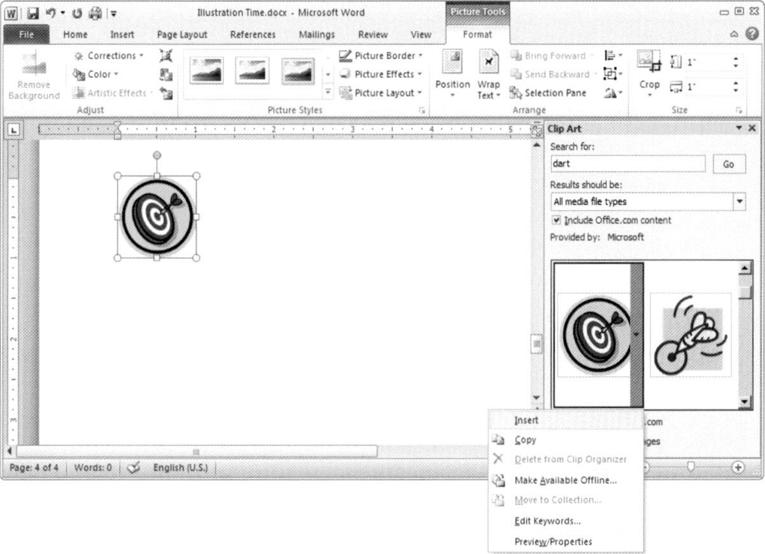

4. Browse through the results. If you can't find anything suitable, then try using different search text. If you find an image you like, click on it and select Insert. It will appear at the current Insertion Point

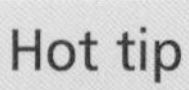

Hot tip

When you click on the image in the Clip Art results list, you also have the option Make Available Offline. This will copy the file to your PC, so you can access it even when you are not connected to the Internet.

Shapes

Word offers a large selection of standard graphic shapes that can be drawn and then customized.

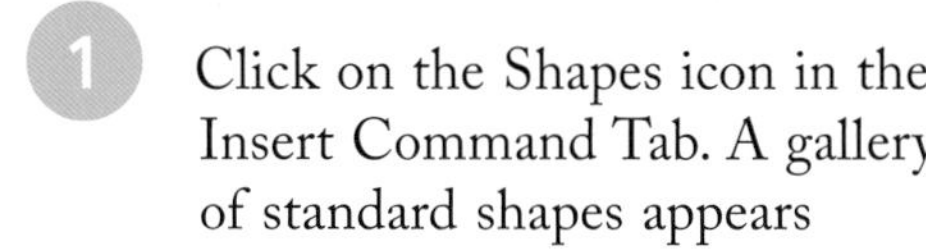

1. Click on the Shapes icon in the Insert Command Tab. A gallery of standard shapes appears

2. Select one of these. This example uses “Down Arrow Callout”

3. Now click and drag diagonally on the page to create the initial shape. Don't worry if it's the wrong size or position, both of these can be changed easily

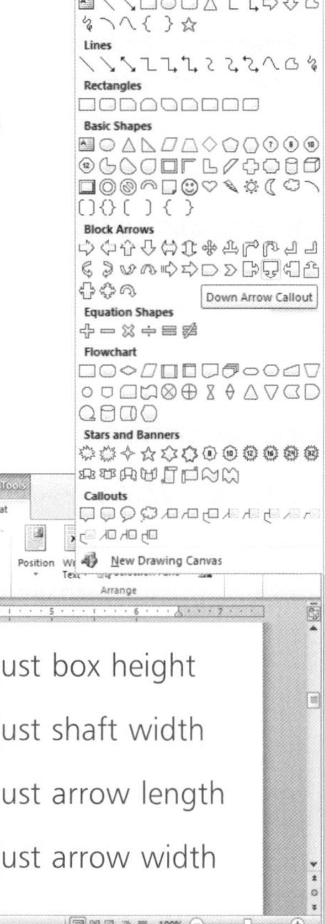

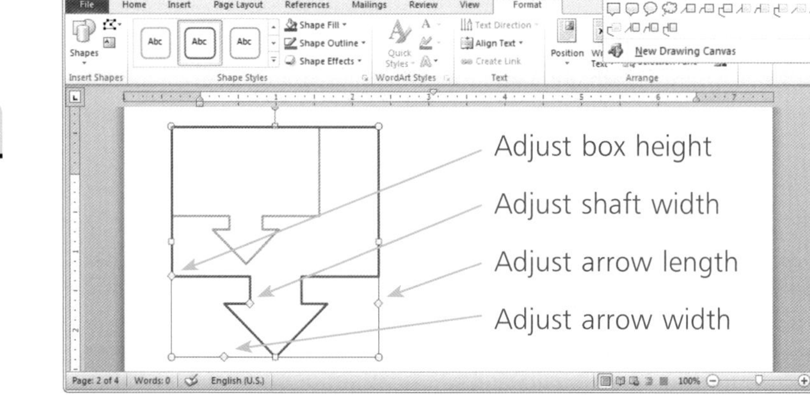

4. You can move the object by dragging directly on it. Drag on a blue square or circular handle to resize it

5. Drag on a yellow diamond-shaped handle to change a single aspect of the shape. Precisely what this changes depends on the shape you drew, so it's worth experimenting to see what you can do in each case. In the above example, the yellow handles let you customize the dimensions of the box and the arrow part individually

Since Shapes are draw-type graphics, you can resize and manipulate them in other ways without any loss in quality.

Right-click on a shape and choose edit points. You'll then be able to change the shape by dragging its vertices. Click and drag along a line to add a new point. Right-click a point to choose between Smooth, Straight, or Corner.

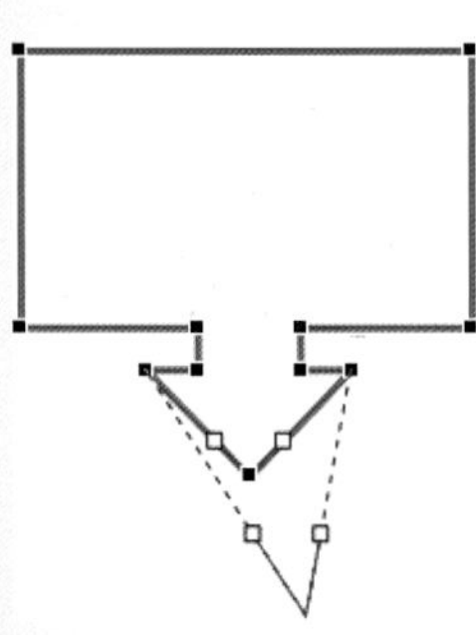

Text Wrap

Text wrap allows you to define how your object interacts with any nearby text. For graphics, the default is usually "In Front of Text", which means you're free to drag it wherever you like. Sometimes, however, it's more useful to treat the object as part of the text – so that, if you edit the text, the graphic moves with it.

1. Select your graphic and click on Wrap Text in the Arrange section of the Format Command Tab. If you select Square, Tight, or "Top and Bottom", then Word will apply a boundary to your object, and nearby text will keep outside that boundary

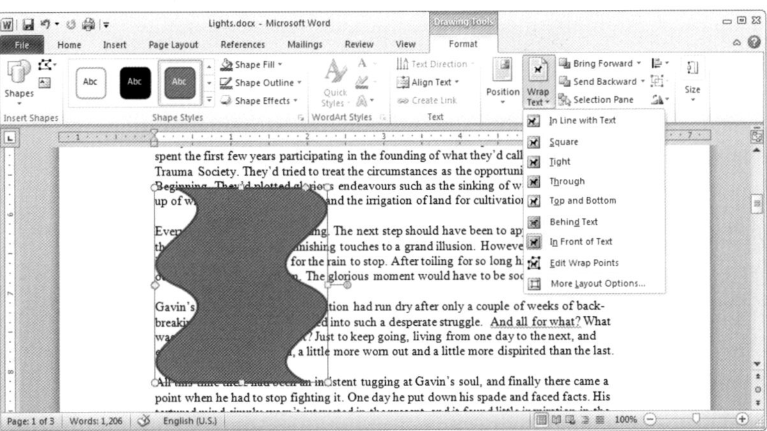

2. Choosing Tight is sometimes all you need for Word to create a Text Wrap, which allows the surrounding text to closely follow the contours of the shape. Sometimes, however, you'll want finer control over things

3. Choose Edit Wrap Points from the same pop-up menu to edit the wrap border. As soon as you do this, you'll be able to see the Text Wrap border defined as straight black lines, connected by small black squares known as "handles"

4. Drag one of these handles to move the boundary line. If there's text nearby, then you'll see it move so that it's always outside the perimeter

Hot tip

If you select a graphic then click on the Position icon, you can choose between a number of preset layouts. This can save you time positioning and applying Text Wrap manually.

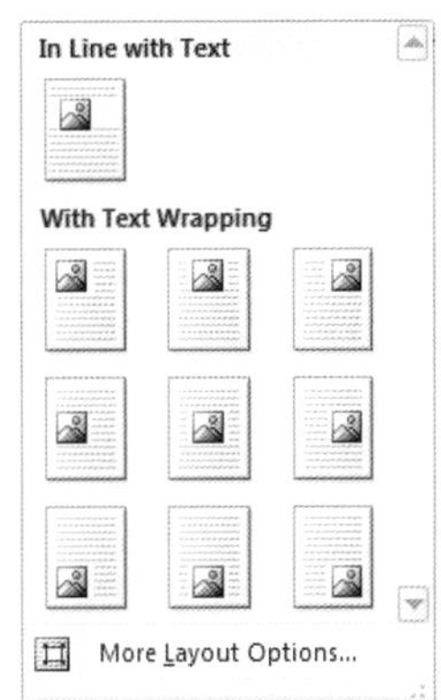

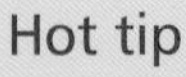

Hot tip

To delete a text wrap handle, hold down the Ctrl key and click directly on the handle.

...cont'd

5. Click and drag on the border, but not on an existing handle, to create a new handle. Using these controls, you can alter the way text flows around any irregular shape

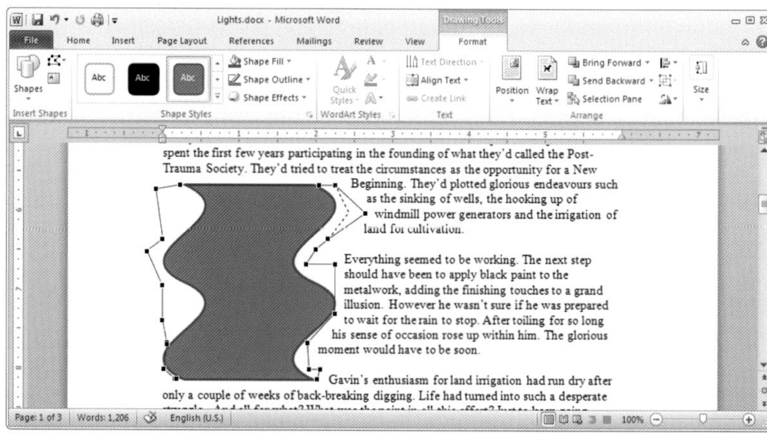

Lights.docx - Microsoft Word
Drawing Tools
File
Home
Insert
Page Layout
References
Mailings
Review
View
Format
Shapes
Insert Shapes
Shape Fill
Shape Outline
Shape Effects
Shape Styles
Quick Styles
WordArt Styles
Text Direction
Align Text
Create Link
Text
Position
Wrap Text
Bring Forward
Send Backward
Selection Pane
Arrange
Size
spent the first few years participating in the founding of what they'd called the Post-Trauma Society. They'd tried to treat the circumstances as the opportunity for a New Beginning. They'd plotted glorious endeavours such as the sinking of wells, the hooking up of windmill power generators and the irrigation of land for cultivation.
Everything seemed to be working. The next step should have been to apply black paint to the metalwork, adding the finishing touches to a grand illusion. However he wasn't sure if he was prepared to wait for the rain to stop. After toiling for so long his sense of occasion rose up within him. The glorious moment would have to be soon.
Gavin's enthusiasm for land irrigation had run dry after only a couple of weeks of back-breaking digging. Life had turned into such a desperate
Page: 1 of 3
Words: 1,206
English (U.S.)
100%

Adding Text Inside a Shape

Most shapes can be used as Text Boxes, and all the normal text formatting options are available within these.

1. If there's currently no text in the shape, then right-click and choose Add Text

2. Enter the text (or paste if you've got the text in the Clipboard)

3. Format using the Mini Toolbar or the other tools

4. You can still apply effects to the shape itself. If you rotate, for example, the text will rotate as well (when you edit the text it will temporarily switch back to horizontal, so you can see what you are trying to change)

Calibri (E
16
This way down..
do not hesitate

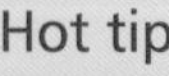

Hot tip

The Arrange Tools on the right of the Format Tab can be used to align objects, and move them in front of or behind other objects.

SmartArt

SmartArt graphic items allow you to present concepts and information in a visual way.

1. Click on the SmartArt icon in the Insert Tab. The following dialog appears. Choose an item and click OK

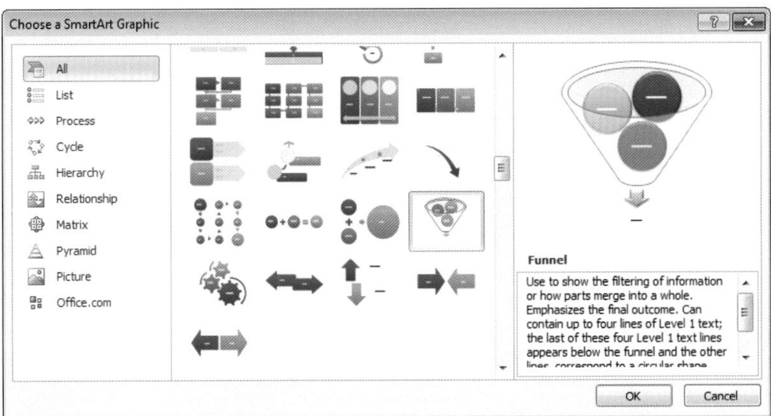

2. Enter your text in the window on the left, and it will appear in the diagram. If you right-click anywhere within the object, you can choose to add a caption

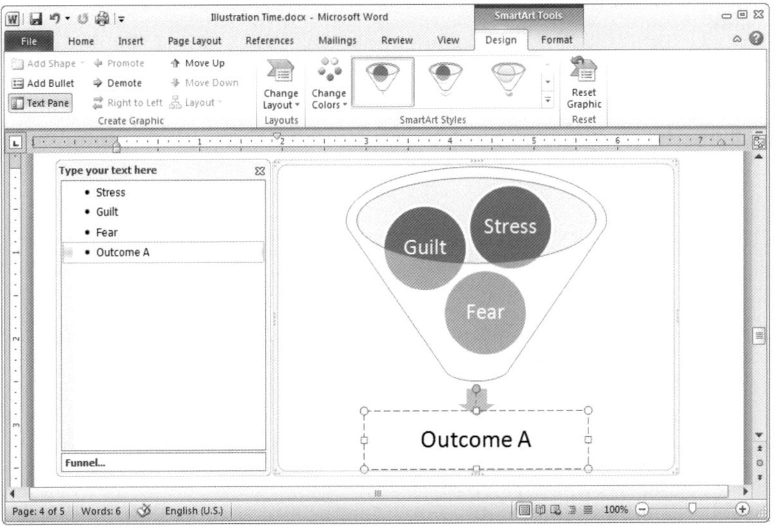

3. You can customize parts of the object if you click on them

Hot tip

You can radically change your design at any time, by changing the selection from the Layouts and SmartArt Styles in the Design tab.

...cont'd

The SmartArt Tools

Whenever SmartArts objects are selected, the SmartArt Tools appear, divided into two tabs: Design and Format.

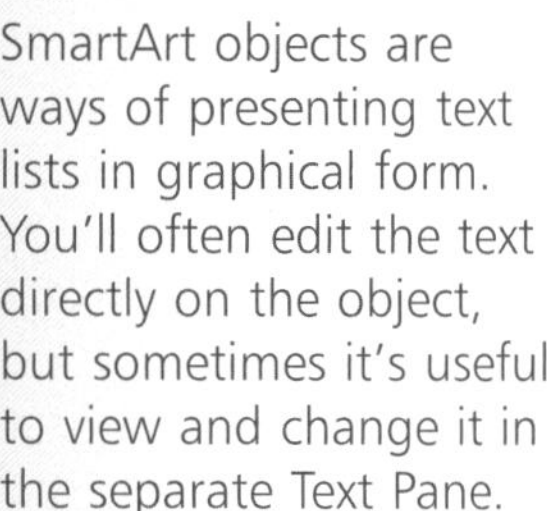

Don't forget

SmartArt objects are ways of presenting text lists in graphical form. You'll often edit the text directly on the object, but sometimes it's useful to view and change it in the separate Text Pane.

1. In the Design tab, click the Text Pane icon to activate it. Now you can edit the text content, which may be structured as a multilevel list, as in the example below

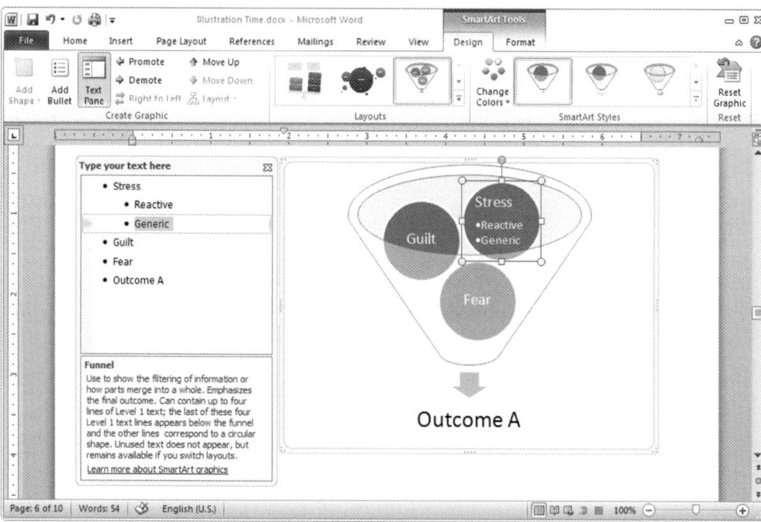

2. With the Format tab, apply styles to parts of the object

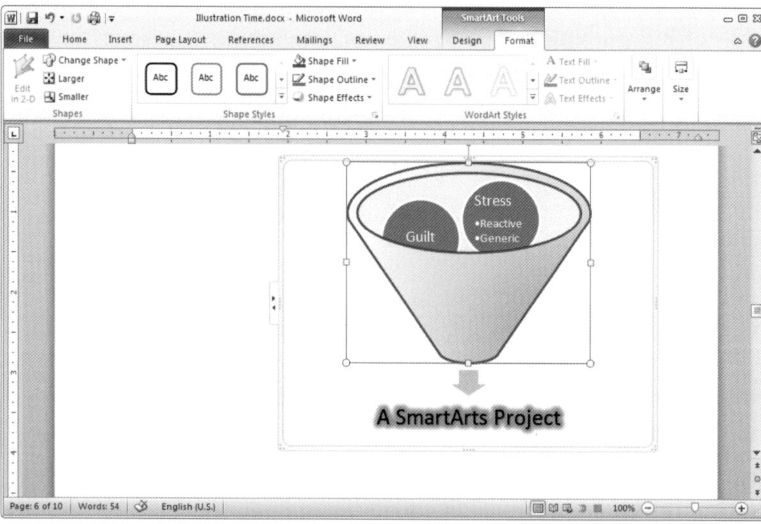

Charts

If you've used Microsoft Excel, you may be familiar with the concept of presenting tables of figures in chart form.

1. Click on the Chart icon in the Insert Tab. The following dialog appears, with a large selection of chart variants:

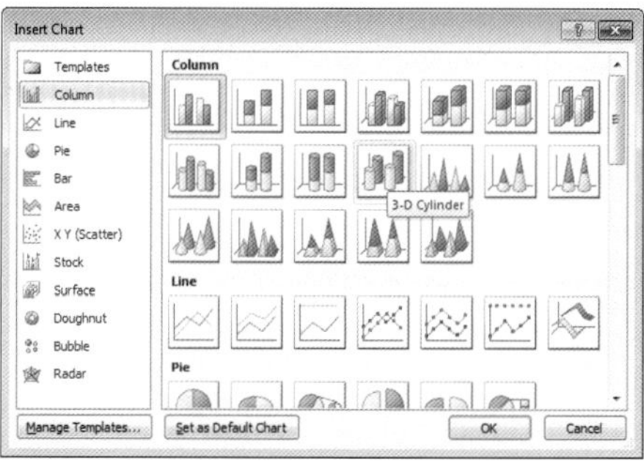

2. Choose a chart type and click OK

Beware

If Microsoft Excel isn't installed on your PC, then clicking on the interface will be slightly different. However, you'll still be able to change chart types and edit the underlying data.

3. A default chart appears. You can select and customize this using the Chart Tools Tab, which appears automatically

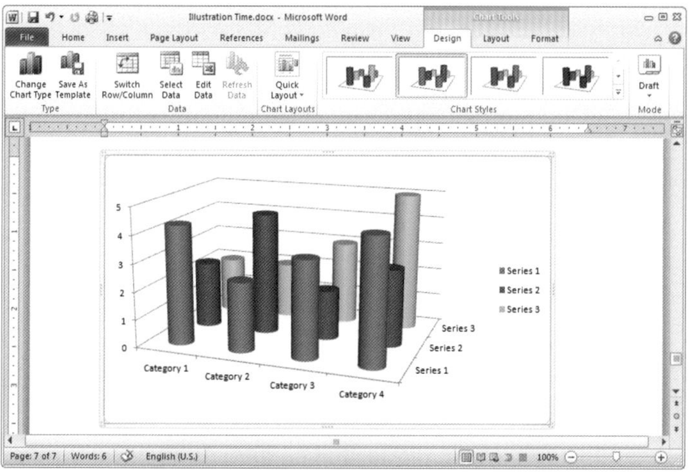

A separate Excel window opens, displaying sample chart data. You'll want to edit this to use your own data.

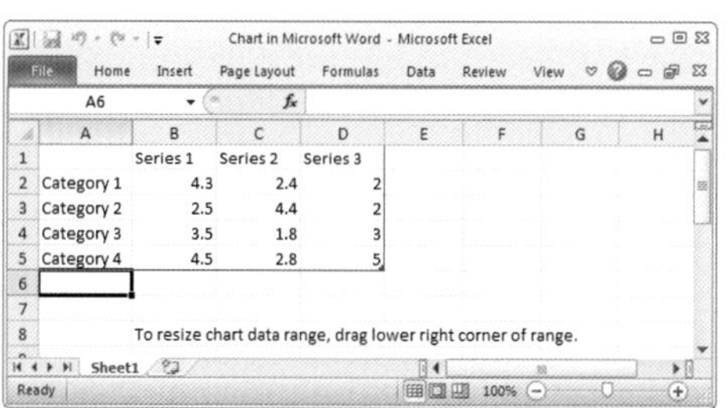

Don't forget

If you don't like the chart type you selected, it's easy to go back and select another, so enjoy the freedom to experiment.

Screenshots

Many technical and training documents make use of screen shots, which are images taken directly from the computer screen, perhaps demonstrating a particular task within a program. Some people use the Prt Sc key, which places an image of the entire current screen in the Clipboard (Alt+Prt Sc snapshots just the currently selected window). Since this functionality is rather limited, others might use special utility software. Now there's support for doing this directly within Word.

1. Click on the Screenshot icon in the Insert Tab. The popup will show you the thumbnails of the current windows – either choose one of these or select Screen Clipping

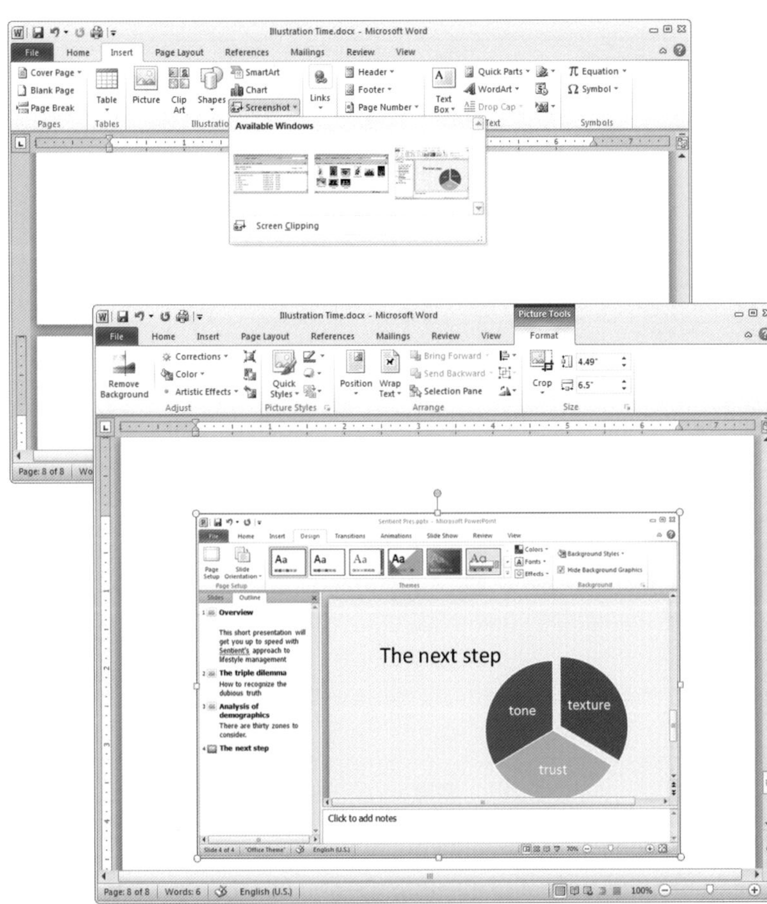

2. The screenshot is inserted into your document as a picture

Hot tip

If you choose Screen Clipping, then you'll be able to click and drag it to define a rectangular area to crop within a window.

The Page Layout Tab

This chapter looks at features that help you work on the design and organization of longer documents.

Themes

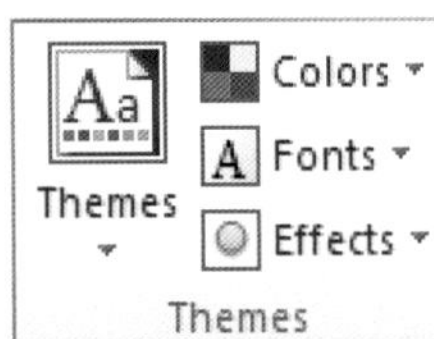

Themes can control your overall document design, by defining its main colors, fonts and effects. If you use a Theme's colors, for example, then changing Themes will change these automatically.

Selecting a Theme

1. Make the Page Layout Command Tab active

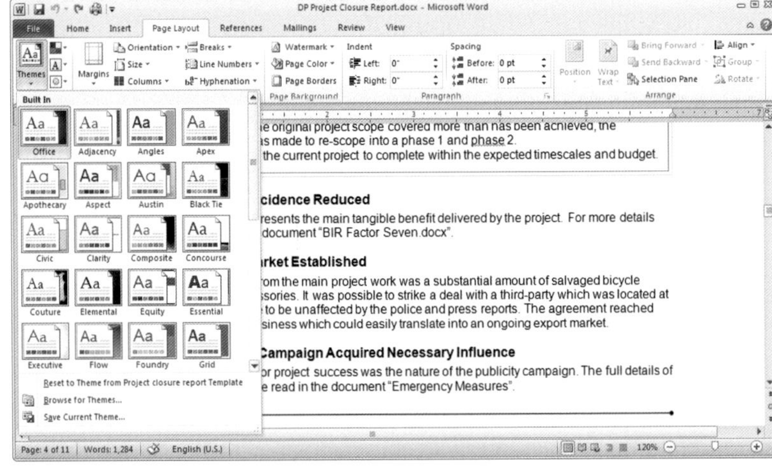

2. Click the Themes button and browse through the Themes in the Gallery. As you hover over a Theme, your document will preview its settings. Click once to set the Theme

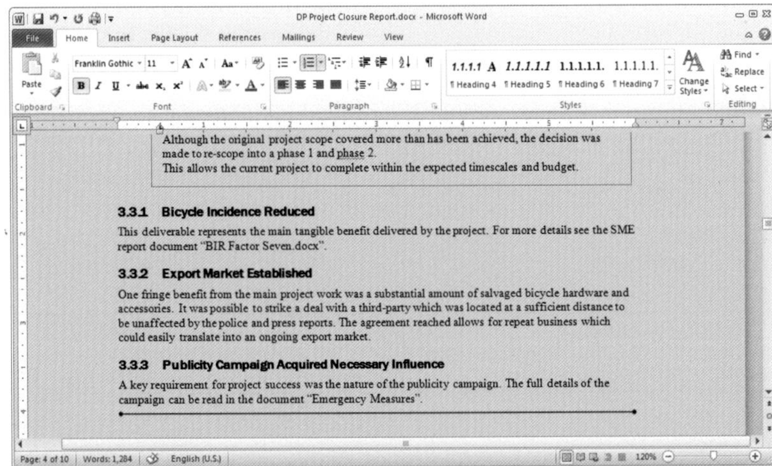

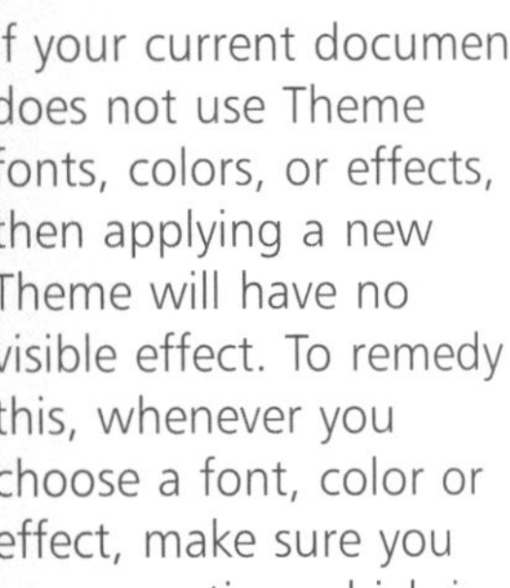

Beware

If your current document does not use Theme fonts, colors, or effects, then applying a new Theme will have no visible effect. To remedy this, whenever you choose a font, color or effect, make sure you use an option which is listed under Themes.

Using a Theme's Colors

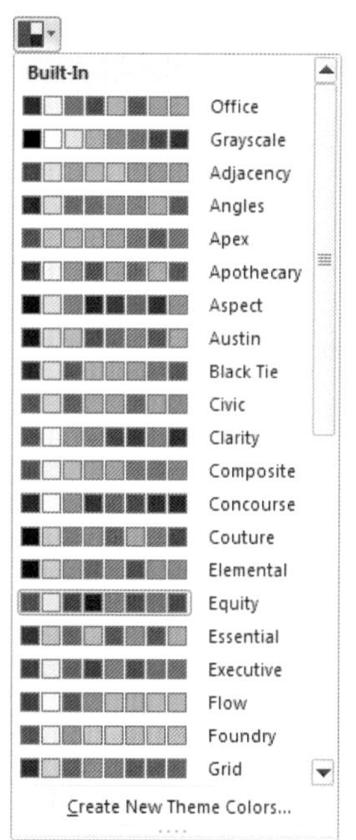

1. To just change the colors that belong to the Theme, click on the Theme Colors icon in the Themes area. A gallery of color swatches appears

2. Choose a different option. If your document used Theme colors, then these will be changed automatically

3. From now on, whenever you select a color, you will be able to choose one from the Theme's current selection

Using a Theme's Effects

1. You can also change a Theme's effects independently of its fonts and colors. To do this, click on the Effects button in the Themes area and select a different option

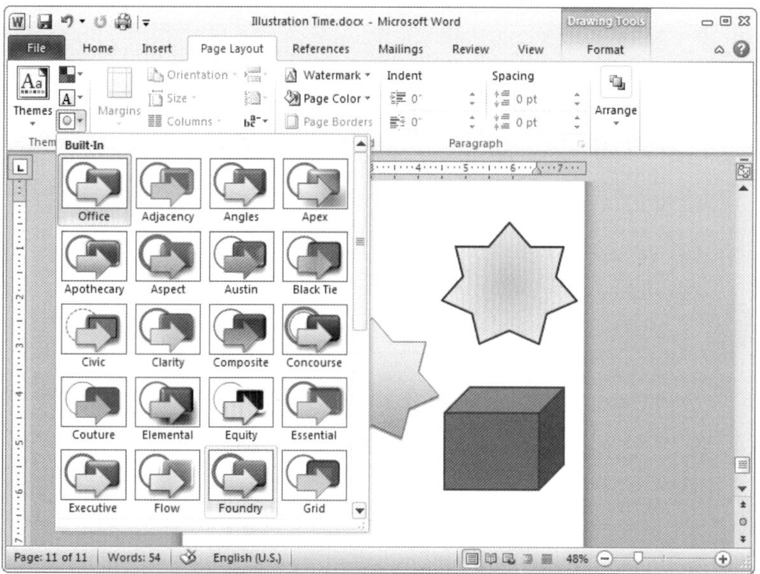

...cont'd

Using a Theme's Fonts

1. Click on the Fonts icon in the Themes area. A gallery of fonts appears. Each theme contains one font defined for headings, and a second for main body text

2. Choose a different option. If your document used Theme fonts, then these will be changed automatically

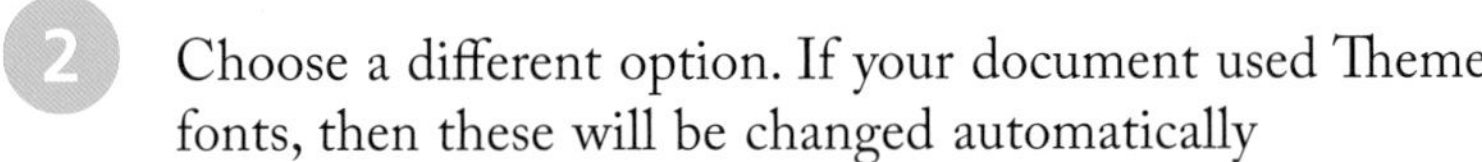

Hot tip

As you hover over an option, any text currently using Theme fonts will preview the new settings.

3. Now switch back to the Home Command Tab and open the Fonts menu. At the top you will see the two Theme fonts. If you use these, you can easily switch Themes later – your text will change accordingly

4. It's a very good idea to make sure your text Styles are defined using Theme fonts – if your document uses those Styles throughout, then it's very easy to experiment with different designs

Page Setup

This area contains controls for margins, size and orientation, as well as line numbering, adding breaks, and adjusting hyphenation.

Margins

1. Click on the Margins icon to choose from the gallery, or click Custom Margins to define these via a dialog box

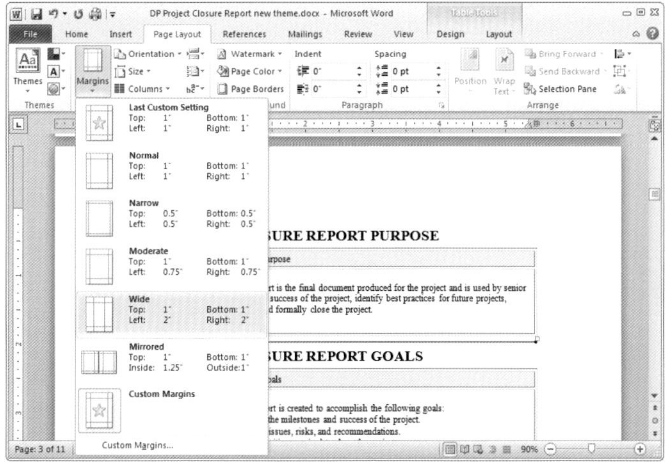

Columns

1. By default your text is set out in a single column spread across the page. To change to a multi-column layout, click the Columns icon and choose the number you want. Your text will be reformatted in the new layout

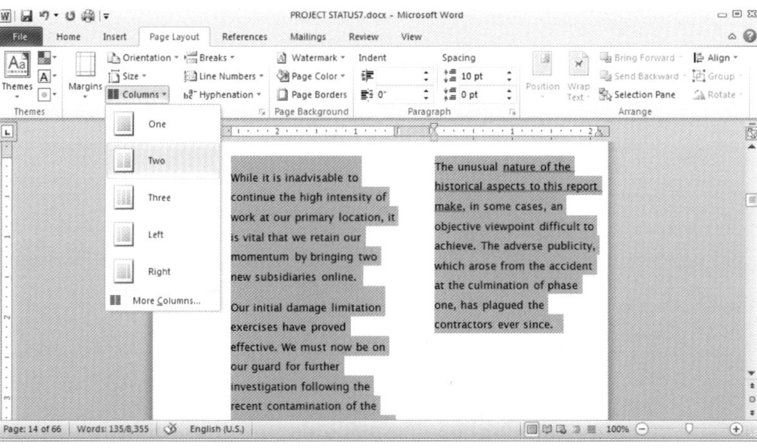

Breaks

Different Types of Break

In Chapter Two "The Home Tab", we saw how to add a simple page break. The Page Layout Tab also has a tool for this, but it's much more powerful.

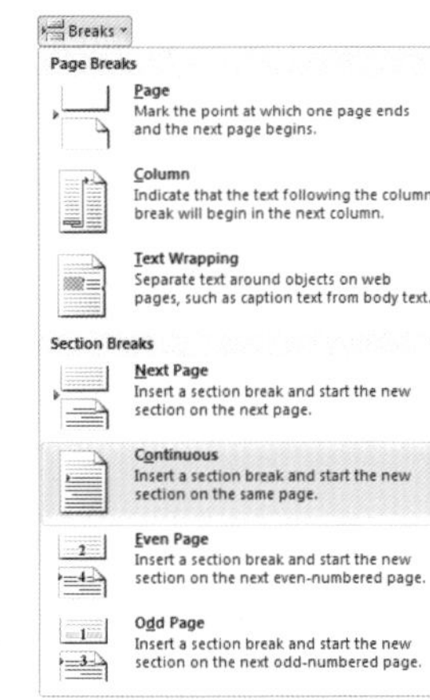

Breaks
Page Breaks
Page
Mark the point at which one page ends and the next page begins.
Column
Indicate that the text following the column break will begin in the next column.
Text Wrapping
Separate text around objects on web pages, such as caption text from body text.
Section Breaks
Next Page
Insert a section break and start the new section on the next page.
Continuous
Insert a section break and start the new section on the same page.
Even Page
Insert a section break and start the new section on the next even-numbered page.
Odd Page
Insert a section break and start the new section on the next odd-numbered page.

Don't forget

The quickest way to add a simple page break is to type Ctrl+Return.

1. Position your Insertion Point, then click the Breaks tool

2. As you can see, there's a number of different options. In this example, we'll create a Section break – choose the Continuous type

3. At first glance, nothing seems to change. However, if you click on the ¶ tool in the Home Tab you'll see the break

4. Now click in the text after the break and change the number of columns. Note that this just affects the current section, i.e. the text after the break

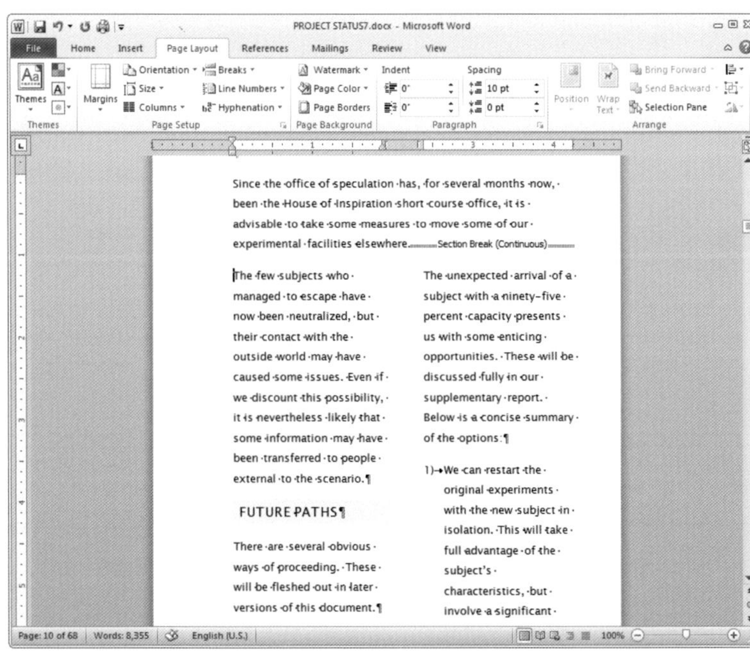

PROJECT STATUS7.docx - Microsoft Word
File
Home
Insert
Page Layout
References
Mailings
Review
View
Since the office of speculation has, for several months now, been the House of Inspiration short course office, it is advisable to take some measures to move some of our experimental facilities elsewhere.
Section Break (Continuous)
The few subjects who managed to escape have now been neutralized, but their contact with the outside world may have caused some issues. Even if we discount this possibility, it is nevertheless likely that some information may have been transferred to people external to the scenario.¶
FUTURE PATHS¶
There are several obvious ways of proceeding. These will be fleshed out in later versions of this document.¶
The unexpected arrival of a subject with a ninety-five percent capacity presents us with some enticing opportunities. These will be discussed fully in our supplementary report. Below is a concise summary of the options:¶
1) We can restart the original experiments with the new subject in isolation. This will take full advantage of the subject's characteristics, but involve a significant
Page: 10 of 68
Words: 8,355
English (U.S.)

Sections

Dividing a Document Into Sections

It's useful to divide your document into Sections using the Next Page Section Break, so that the next Section starts on a new page. This helps organise your work, and different Sections can have their own page numbering, plus different headers and footers.

1. Divide your document into Sections. On the first page after a Section Break, double-click anywhere within the Footer to see the Header and Footer Tools

2. Click the Link To Previous icon to deactivate it. You can now set a different Footer for this Section

3. If you have an automatic page number, then right-click on it and choose Format Page Numbers

4. Change the Page Numbering option to restart at page 1

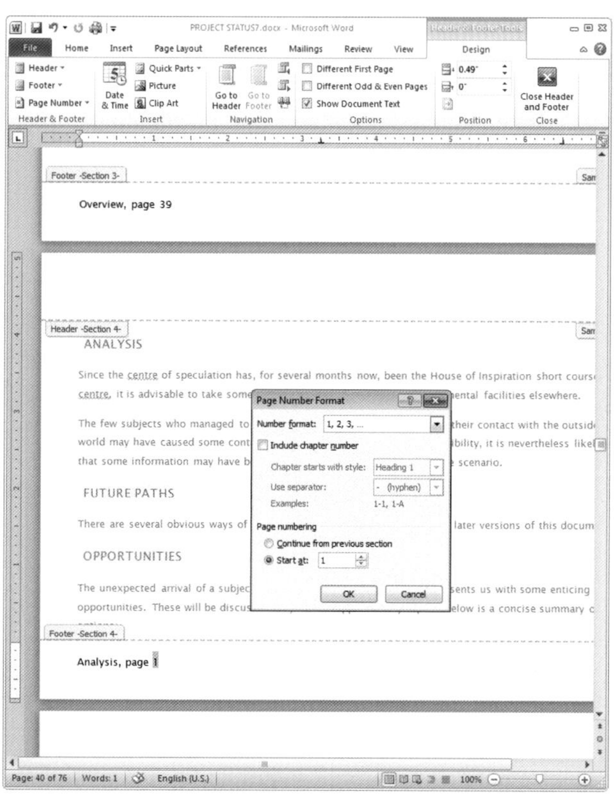

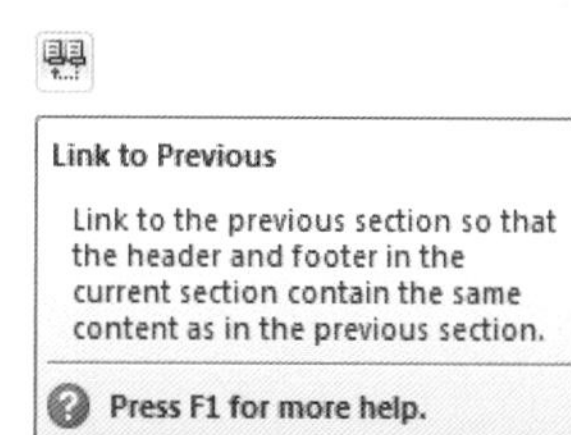

Link to Previous
Link to the previous section so that the header and footer in the current section contain the same content as in the previous section.
Press F1 for more help.

Hot tip

It's worth spending some time customizing each Section. In this example, the Footer text in the new Section has been changed. Note that the previous Footer is "Overview, page 39", while the current one is "Analysis, page 1".

Line Numbers

You can add line numbers to your whole document, or just to sections, and you can also switch it off for individual paragraphs.

1. Either select your whole document, or just click within a section, depending on where you'd like line numbering

2. Click on Line Numbers and select an option

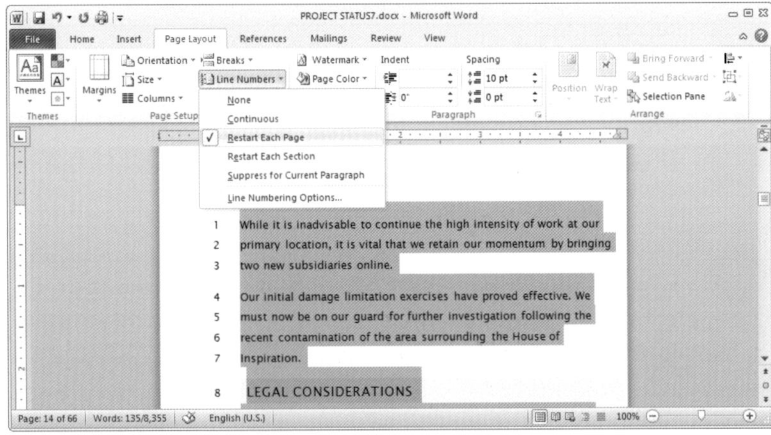

The Page Setup Dialog

1. Click on the small ▾ icon in the lower right corner of the Page Setup tools area

2. This dialog contains controls for adjusting the margins and page orientation, as well as advanced settings for setting multiple pages per printed sheet

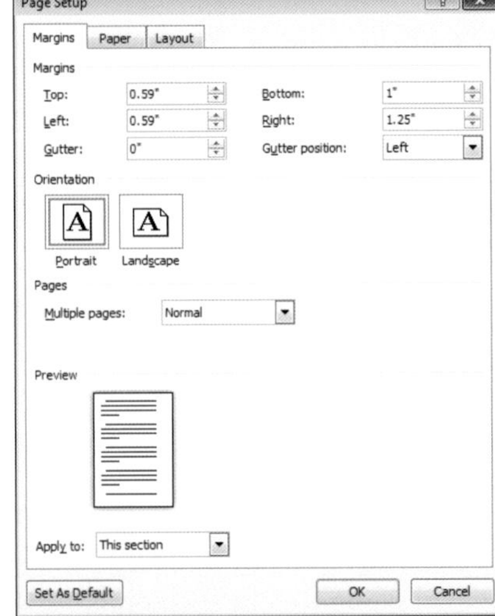

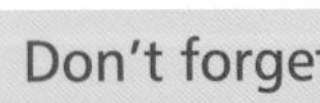

Don't forget

If your screen doesn't match this illustration, then make sure the Margins tab within the dialog is active.

3. Click the Paper tab to define the size and printing options

4. The Layout tab lets you make settings for either the whole document or individual sections. You can also access line numbering and border options

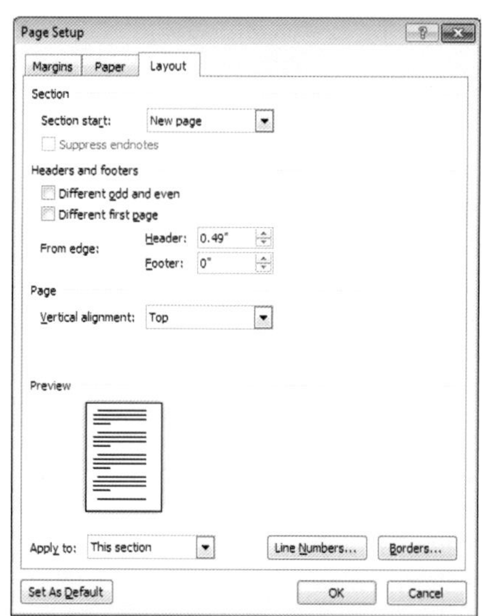

Hyphenation

Word can automatically hyphenate your text for you. This can allow more text to fit on the page – particularly if you're working in narrow columns. You can also choose manual hyphenation, where Word will prompt you for each potential instance.

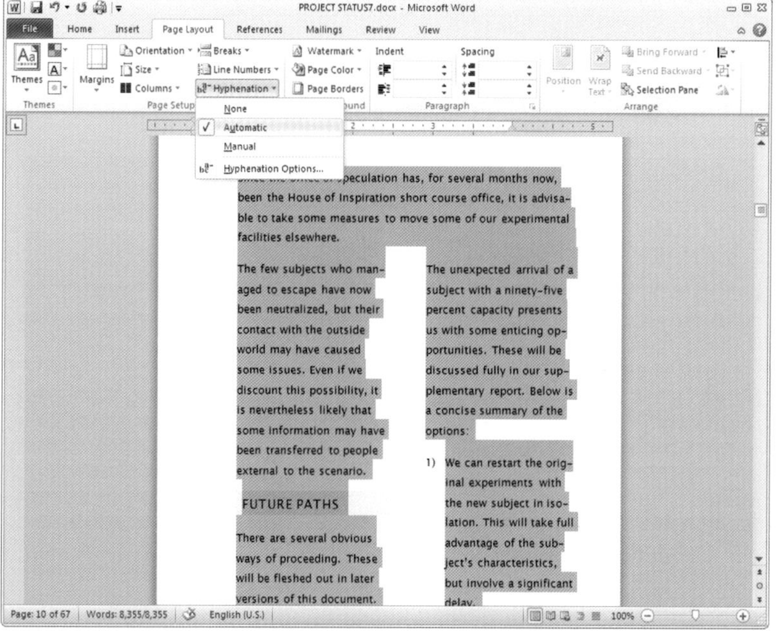

Hot tip

Click the Hyphenation tool and choose Hyphenation Options... to see the following dialog. This gives you finer control over exactly how much hyphenation takes place.

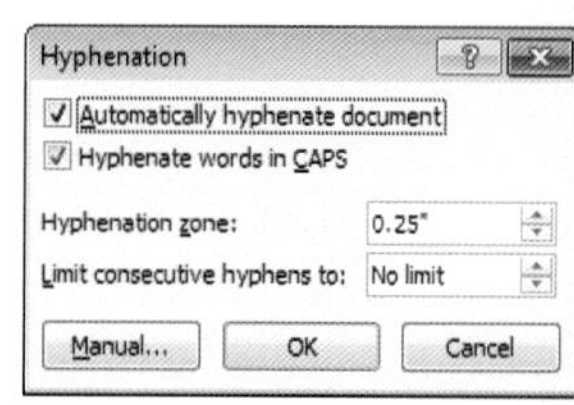

Page Background

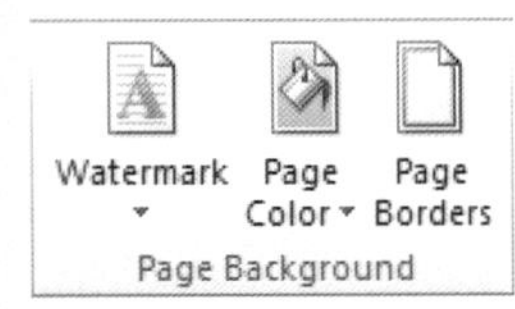

This contains controls for Watermarks, Page Color, and Borders.

Watermark

1. Click on the Watermark icon and either choose one of the preset designs or click on Custom Watermark...

2. From this dialog, you can either use your own text or a graphic. For text, click on the option "Text watermark", for a graphic, click on "Picture watermark" and locate the appropriate file

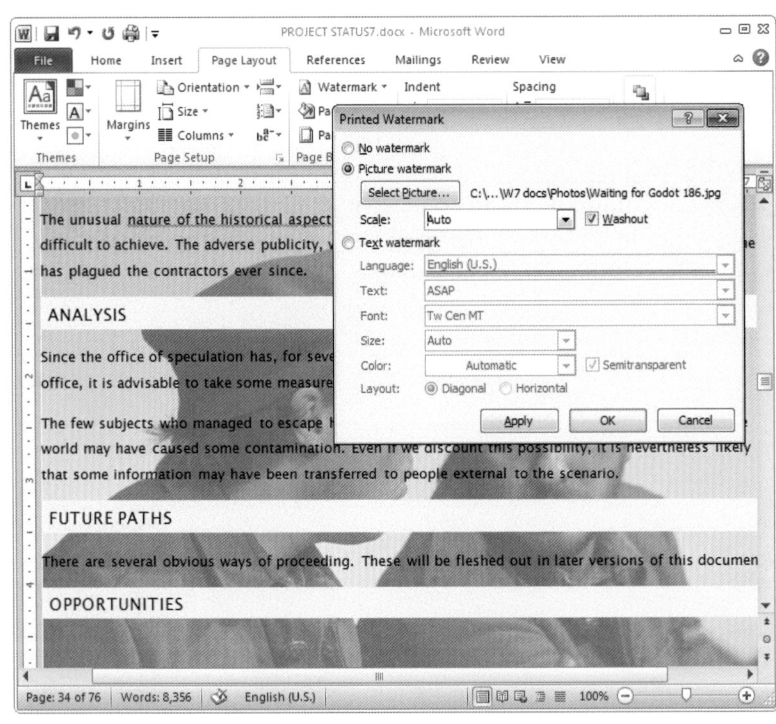

3. Choose a scale – Auto is probably best if you want to fill the entire page

4. It's usually a good idea to select Washout. This lightens the image considerably, which means that the page's text and other elements will still be easy to read

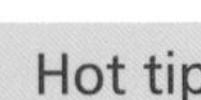

Hot tip

To delete the Watermark, click on the Watermark icon and select Remove Watermark.

Page Color

1. Click on the Page Color icon and choose a color from the range of defined Theme Colors

2. For a more interesting effect, click the Page Color icon and choose Fill Effects...

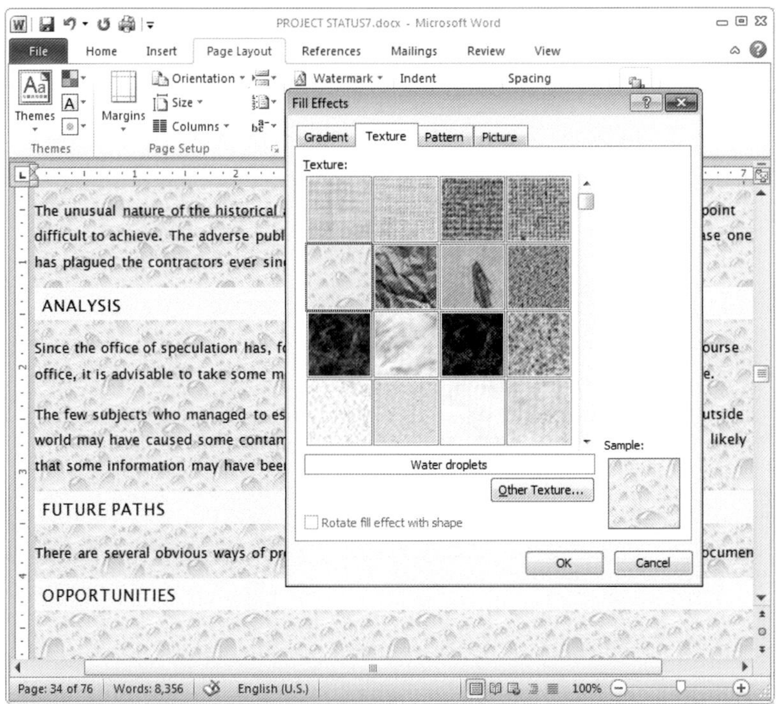

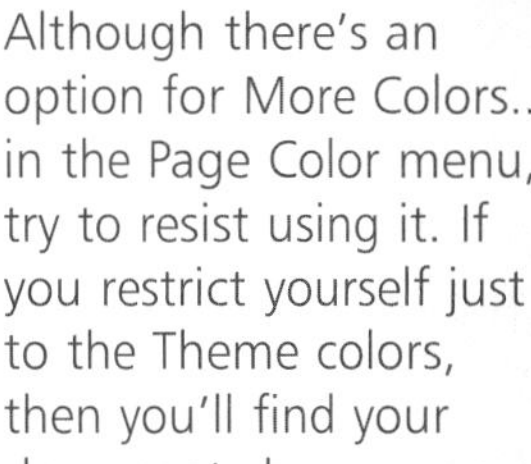

Although there's an option for More Colors... in the Page Color menu, try to resist using it. If you restrict yourself just to the Theme colors, then you'll find your documents have a more consistent design feel.

3. From this dialog, you can choose a gradient (where one color slowly changes into another), a texture, a pattern, or even a picture, from a file on disk

4. In this example, the "Water droplets" texture was chosen. A texture is a small image that is repeated across and down to fill the page. A well-designed texture will join or "tile" seamlessly, so that it's impossible to see exactly where one tile begins and another ends. If you're able to design your own texture (perhaps in a dedicated graphics program) then click Other Texture and locate its file

...cont'd

Page Borders

Word gives you a range of options for adding borders to the edges of your page.

1. Click on the Page Borders icon

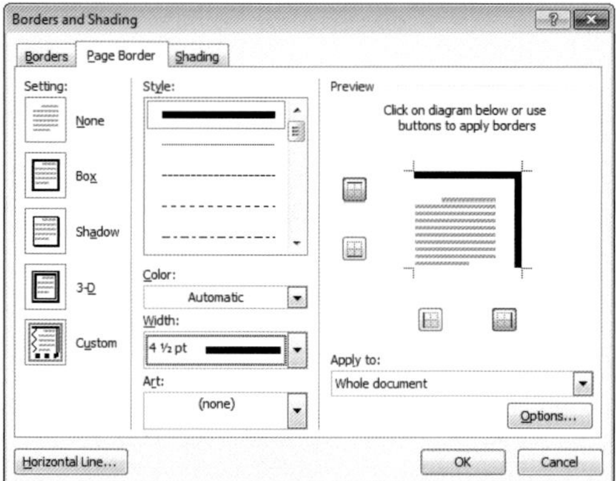

2. Choose your setting and experiment with the line style, color, and width. The Art popup lets you select from a range of graphic designs. As you work, the Preview section on the right will give you some visual feedback

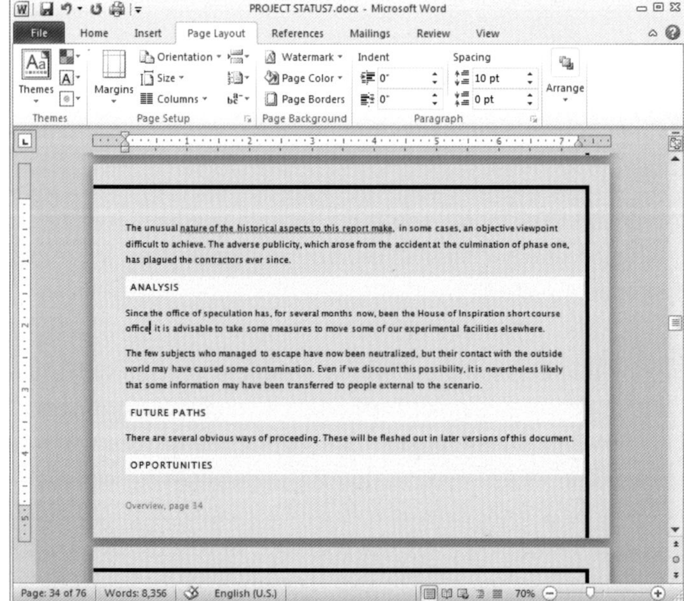

Hot tip

The Page Layout Tab also reproduces two sets of tools, which we've already seen in other Tabs. These are the Paragraph tools (which are also in the Home Tab) and the Arrange tools (also in the Format Tab, which appears when you select a chart or graphic element).

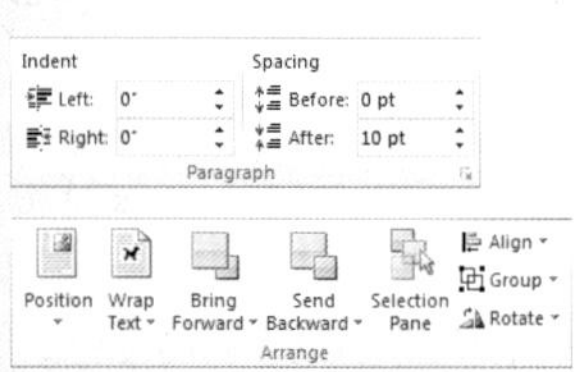

6 The References Tab

The References Tab helps you work with longer, more formal documents. You will see how to add an index, a table of contents, footnotes, captions, and a bibliography.

Table of Contents

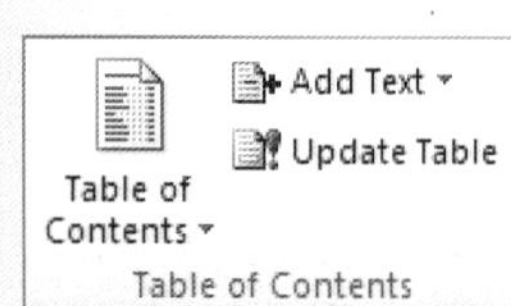

You can automatically create a Table of Contents by asking Word to look for instances of particular styles, or by using entries that you created manually.

Creating a Table of Contents

1. Open a suitably long document that uses a structure of style headings. Make sure the References Command Tab is active, so you can see the Table of Contents controls area on the left

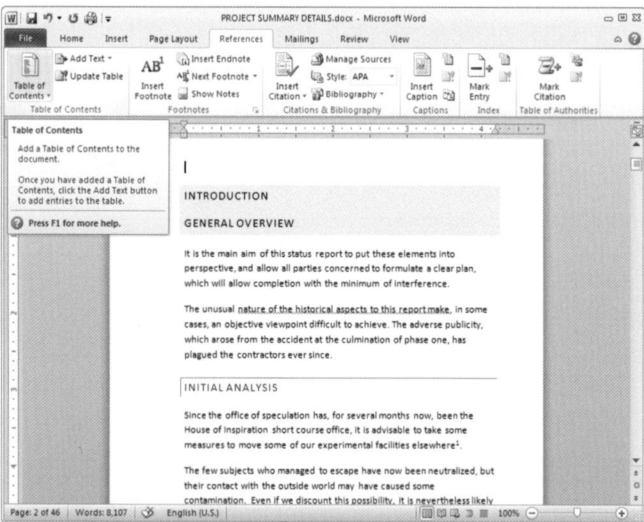

2. Click the "Table of Contents" tool and choose one of the preset styles

3. Word looks through your document and uses the headings to generate the Table of Contents. It calculates the correct page number reference, and adds it to each entry

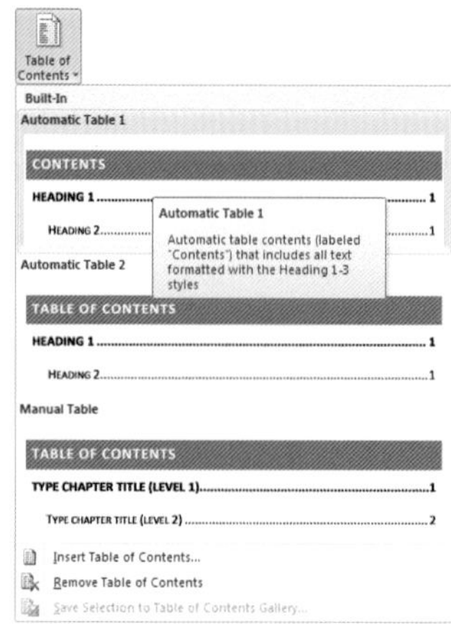

4 The entries in the Table of Contents behave like hyperlinks: Ctrl+Click on any of these to jump straight to the relevant page

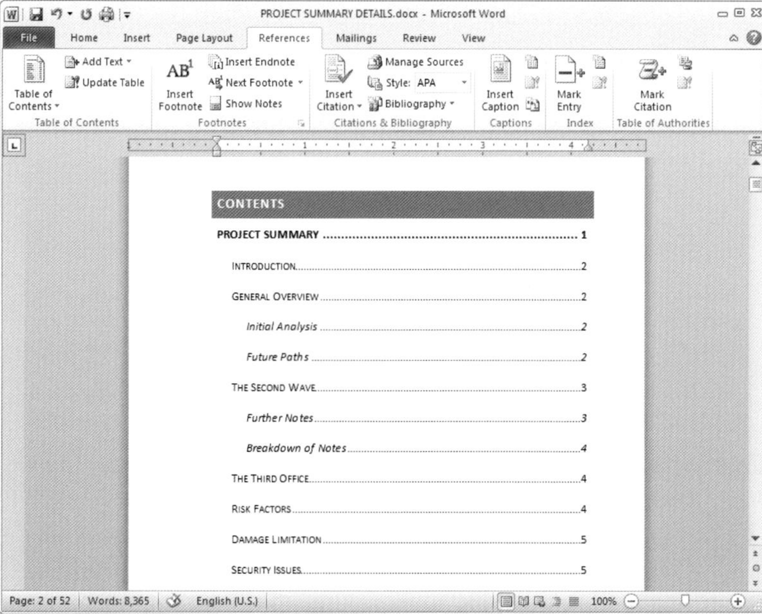

Manually Adding or Removing Items

1 Select some text that is not already in the Table of Contents, then click the Add Text button and choose a Level number

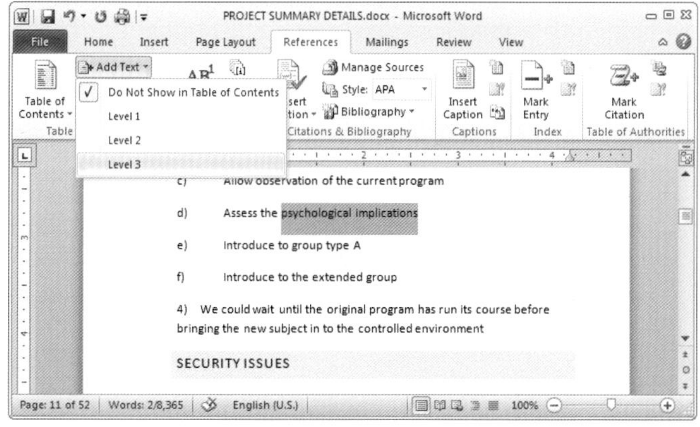

Hot tip

If you are using Web view, then the Table of Contents will be displayed using hyperlinks rather than page numbers.

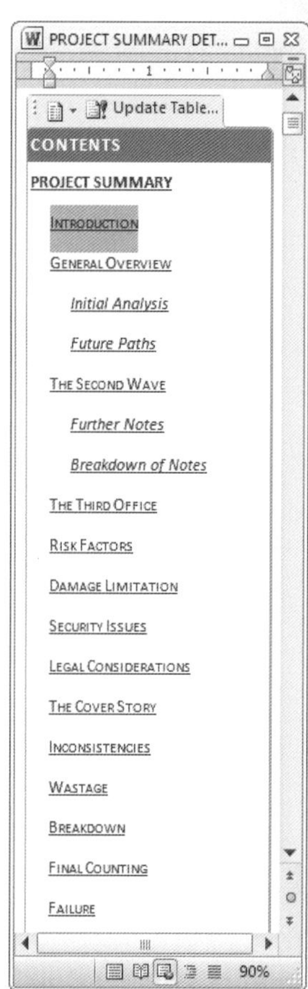

...cont'd

2. To remove an item, select some text that is already in the Table of Contents, then click the Add Text button and select "Do Not Show in Table of Contents"

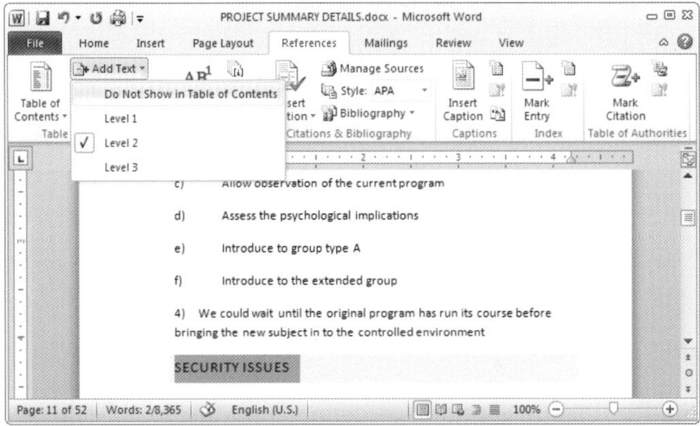

Hot tip

You can check whether a piece of text is currently included in the Table of Contents at any time. To do this, select the text, then click the Add Text tool to see if it's currently assigned to any particular level.

Customizing Your Table of Contents

1. Select a line in the Table of Contents and use the Styles Inspector to view its Style. If you redefine this Style, you automatically change all the entries of the same level

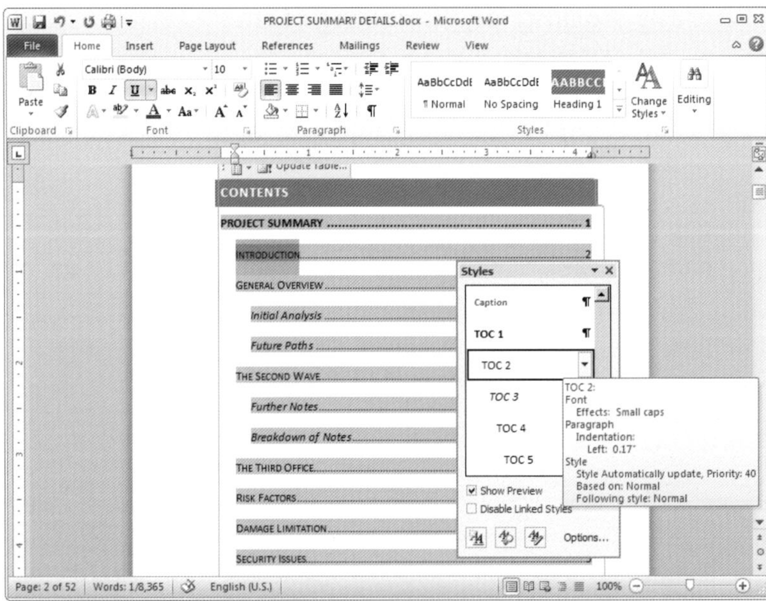

Updating Your Table of Contents

1. As you continue to work with your document, text may move to different pages, pages may be inserted or deleted, and new headings may be added

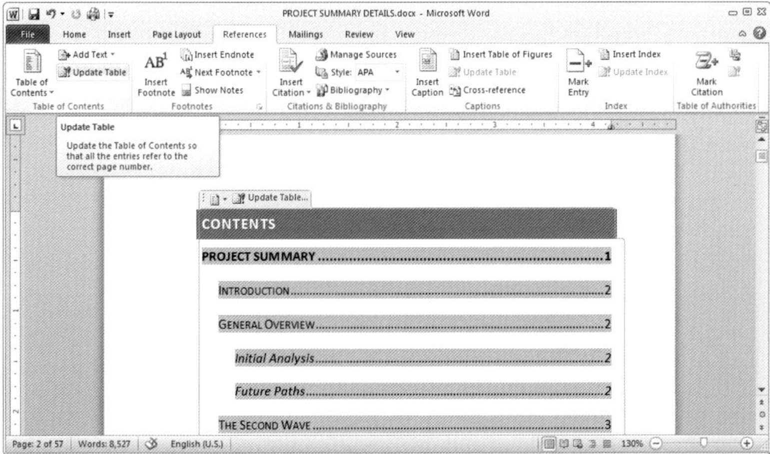

2. Click Update Table to rebuild the Table of Contents. You'll be given the choice of updating the entire table, or just the page numbers of the existing entries

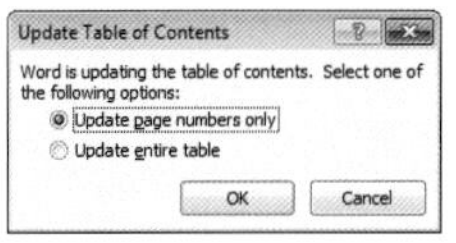

Manually Defining Your Table of Contents

When you click the "Table of Contents" tool to create the Table of Contents, as well as the predefined styles, there's an option "Insert Table of Contents". This will display a dialog where you can choose which text styles to use.

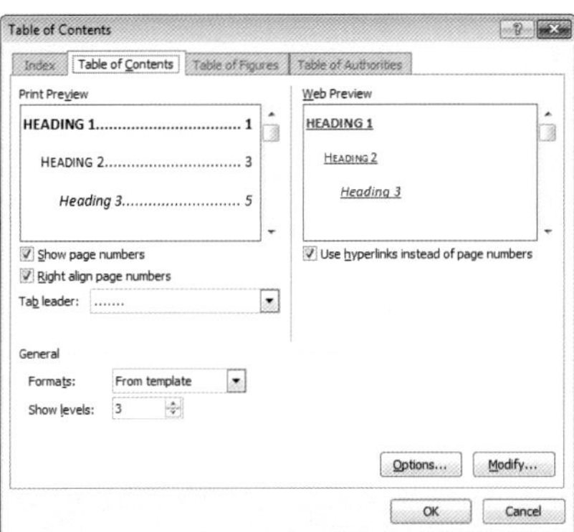

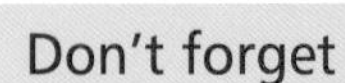

If you've added or removed items from your Table of Contents, then make sure you select "Update entire table" rather than "Update page numbers only."

Footnotes and Endnotes

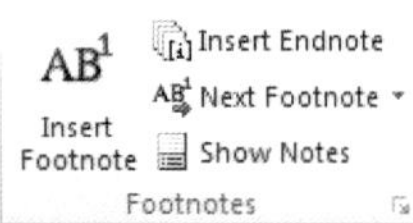

These allow you to add a superscript number to a piece of text that relates to explanatory text at the bottom of the page (for footnotes), or the end of the document, or section (for endnotes).

Adding a Footnote

1. Select the desired text and click Insert Footnote, or press Ctrl+Alt+F

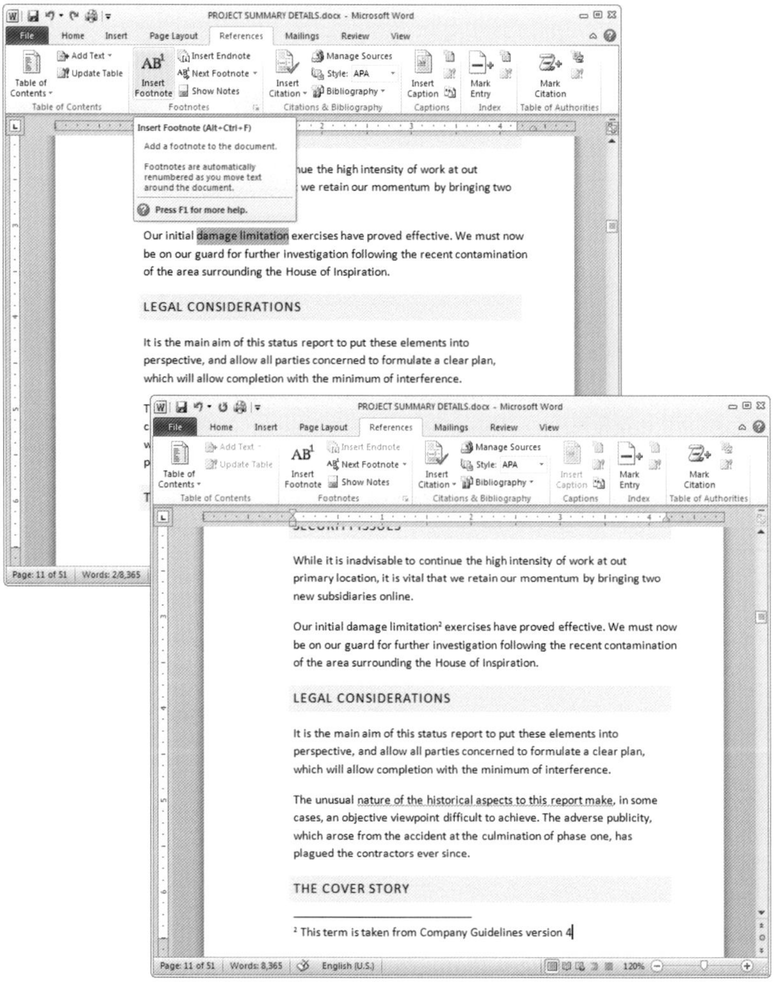

2. Next add the footnote text at the bottom of the page

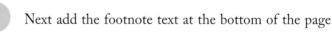

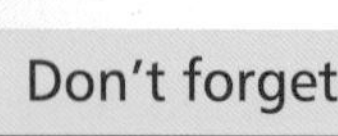

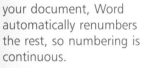

If you add new footnotes earlier on in your document, Word automatically renumbers the rest, so numbering is continuous.

Adding an Endnote

1. Select the text and click Insert Endnote

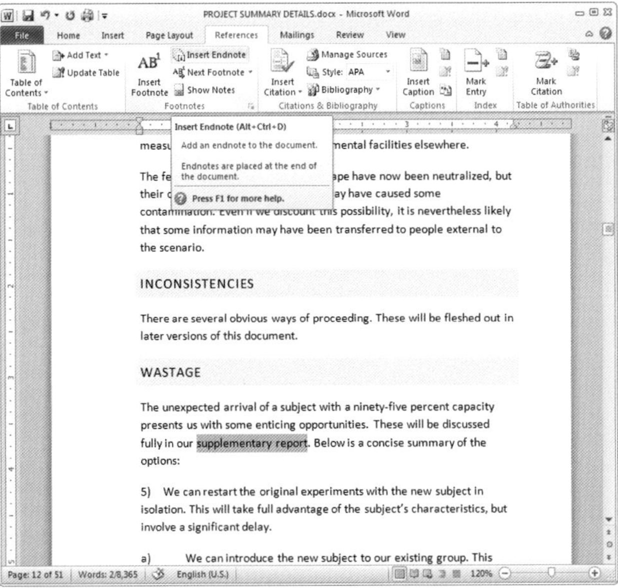
PROJECT SUMMARY DETAILS.docx - Microsoft Word
File
Home
Insert
Page Layout
References
Mailings
Review
View
Add Text
Update Table
Table of Contents
Insert Footnote
Insert Endnote
Next Footnote
Show Notes
Footnotes
Insert Citation
Manage Sources
Style: APA
Bibliography
Citations & Bibliography
Insert Caption
Captions
Mark Entry
Index
Mark Citation
Table of Authorities
Insert Endnote (Alt+Ctrl+D)
Add an endnote to the document.
Endnotes are placed at the end of the document.
Press F1 for more help.
mental facilities elsewhere.
ape have now been neutralized, but
ay have caused some
possibility, it is nevertheless likely
that some information may have been transferred to people external to
the scenario.
INCONSISTENCIES
There are several obvious ways of proceeding. These will be fleshed out in
later versions of this document.
WASTAGE
The unexpected arrival of a subject with a ninety-five percent capacity
presents us with some enticing opportunities. These will be discussed
fully in our supplementary report. Below is a concise summary of the
options:
5) We can restart the original experiments with the new subject in
isolation. This will take full advantage of the subject's characteristics, but
involve a significant delay.
a) We can introduce the new subject to our existing group. This
Page: 12 of 51
Words: 2/8,365
English (U.S.)
120%

2. Enter the text for your endnote in the space provided

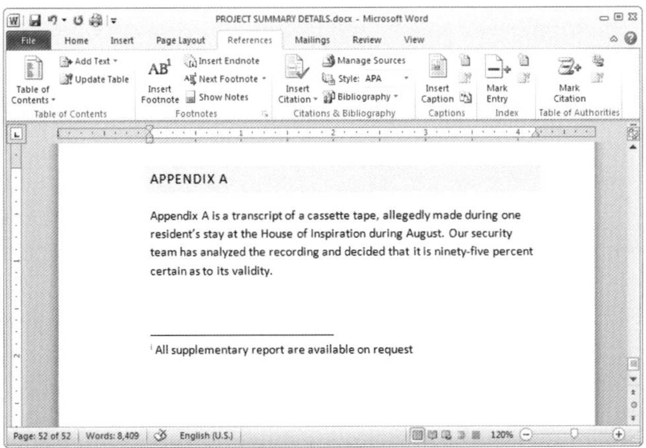
PROJECT SUMMARY DETAILS.docx - Microsoft Word
APPENDIX A
Appendix A is a transcript of a cassette tape, allegedly made during one
resident's stay at the House of Inspiration during August. Our security
team has analyzed the recording and decided that it is ninety-five percent
certain as to its validity.
i All supplementary report are available on request
Page: 52 of 52
Words: 8,409
English (U.S.)
120%

3. The Show Notes button will take you to the footnote, or endnote area, or, if you're already there, to the location within the main page of the current selection

Hot tip

The keyboard shortcut for Insert Endnote is Ctrl+Alt+D.

Hot tip

When you insert a footnote or endnote, the display automatically scrolls to the footnote or endnote area, ready for you to type in the text.

...cont'd

Navigating Through Footnotes and Endnotes

1. Click the Next Footnote icon to see its popup menu

2. There are four options, allowing you to jump straight to the next, or the previous footnote or endnote

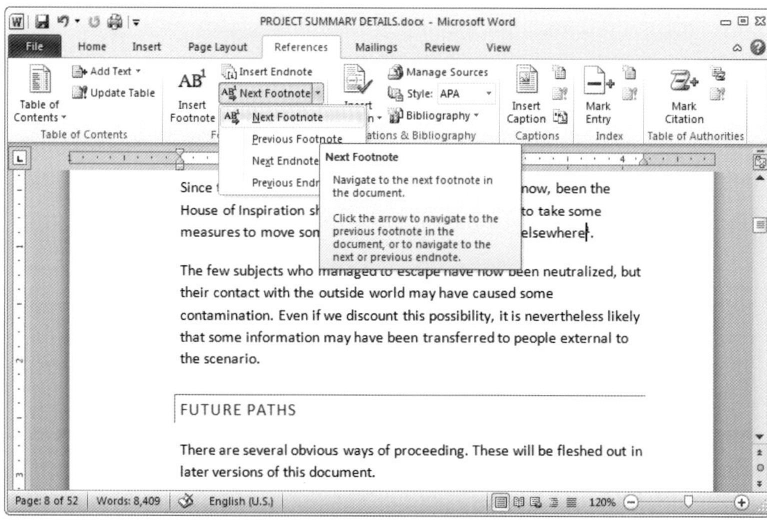

The Footnote and Endnote Dialog

1. Click the ⊽ icon in the lower right corner of the Footnotes area to see the Footnote and Endnote dialog

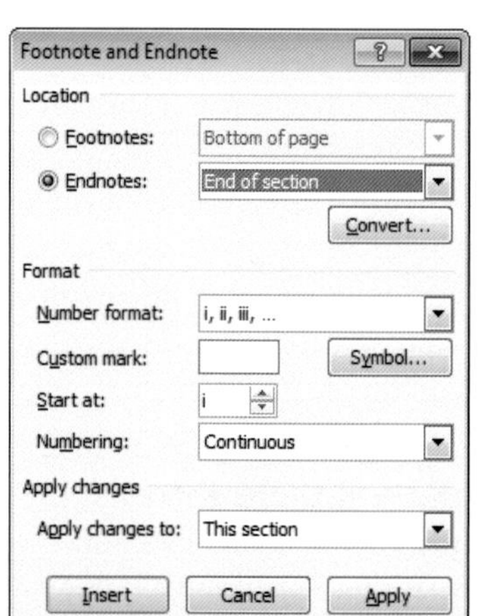

Here you can specify where the notes are positioned – note that endnotes can go either at the end of the document or just at the end of the current section.

The number format defaults to Roman numerals, but there's a number of options available.

You can also have different dialog settings for each section, if you need that level of control.

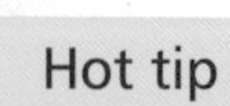

Hot tip

Click the Convert... button to switch around footnotes and endnotes, or to convert all notes to just one type

Convert Notes
- Convert all footnotes to endnotes
- Convert all endnotes to footnotes
- Swap footnotes and endnotes

OK Cancel

Citations

Citations are useful, if you need to add a reference to another author or publication within your text. Later on, you can compile a standard bibliography that collects together all your citations.

Adding a Citation

1. Click just after the reference in your main text. Click the Insert Citation button and choose Add New Source

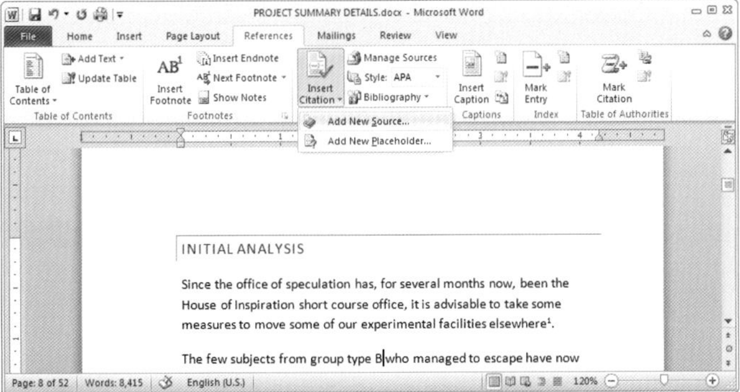

2. The Create Source dialog appears. Choose the Source, then enter the details and click OK

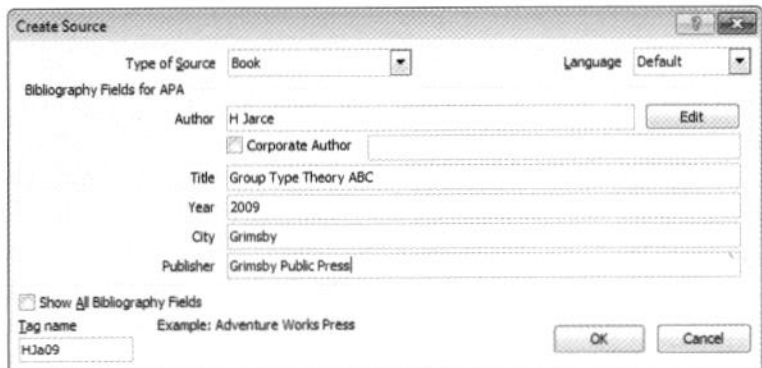

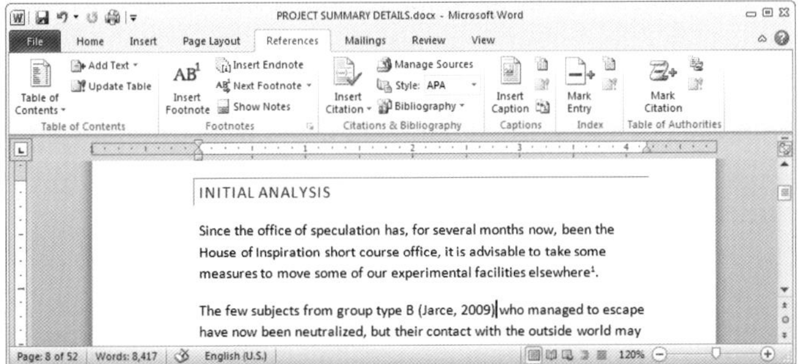

3. A short citation reference now appears next to your text. If you need to change any of the details you entered, click the Manage Sources button

Beware

Don't select the text, or the Insert Citation button will replace your text with the Citation. Instead, make sure you click after the main text, where you'd like the citation inserted.

Hot tip

If you've already added sources to your document, then you can select one of these from the pop-up menu attached to the Insert Citation button. This allows you to refer to the same source several times, without rekeying the details.

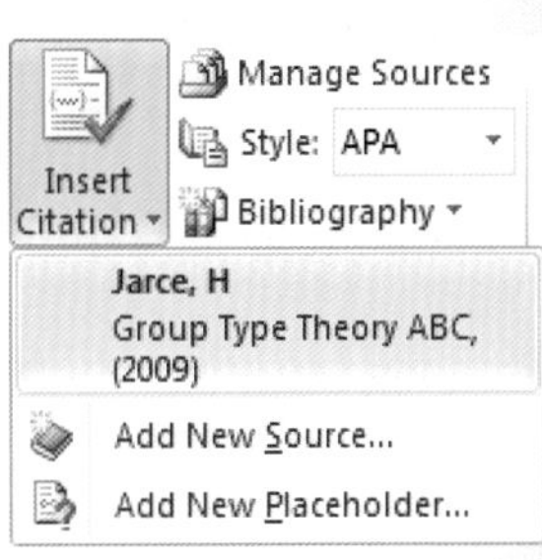

Bibliography

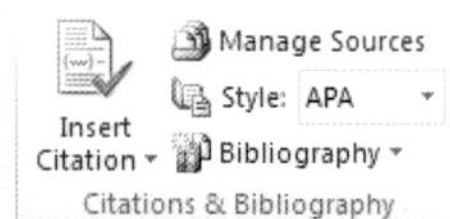

Word can generate bibliographies in a number of formal styles.

Creating a Bibliography

1. Make sure you've inserted citations throughout your document

2. Click on Bibliography, and then select from the gallery

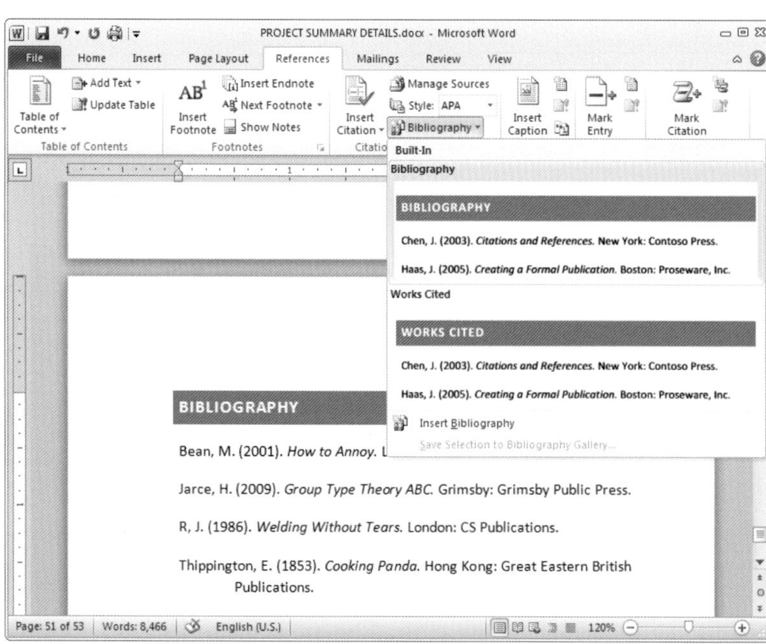

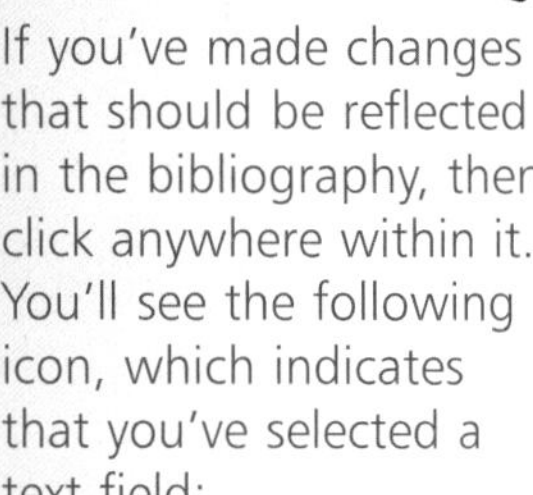

If you've made changes that should be reflected in the bibliography, then click anywhere within it. You'll see the following icon, which indicates that you've selected a text field:

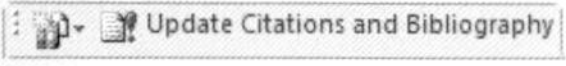

Click on the Update button to refresh your bibliography. You can also change the design by clicking on the small icon on the left.

Word will use the sources you previously defined to build the complete bibliography.

You can continue to work with your document, adding more citations and editing the sources using the Manage Sources button.

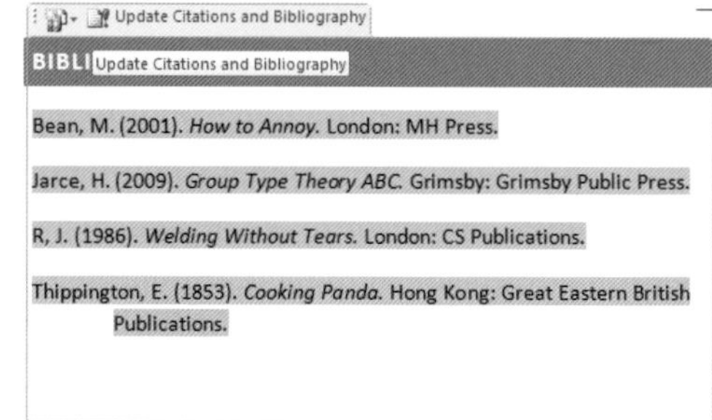

Adding Captions

1. Select your element, then click on Insert Caption

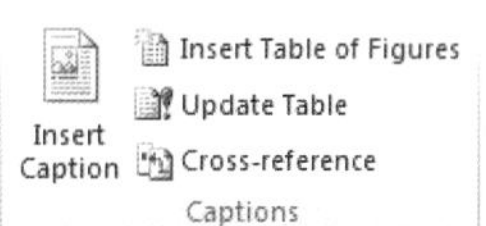

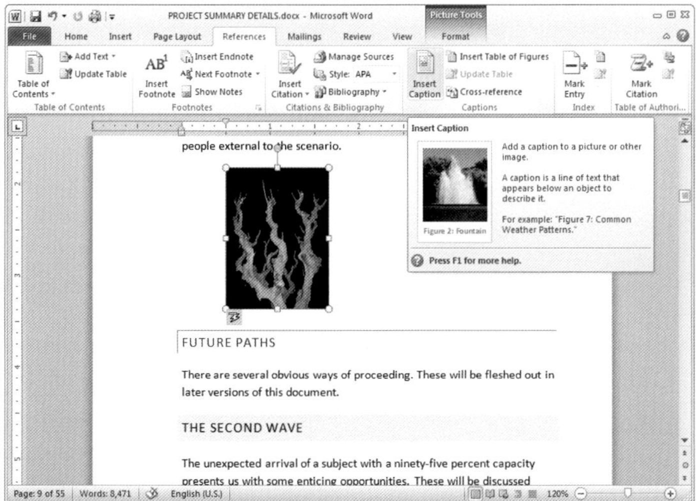

Hot tip

You can also add captions to equations and tables – follow exactly the same procedure.

2. Add the caption text in the dialog. There are three label options – Equation, Figure and Table (you can also use the New Label button to add more options). Choose Figure for this example

3. Captions will normally be numbered 1, 2, 3 and so on, but this can be changed by clicking on Numbering

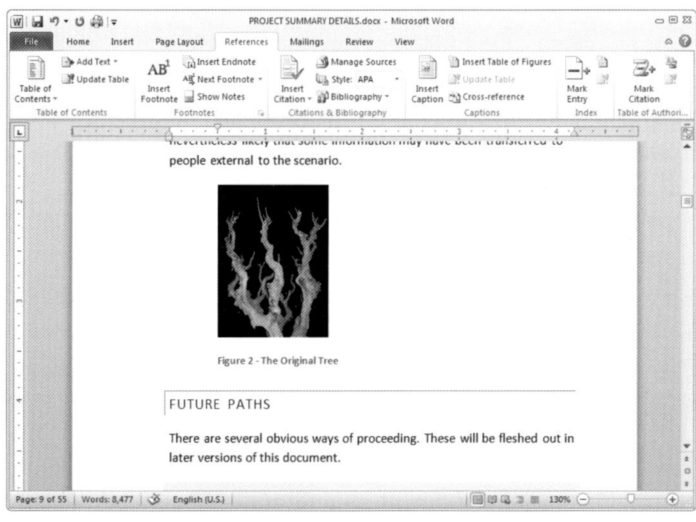

Table of Figures

Once you've created captions throughout your document, you can ask Word to build a Table of Figures.

1. Make sure your Insertion Point is placed where you want the Table of Figures

2. Click on Insert Table of Figures

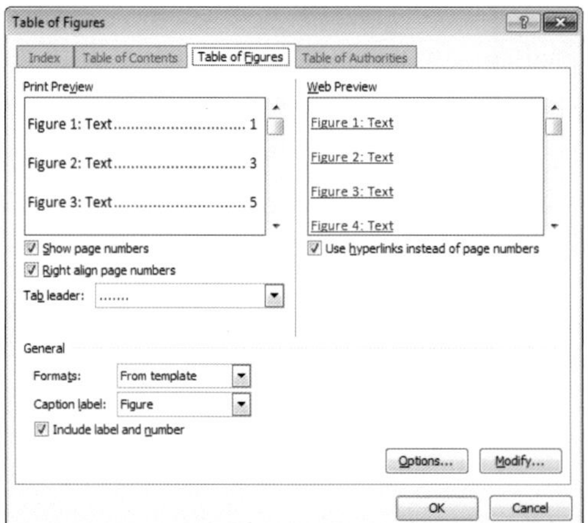

The Table of Figures dialog appears as shown.

3. Choose a format from the pop-up list. The Print and Web Preview areas will show you how this will look. Click OK to generate the table

4. If you make changes to your document, you might want to refresh the table. To do this click Update Table

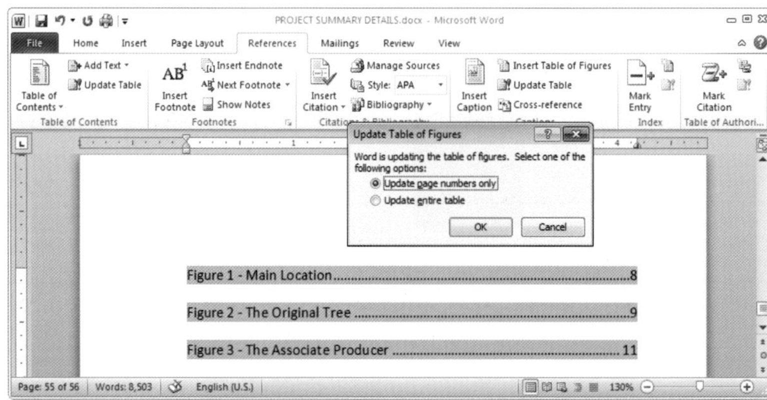

Don't forget

As with footnotes, seen earlier, Word automatically renumbers captions as you add to or delete them from your document.

Indexing

Longer documents benefit greatly from a well-organized index. Word makes the process of creating an index fairly easy.

1. Select the text you want to appear in the index, and click on Mark Index Entry, or press Shift+Alt+X

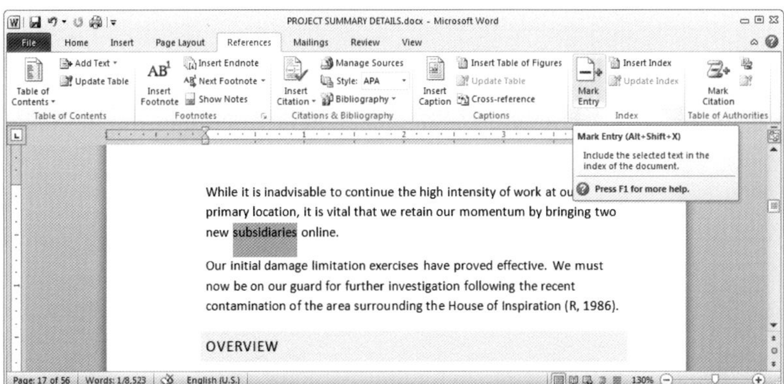

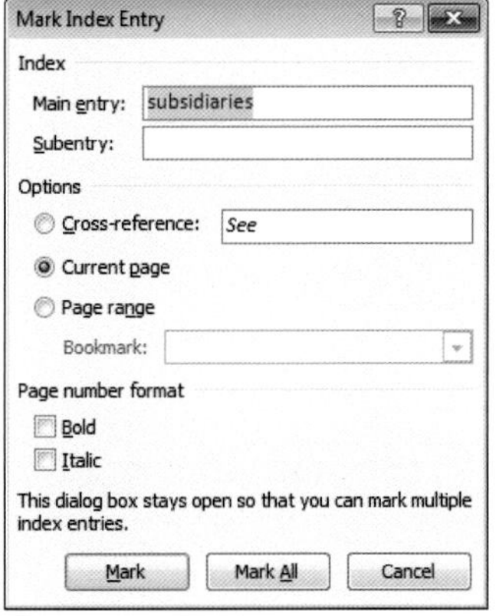

2. You can now edit the entry text, add a subentry, and choose whether the index will show the current page, a range of pages, or a cross reference to another index entry

3. Use the Bold and Italic checkboxes if you want your index entry to be emphasized

4. When you have finished making your settings, click Mark

5. This dialog is *non-modal*, which means that you can continue to work on the main page with the dialog still open. In this way, you can work through your document, quickly and easily, marking new entries without having to keep clicking the Mark Entry tool

Don't forget

You can toggle the Show/Hide ¶ feature on and off with Ctrl+*

6. As soon as you mark an entry, Word switches on the Show/Hide ¶ feature, so you can see your index entries marked clearly

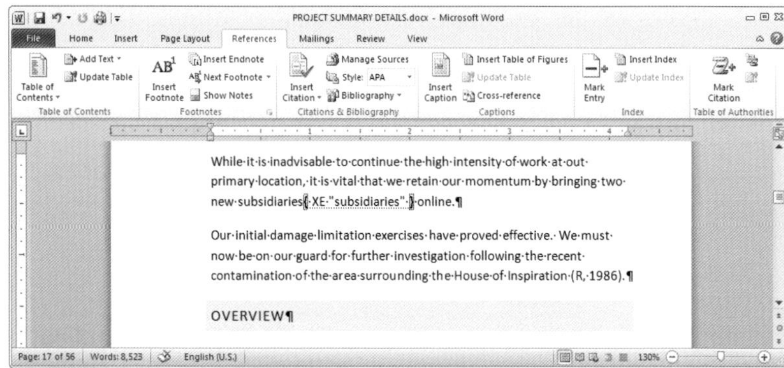

7. Click Insert Index to see the finished result

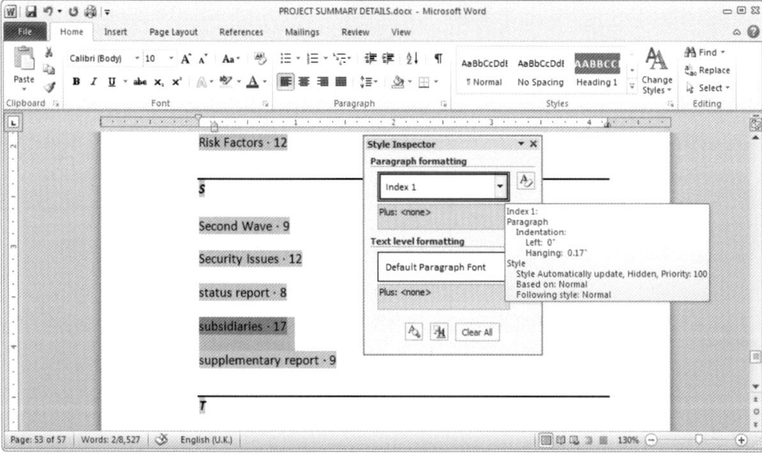

Hot tip

If you edit your document so that the page numbers have changed, or if you have added more index entries, then you will need to rebuild the index. To do this, select the index and then click on Update Index.

8. Word uses special styles (Index Heading, Index 1, Index 2, and so on) to control the formatting. If you edit these styles, rather than the index text directly, then your formatting decisions will be preserved, even if you rebuild the index later on

Tables of Authorities

These are much more flexible than bibliographies, as they allow you to create tables for different categories of citations. They are particularly useful for legal and academic documents.

Marking Citations

Firstly, you must add citations, which will go into your Table(s) of Authorities.

1. Select the text that you'd like to make into a citation

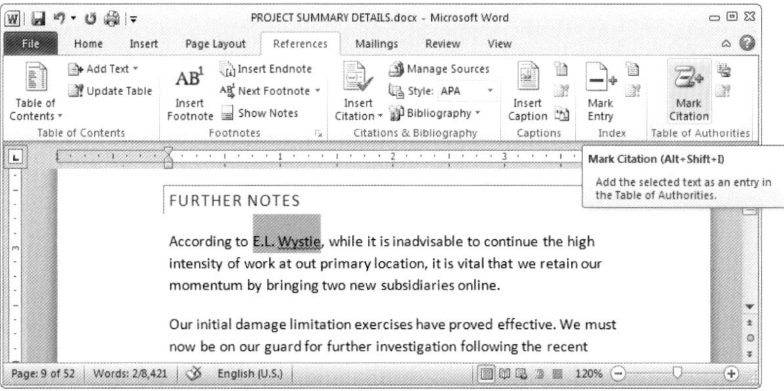

2. Click the Mark Citation button in the Table of Authorities area at the right side of the References Tab

3. In the dialog that appears, choose a citation Category, or use the Category button to define further categories. Click the Mark button, or Mark All to find and mark all instances of your text

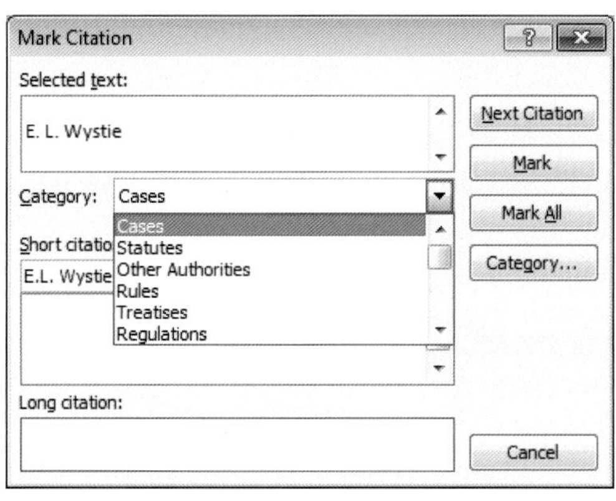

Your text will now be marked as a citation. Later, you will be able to build a Table of Authorities based on one, or all of these categories.

Hot tip

If none of the available categories are suitable, click on the Category button. Select a category you don't need and enter a new name in the "Replace with" field, click Replace and then OK. Your new category name will now be available from the Mark Citation dialog.

...cont'd

Creating a Table of Authorities

1. Go through your document, marking all citations, taking particular note of the category you choose when adding each item

Hot tip

If the option "Use passim" is on, then any citation with five or more page references will appear, using the word "passim" (meaning "everywhere") instead of the long list of page numbers. If you switch this off, you'll get all the page references.

2. When you're ready, click the Insert Table of Authorities tool. The following dialog box appears

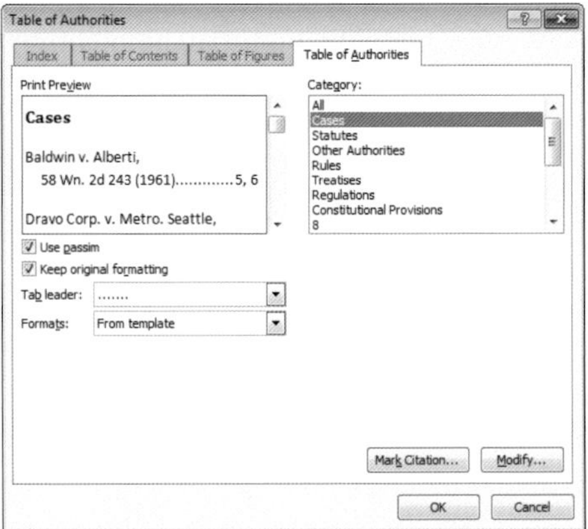

3. Choose the Category, or, if you want to generate a table with all categories one after the other, select All. "Keep original formatting" will copy the text attributes from the source, so switch this off for a neater table

4. Choose a suitable format from the popup menu, checking the Print Preview box for visual feedback on your current selection. Click OK to generate the Table of Authorities

Hot tip

To rebuild the table, click the Update Table button or, alternatively, right click on the table and choose Update Field.

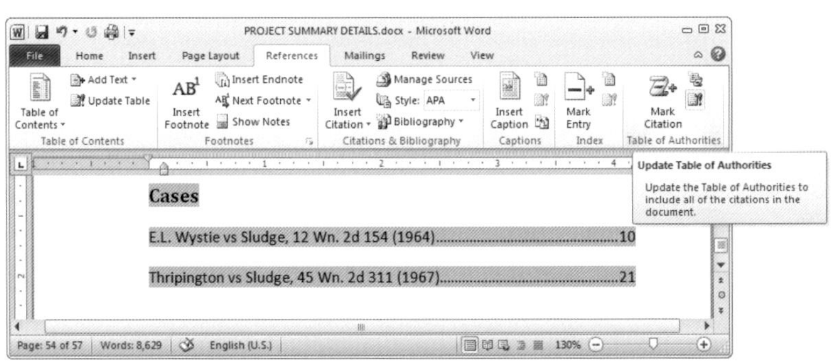

7 The Mailings Tab

This chapter examines the features of the Mailings Tab.

Envelopes

Adding Envelopes to your Document

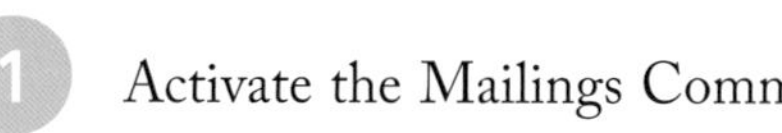

1. Activate the Mailings Command Tab

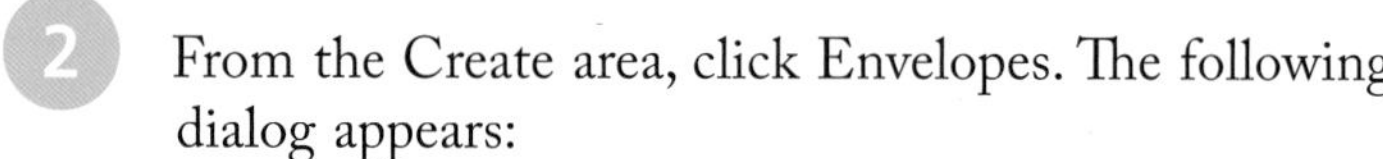

2. From the Create area, click Envelopes. The following dialog appears:

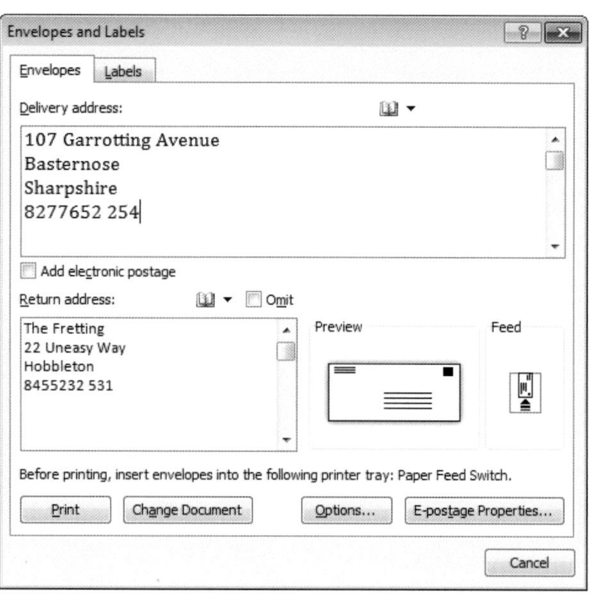

3. Enter the delivery address and, optionally, the return address. Click on the Options button to select the envelope's dimensions from a list of standard sizes

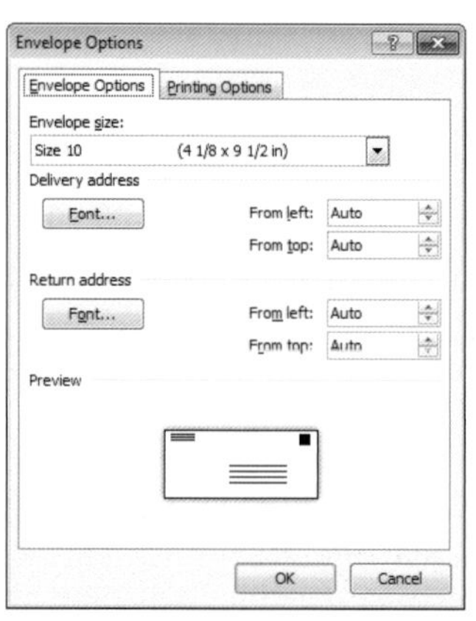

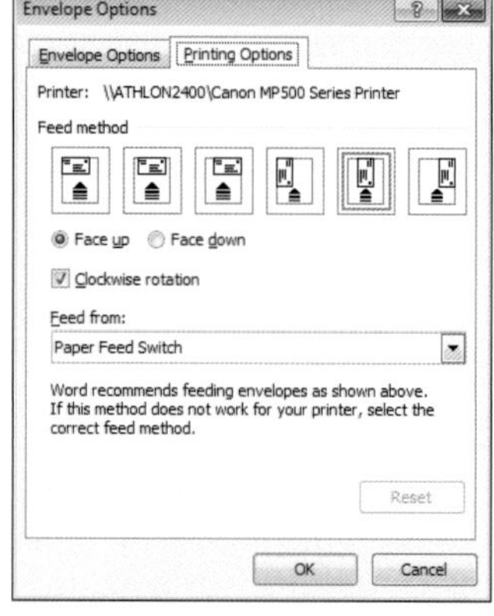

As well as the Envelope Options, this dialog has a tab for Printing Options. This lets you tailor the settings to match the way you load envelopes into your printer.

4. Click Add to Document

5. If you entered a return address, you'll be shown a dialog asking you whether you want to make this the default return address. If you click Yes, then you won't need to retype it the next time you create an envelope

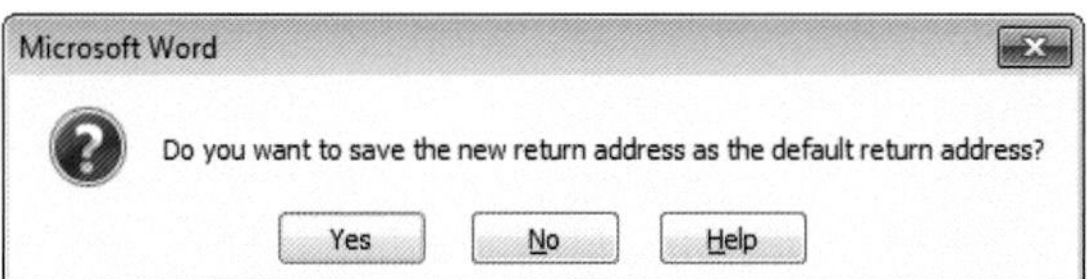

6. Once you've dismissed the dialog box, your envelope will be generated on a new page

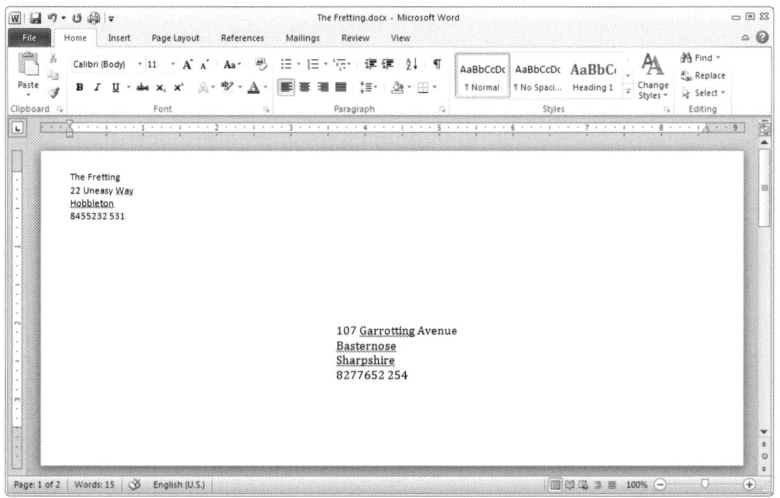

7. Your envelope is now part of the normal document, so you can edit the text, or experiment with different formatting options

8. Choose the Print option from the File Tab when you're ready to print out your envelope

Labels

Word can create labels, using a wide range of standard sizes.

Creating a New Document for Your Labels

1. Click the Labels tool. The following dialog box appears

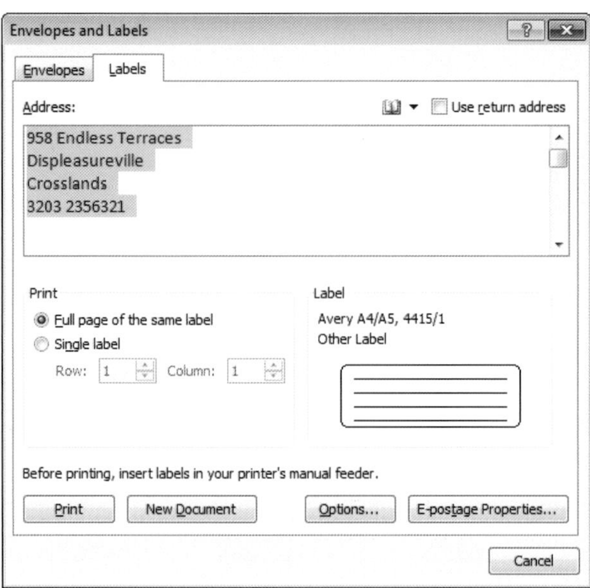

2. Enter the text (usually an address) and choose between creating a single label, or a full page of the same label

3. Click the Options button and select the label vendor, and then select the label from the product numbers listed

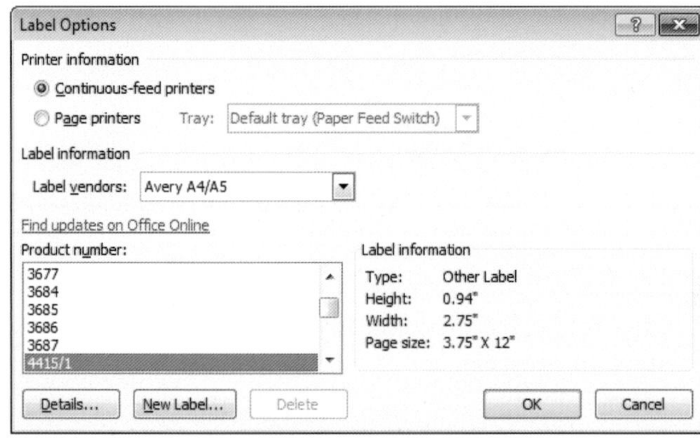

If the label you require isn't listed in the Label Options dialog, click the New Label button. This will let you define your own label design by entering all its dimensions numerically.

4. Click the Details button to review the attributes of the currently selected label

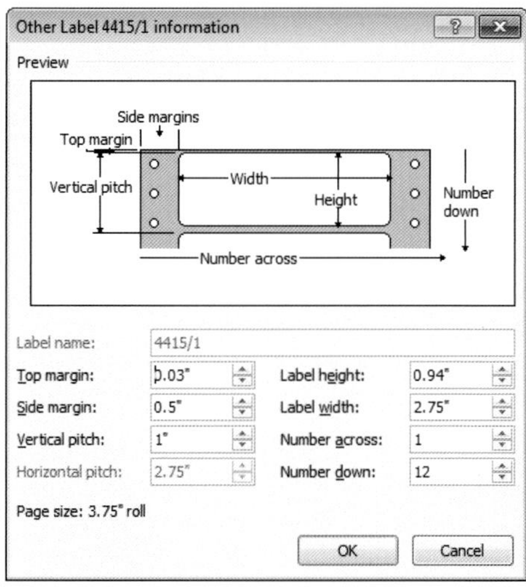

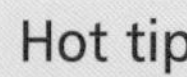

Hot tip

You can also Print directly from the Envelopes and Labels dialog box

5. If you can't find the right label, then click Cancel to return to Label Options dialog, then click on Create New Label

6. Click OK to return to the Envelopes and Labels dialog, then choose New Document to generate your labels

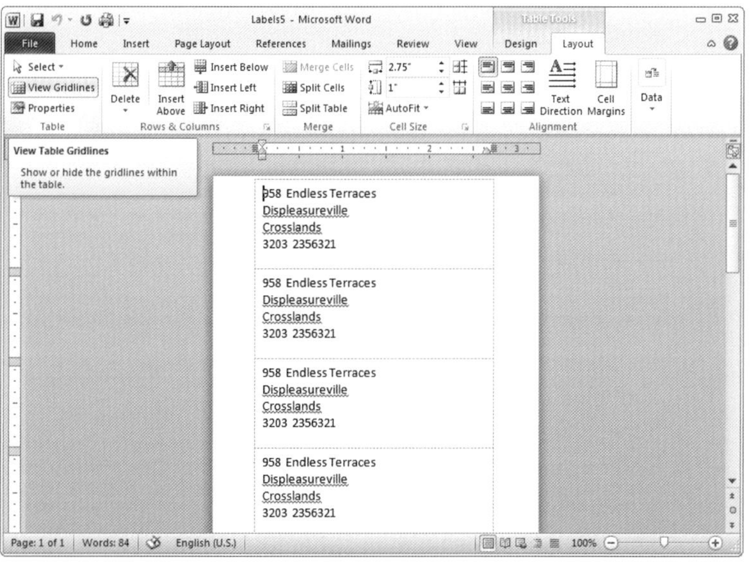

Mail Merge

There are several ways of setting up mail merging in Word, but the easiest is to use the Wizard, which guides you through the various stages of the process.

Using the Mail Merge Wizard

1. Click on Start Mail Merge and select "Step by Step Mail Merge Wizard"

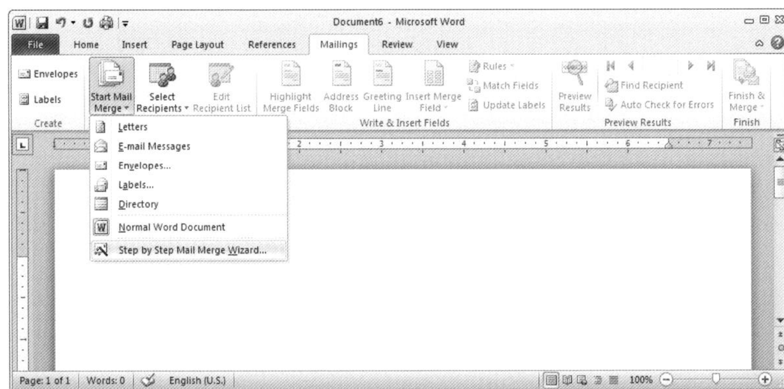

2. The Mail Merge window appears at the right-hand side of the screen. If you drag on its title bar, you can make it into a floating window

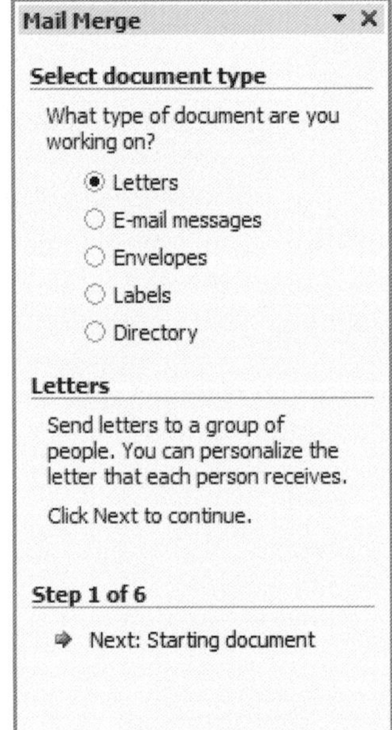

3. The first step is to choose the document type. In this example, we'll produce a single letter design, and then print out a copy for each person in a preset list of addresses. Make sure Letters is selected, and then click on the hyperlink "Next: Starting document" at the bottom of the Mail Merge Window

Don't forget

Mail Merge can be a real time saver, if you've a long list of recipients. However, if you've only got one or two, then it's probably easier just creating your documents manually.

4 At the next step, choose "Use the current document" if you are happy to write the letter using the current document. Alternatively, you can open a document previously saved, or even create a new document based on a template design

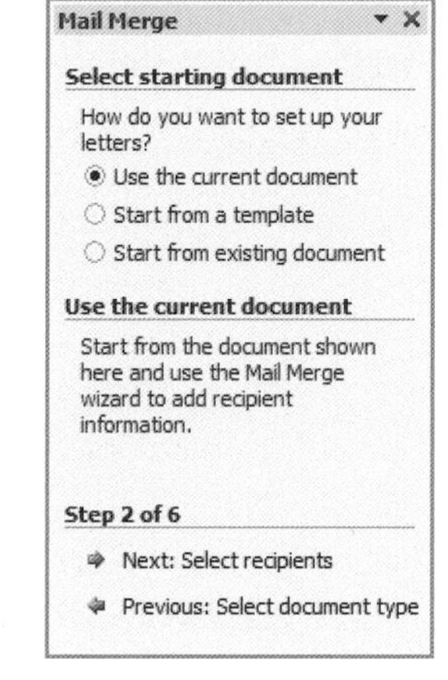

5 Click the hyperlink "Next: Select recipients" to proceed to the next stage

6 There are several ways to define the letter's recipients. If you have previously defined a list, then select "Use an existing list". If you use Microsoft Outlook and have created contacts you'd like to use, then choose "Select from Outlook contacts". This will allow you to choose which of your Outlook contacts you'd like to use. In this example, we will create our own new list, so select "Type a new list"

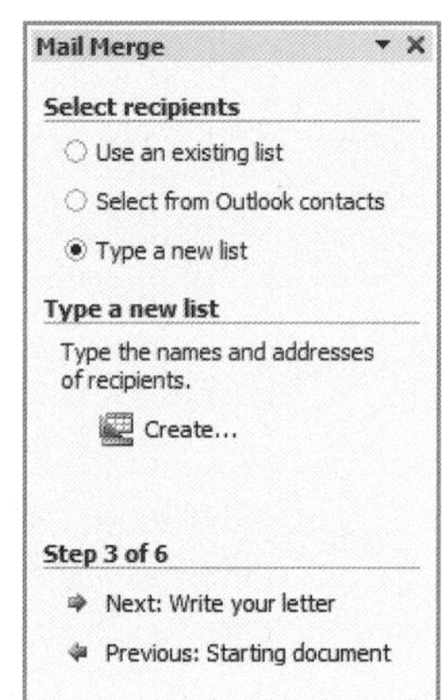

7 Click on the "Create" hyperlink

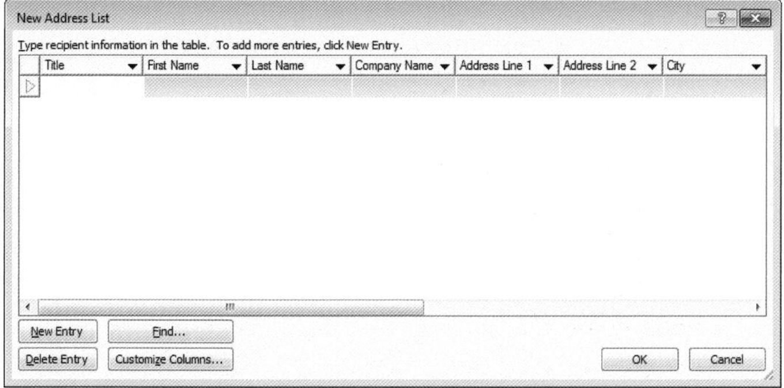

...cont'd

8 Enter the details of each recipient into the table provided

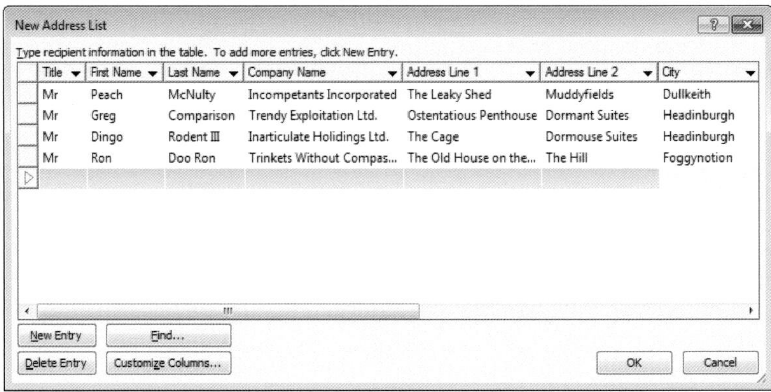

9 If you don't like the headings provided, click the Customize Columns button and add, delete, or edit, as necessary. Click OK when done

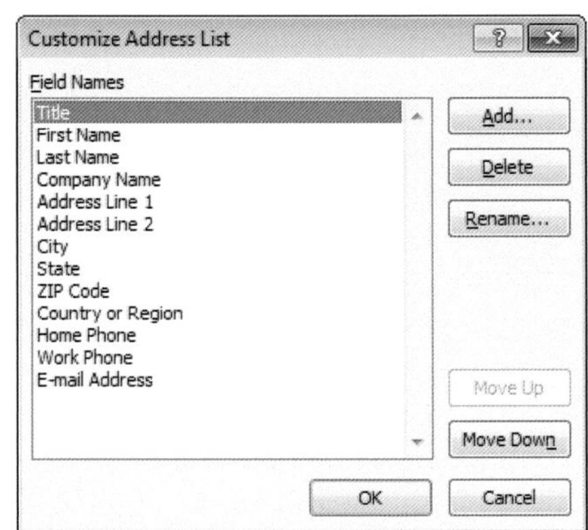

10 You're then given the option to save your list to disk, which is worth doing if you plan to use it again

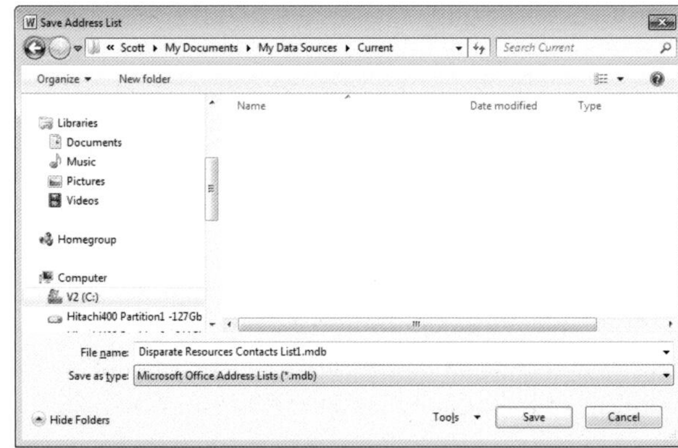

11 In the MailMerge Recipients dialog, make sure all of the lines are selected

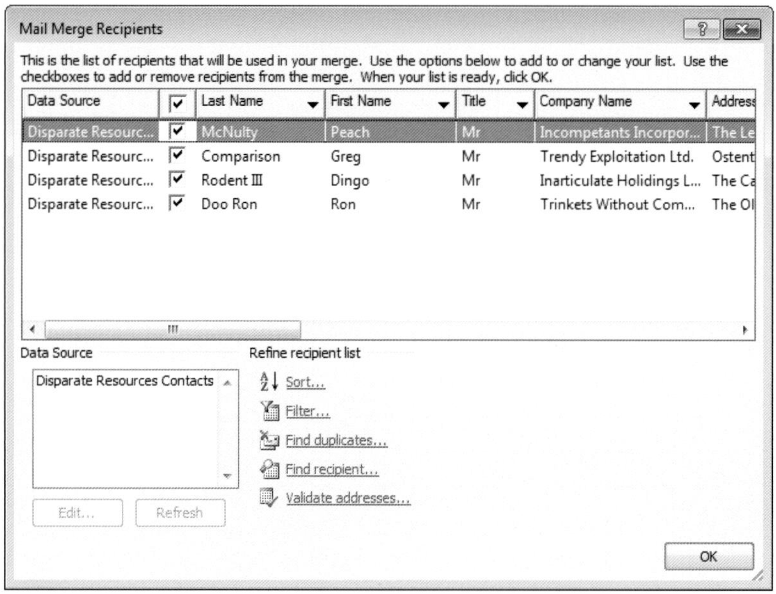

12 If your data source was a previously-saved list, or your Outlook contacts, then you might decide to select some of, rather than all, the items. If the list is very long, then the controls under the heading "Refine recipient list" are useful. Click on Filter

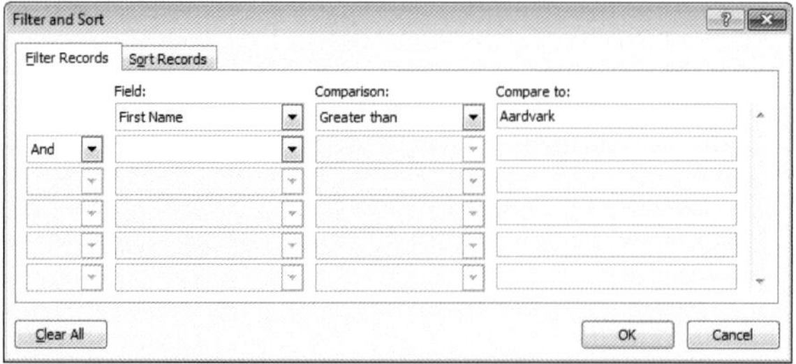

13 From this dialog, you can build up one or more filter criteria by comparing fields with known values. In this example, the field First Name is being checked to see if it comes (alphabetically) after the value "Aardvark"

Hot tip

The "Find duplicates..." feature is useful if you've imported your list from several combined sources, or if your list has been badly maintained.

...cont'd

14 Click OK. Back in the main screen, the Mail Merge window now displays a summary of the recipients selected

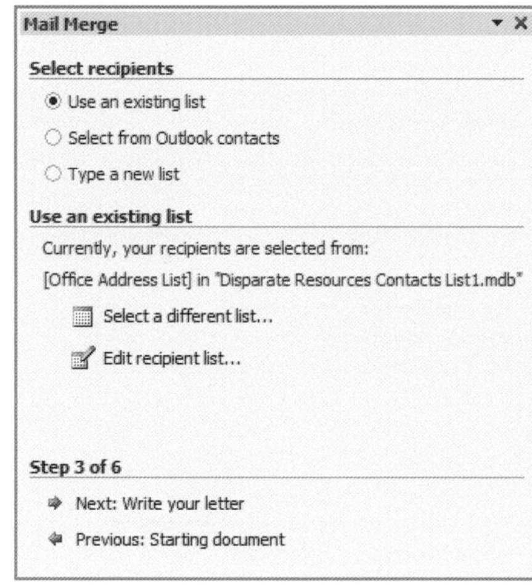

15 From this page of the Wizard, you can edit the recipient list, or even select a different list altogether

16 When you're happy with your choice of recipients, click the hyperlink marked "Next: Write your letter"

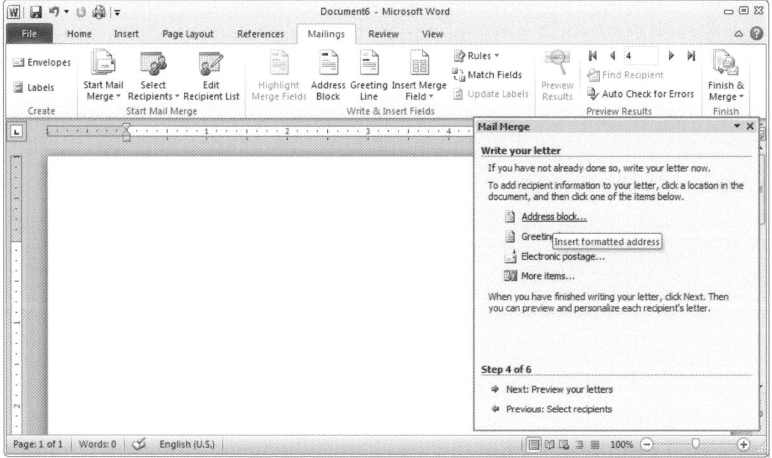

17 You can now start working on your letter, typing in and formatting text as usual. In addition to this, you'll want to add one or more special Mail Merge fields. Place your Insertion Point where you'd like the address, and click the Address Block icon in the Mail Merge window

The following dialog box appears:

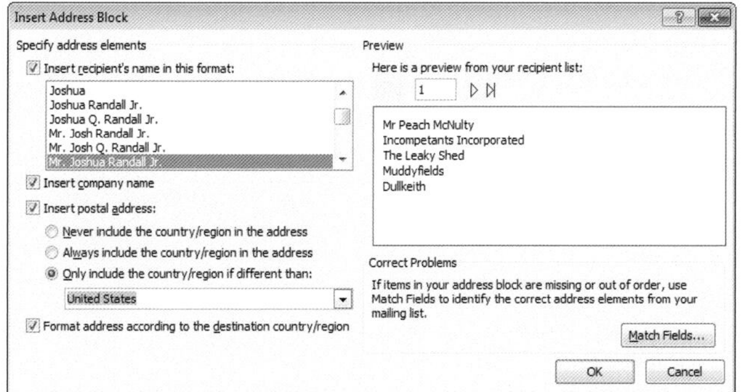

18 Choose a format style, check the preview area to see the effect of different choices. When you click OK, you'll see the placeholder <<AddressBlock>> appear

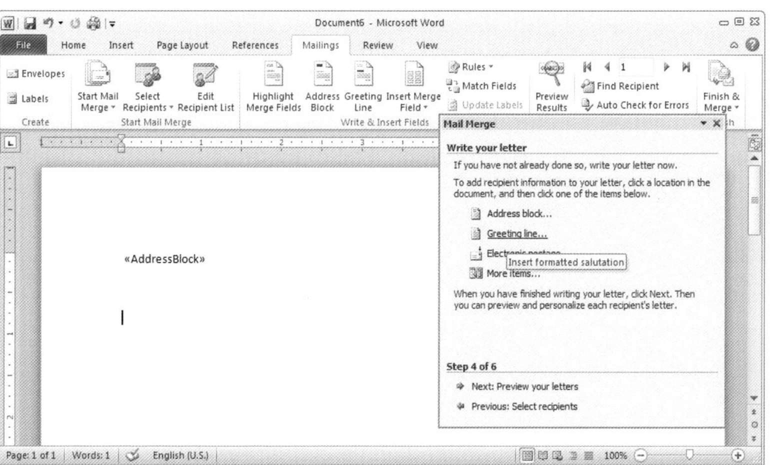

19 If you add normal text into your document by typing manually (for example your own address, or the main body of the letter), then this will be "static", i.e. it will be exactly the same for each version of the letter printed

20 You can format your text in the normal way. If you select <<AddressBlock>> and change its font and size, then this will affect each literal address that will be substituted when the Mail Merge is performed

Fields within Word appear as a name surrounded by angle brackets, for example <<AddressBlock>>. Although you do not yet see the text that will be substituted for this placeholder, you can still control its positioning and formatting, using the normal editing controls.

...cont'd

21 Add an automatic Greeting Line near the top of your letter. Word will substitute each name and salutation when the document is printed. Click your Insertion Point is in the correct place and then choose Greeting Line.

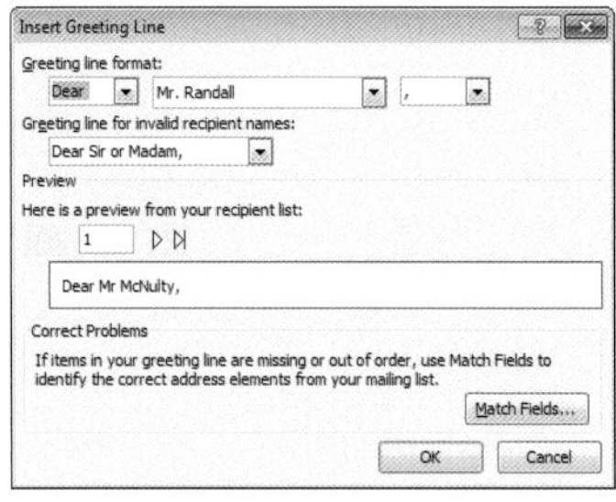

22 Select the appropriate format and click OK

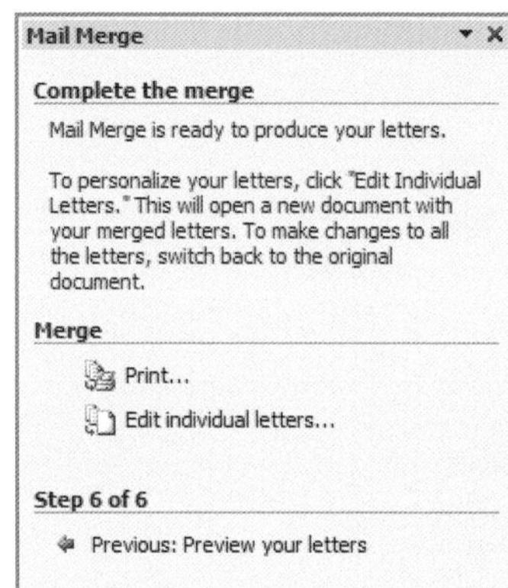

23 Click on "Preview your letters" to see how they will print. You can now choose between generating individual letters, or simply printing the results of the merge

Hot tip

When previewing the Mail Merge results, you can move to each recipient to check that each instance of your letter looks OK. The controls for moving back and forth are in the Preview Results area of the Mailings tab, and also on the fifth page of the Mail Merge Wizard screen, as shown here.

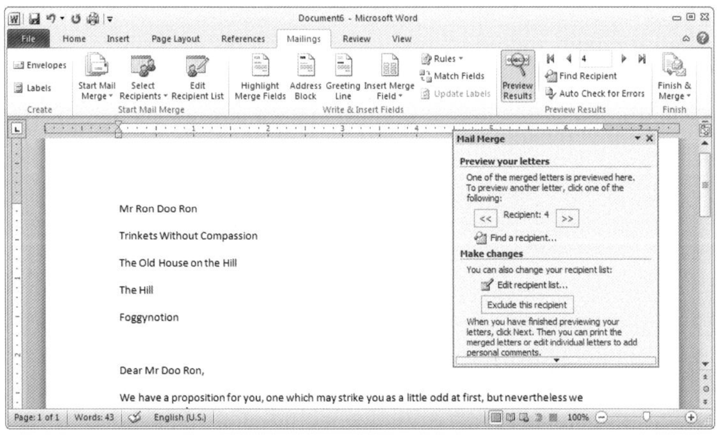

24 Complete the merge and output your results by clicking on Print in the Mail Merge window

8 The Review Tab

The Review Tab gives you various ways of checking your work, as well as tracking and controlling changes that may need to be worked on by you or others.

Spelling and Grammar Check

Word has access to a number of English and non-English dictionaries, which it uses when running spelling checks.

Checking Selected Text

1. Select the text you want to check

2. Make sure the Review Command Tab is active. Click on the Spelling & Grammar icon in the Proofing area

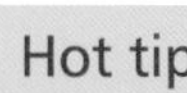

To run a spelling check on the entire document, make sure that no text is selected at all when you click the Spelling & Grammar icon.

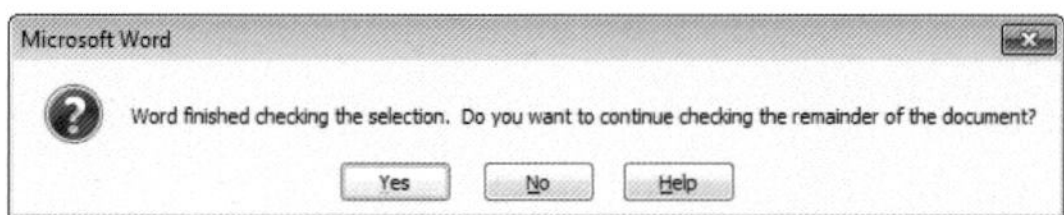

Once the check is completed, you'll be asked whether you want to check the rest of the document.

3. If Word detects any errors in your text, you'll see the Spelling and Grammar dialog box

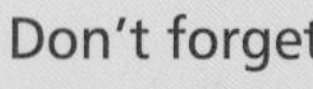

In this example, the dictionary language is English (United States). Language is one of the editable attributes of a Text Style – so you may decide to define particular styles to use particular languages. See Chapter Two, "The Home Tab", for more information on working with styles.

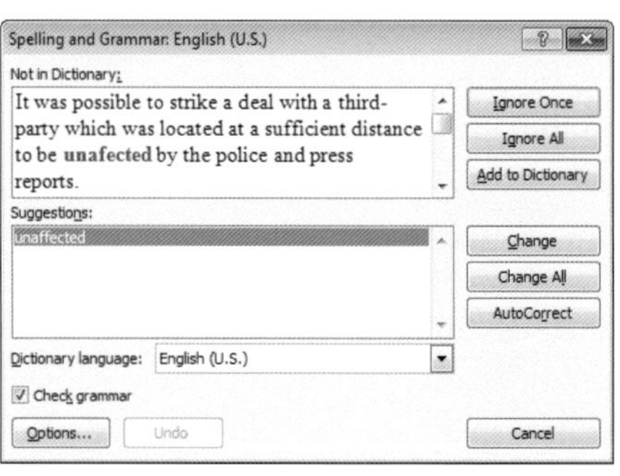

Word will show you suggestions for spelling corrections – select one and click on Change, or Change All. If the word is correct, but not in Word's dictionary, you can click on the "Add to Dictionary" button.

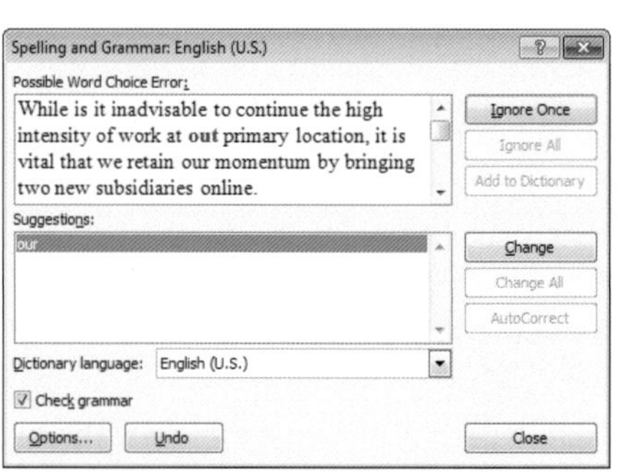

In this example, the spelling checker has found a word which, while spelled correctly, may be an incorrect choice (based on the surrounding text). In this case, it correctly suggests the replacement word.

If the "Check grammar" checkbox is selected, Word will apply a set of predefined grammar rules to your text. In this example, the rule "Subject-Verb Agreement" was violated.

4 If Word finds a possible grammatical error, you can either accept one of its suggestions by clicking the Change button, or ignore the recommendation (click Ignore Once, or Ignore Rule, if you don't want Word to apply this rule in future)

If you click the Explain button, Word's Help window appears with a description of the current rule.

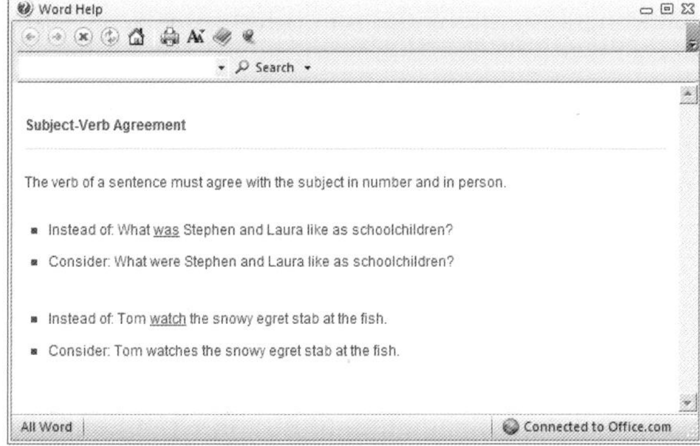
Word Help
Search
Subject-Verb Agreement
The verb of a sentence must agree with the subject in number and in person.
Instead of: What was Stephen and Laura like as schoolchildren?
Consider: What were Stephen and Laura like as schoolchildren?
Instead of: Tom watch the snowy egret stab at the fish.
Consider: Tom watches the snowy egret stab at the fish.
All Word
Connected to Office.com

5 If you want to stop the spelling and grammar check before it's finished, click the Close button, or manually close the dialog window by clicking the "x" icon in its top right corner

6 From within the Spelling and Grammar dialog, click on Options to review or customize the way the check runs

Don't forget

If Word comes up with multiple suggestions for correcting your grammar, it will list them with the word OR between each item and the next. If one of these suggestions is acceptable to you, select the item and then click the Change button.

...cont'd

You can also access this dialog from the File Tab – click the Options button and then choose Proofing.

The following dialog box appears.

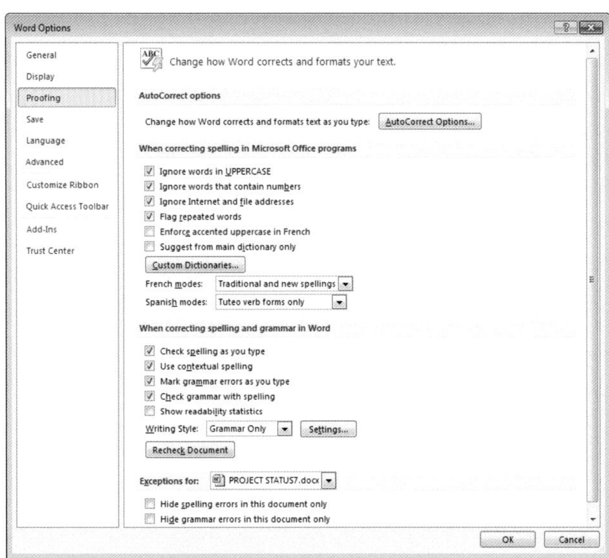

This gives you access to a range of settings, grouped separately into spelling and grammar sections.

7. Click the Custom Dictionaries button to check where your user dictionary file is kept

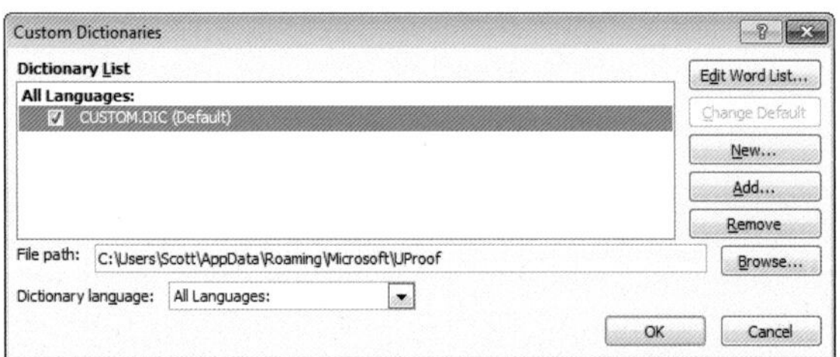

8. Choose Edit Word List to see the list of words you've added when spell checking. When done, click OK twice to return to the Word Options' Proofing page

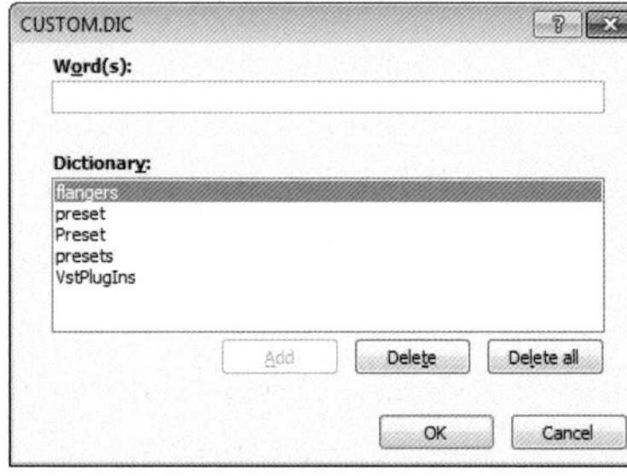

9 Under the "When correcting spelling and grammar in Word" heading, click Settings

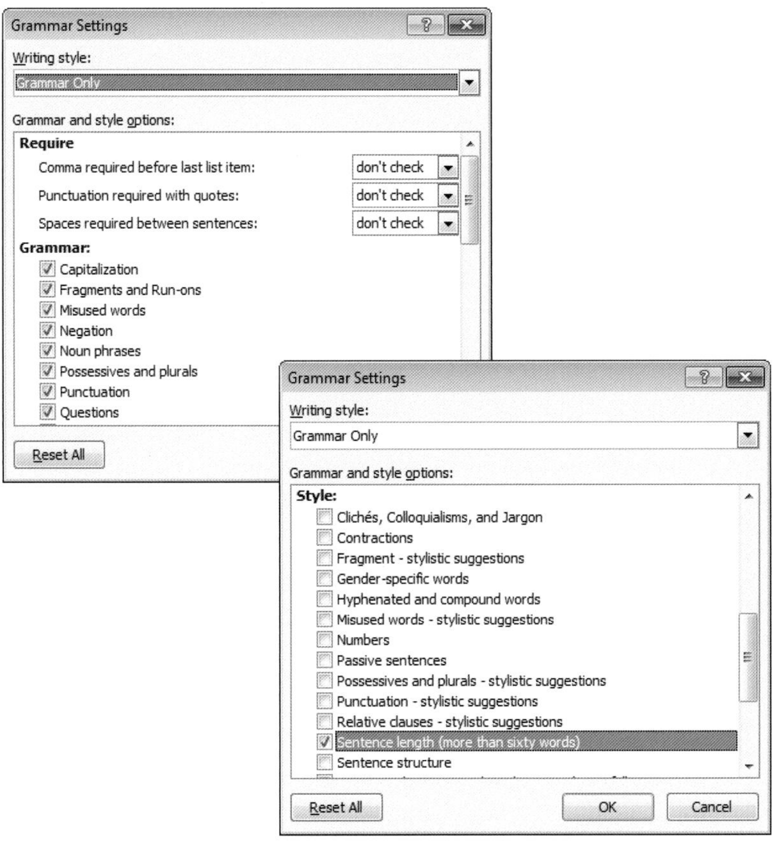

It's worth reviewing all the Grammar Settings to make sure that you are happy with each option, this can save you a lot of annoyance later on, when running Spelling and Grammar checks.

10 The Grammar Settings dialog contains three sets of options. "Require" is for general punctuation and spacing rules. "Grammar" is a list of groups of grammatical rules. "Style" is a list of less strict rules – breaking these is more a matter of taste, and will probably depend on the level of formality in your writing

11 Click OK to this, and to the Word Options dialog, to return to the spelling and grammar checker

12 When Word has finished checking your document, you will see a confirmation dialog

Research

Word provides a range of options for looking up reference information, based on text you select.

Looking Up Information

1. Select the relevant text and then click the Research button

2. In the Research Pane, the “Search for” field should contain your selected text. In the field below this, open the pop-up menu and choose a reference book or site

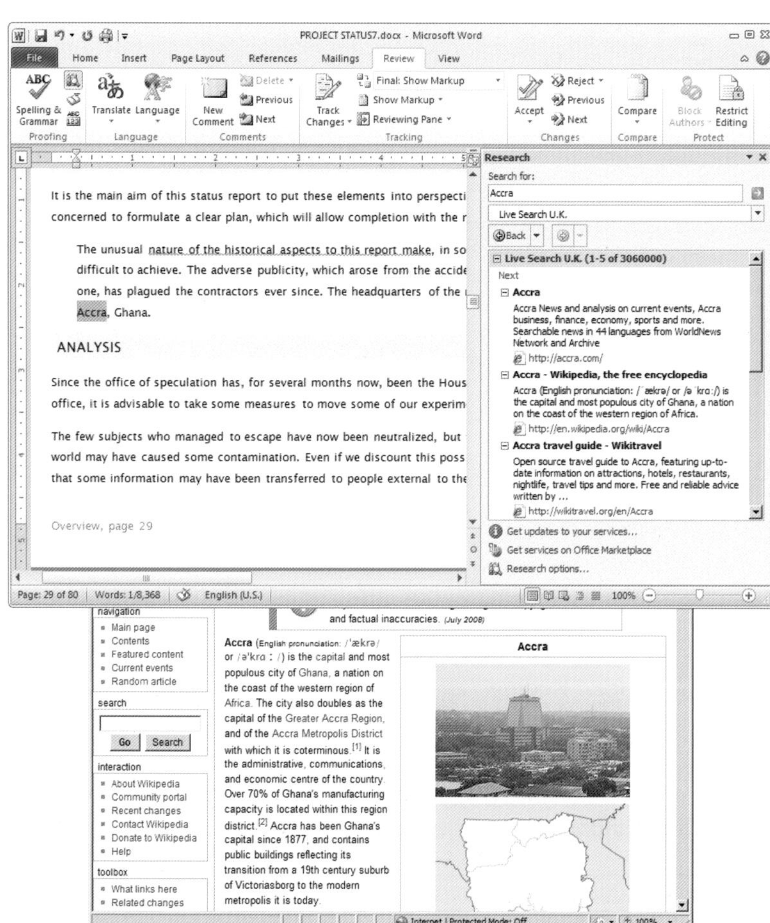

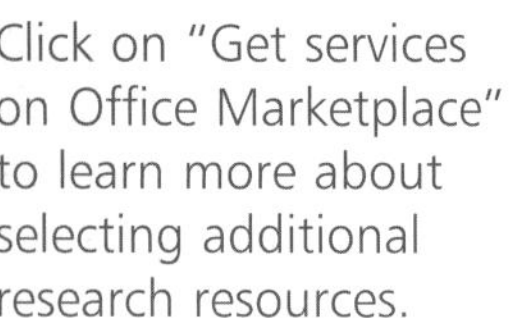

Click on "Get services on Office Marketplace" to learn more about selecting additional research resources.

You can use the hyperlinks in the main area of the Research Pane to access articles from a range of sources on the Web.

3. Click on "Research options..." at the bottom of the Research Pane to see the dialog illustrated below. This lets you control which services and sites are used for research

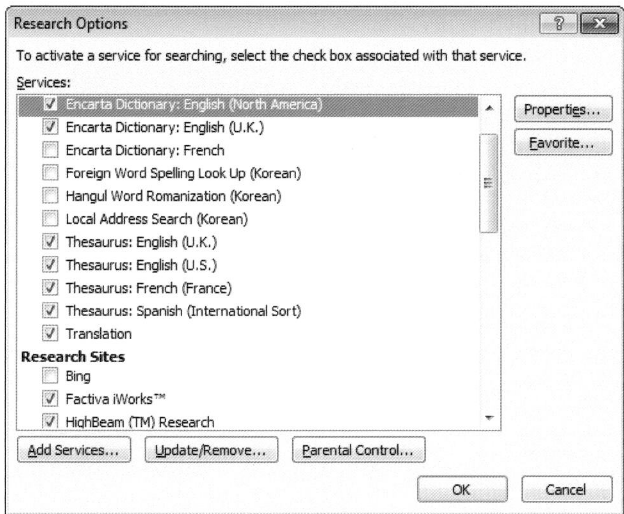

4. Click the Parental Control button

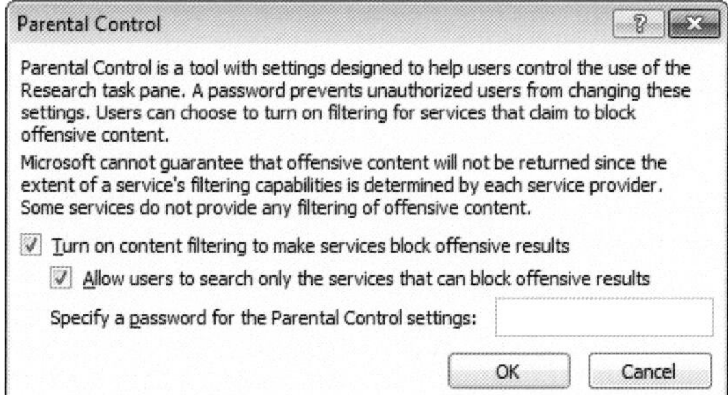

5. Some Web-based services provide a filtering capability for their content, so you can choose to prevent access to material that might be unsuitable for children, or others of a sensitive disposition. If this sounds like a good idea to you, turn on both checkbox options

6. Enter a password if you want to prevent others from changing these settings

Hot tip

Choose any item and click Properties, to see a description plus other details.

Hot tip

Another useful tool in the Proofing area of the Review Tab is Word Count. Although the Status Bar gives you basic information, this shows you much more, via the dialog below.

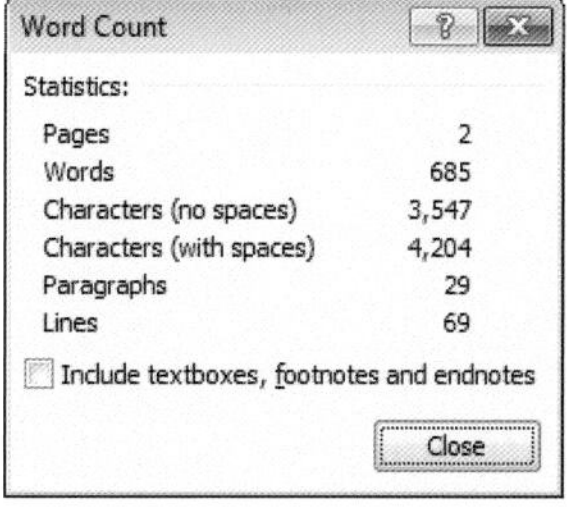

Thesaurus

1. Select a single word and then click on the Thesaurus icon in the Proofing tab

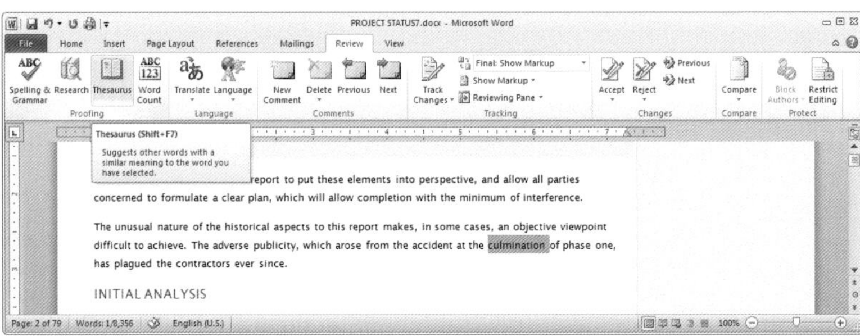

Don't forget

A Thesaurus is a collection of synonyms (words with identical or similar meanings).

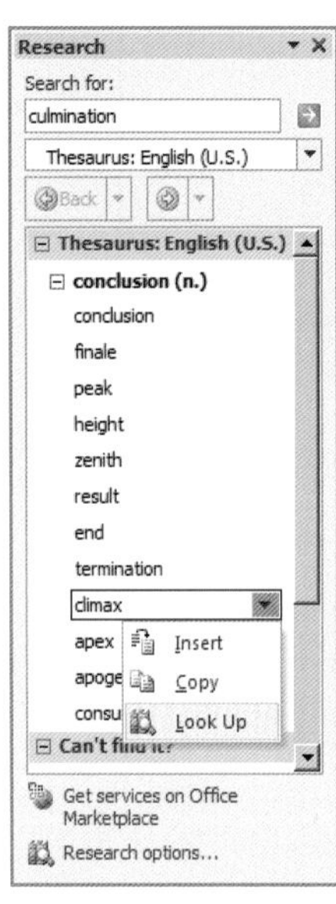

2. The Research pane appears – this can be moved or resized simply by dragging with the mouse. It contains a list of words that have a similar meaning to the one you selected

3. Scroll though and select one of the options

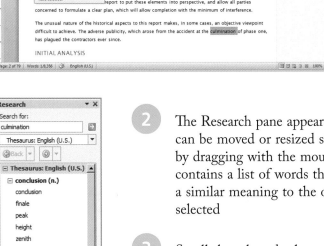

4. From the pop-up menu that appears, you can choose to insert the selected item, or copy it to the Clipboard

5. Alternatively, select Look Up to search the Thesaurus again, this time with the new selected word. You can repeat this process as many times as you like

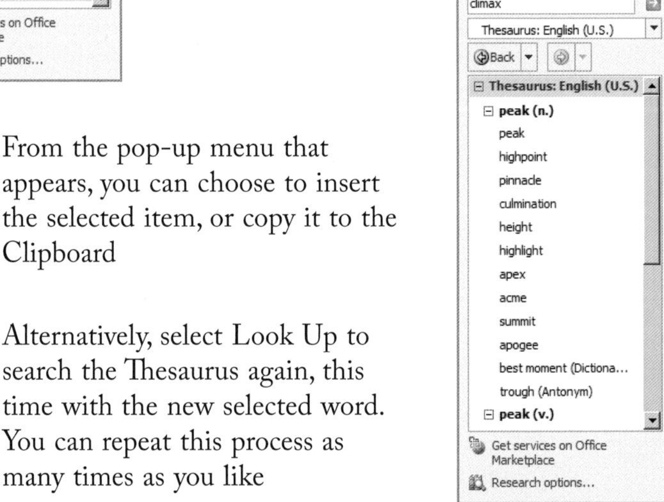

Translation

There are a number of built-in bilingual dictionaries, which allow you to see translations of words or sentences.

Translating Selected Text

1. Select one or more words, and then click on the Translate icon and choose Translate Selected Text

2. In the Research Pane, choose English in the From field, and the desired target language in the To field

3. The translated text appears in the lower half of the Research Pane

4. If you'd like to use the translated text, click Insert

Translating the Whole Document

1. Click the Translate icon and choose Translate Document

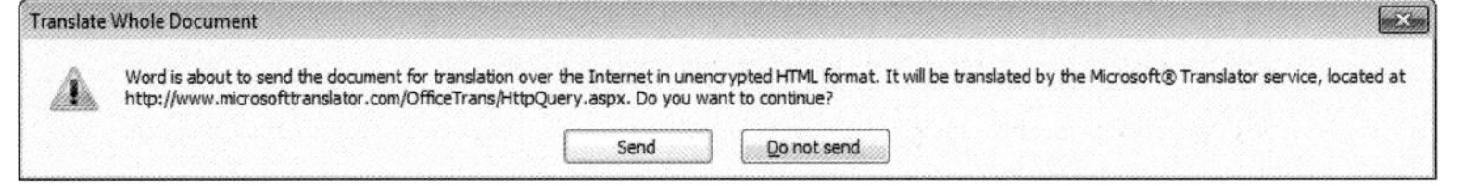

Don't forget

As well as a definition of the word selected, the dictionary also gives you an indication of pronunciation, using standard phonetics.

When translating a document, if you haven't already made the settings, Word will prompt you to specify the langauges to use.

...cont'd

2. Click Send, when the confirmation message appears. You'll be taken to the Microsoft Translator website, where you'll be able to see both the untranslated and the translated versions of your document

Beware

Because the Translate Whole Document feature uses a remote translation service, you need to be connected to the Internet to use this feature.

3. There may be a delay, depending on the amount of text to be translated

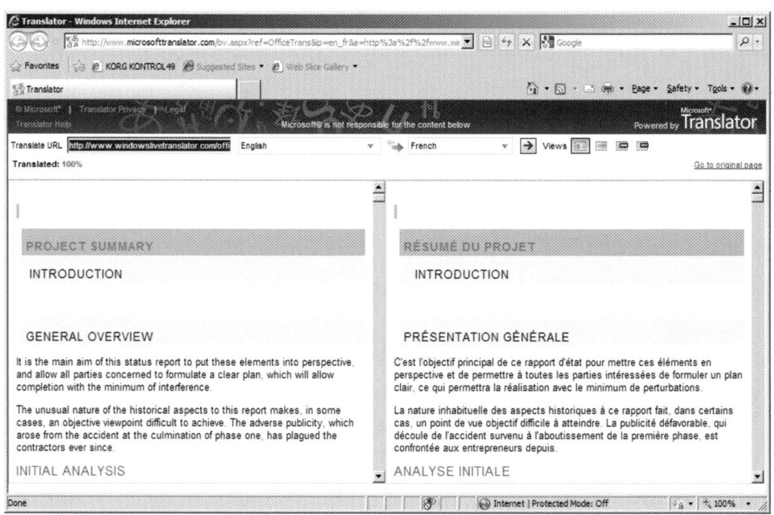
Translator - Windows Internet Explorer
Translate URL
English
French
Translated: 100%
Go to original page
PROJECT SUMMARY
INTRODUCTION
GENERAL OVERVIEW
It is the main aim of this status report to put these elements into perspective, and allow all parties concerned to formulate a clear plan, which will allow completion with the minimum of interference.
The unusual nature of the historical aspects to this report makes, in some cases, an objective viewpoint difficult to achieve. The adverse publicity, which arose from the accident at the culmination of phase one, has plagued the contractors ever since.
INITIAL ANALYSIS
RÉSUMÉ DU PROJET
INTRODUCTION
PRÉSENTATION GÉNÉRALE
C'est l'objectif principal de ce rapport d'état pour mettre ces éléments en perspective et de permettre à toutes les parties intéressées de formuler un plan clair, ce qui permettra la réalisation avec le minimum de perturbations.
La nature inhabituelle des aspects historiques à ce rapport fait, dans certains cas, un point de vue objectif difficile à atteindre. La publicité défavorable, qui découle de l'accident survenu à l'aboutissement de la première phase, est confrontée aux entrepreneurs depuis.
ANALYSE INITIALE
Done
Internet | Protected Mode: Off
100%

4. Although you can't save the translation directly, it's easy enough to copy and paste the translated text into a new or an existing Word document

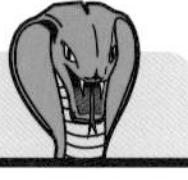

Beware

Although automatic translation software has improved dramatically in recent years, it's still not a perfect mechanism. If your document is important, you should get a human who understands the language to check it carefully.

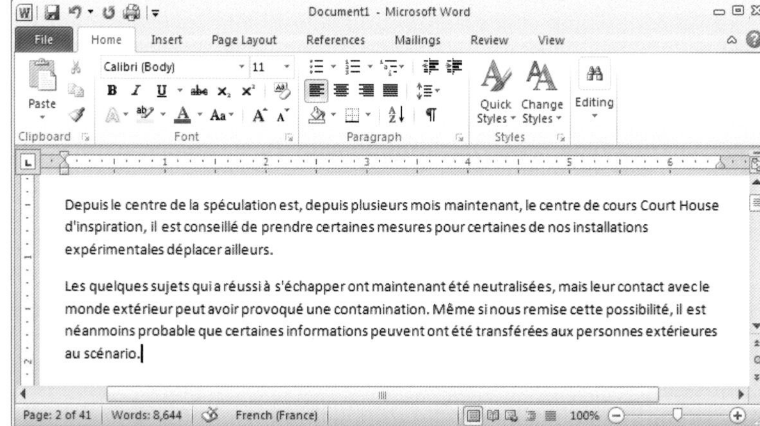
Document1 - Microsoft Word
File
Home
Insert
Page Layout
References
Mailings
Review
View
Calibri (Body)
11
Paste
Quick Styles
Change Styles
Editing
Clipboard
Font
Paragraph
Styles
Depuis le centre de la spéculation est, depuis plusieurs mois maintenant, le centre de cours Court House d'inspiration, il est conseillé de prendre certaines mesures pour certaines de nos installations expérimentales déplacer ailleurs.
Les quelques sujets qui a réussi à s'échapper ont maintenant été neutralisées, mais leur contact avec le monde extérieur peut avoir provoqué une contamination. Même si nous remise cette possibilité, il est néanmoins probable que certaines informations peuvent ont été transférées aux personnes extérieures au scénario.
Page: 2 of 41
Words: 8,644
French (France)
100%

Using ScreenTips for Translation

This feature allows you to quickly see a translation for a small piece of text.

1. Click the Translate icon and choose Mini Translator
2. In the Research Pane on the right of the screen, make sure the correct languages are set for From and To
3. If you allow your pointer to hover over a word for a few moments, a popup window will appear with its translation

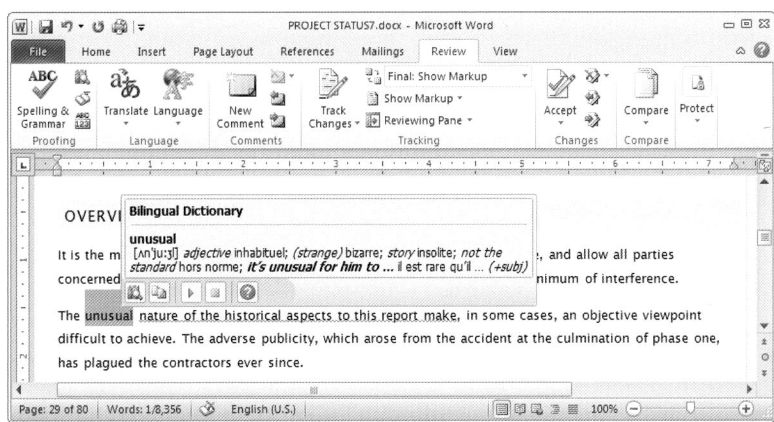
PROJECT STATUS7.docx - Microsoft Word
File
Home
Insert
Page Layout
References
Mailings
Review
View
Spelling & Grammar
Translate
Language
New Comment
Track Changes
Final: Show Markup
Show Markup
Reviewing Pane
Accept
Compare
Protect
Proofing
Language
Comments
Tracking
Changes
Compare
OVERVI
Bilingual Dictionary
unusual
[ʌn'ju:ʒl] adjective inhabituel; (strange) bizarre; story insolite; not the standard hors norme; it's unusual for him to ... il est rare qu'il ... (+subj)
It is the m
, and allow all parties
concerned
nimum of interference.
The unusual nature of the historical aspects to this report make, in some cases, an objective viewpoint
difficult to achieve. The adverse publicity, which arose from the accident at the culmination of phase one,
has plagued the contractors ever since.
Page: 29 of 80
Words: 1/8,356
English (U.S.)
100%

4. If you select a larger amount of text, the popup window will translate this

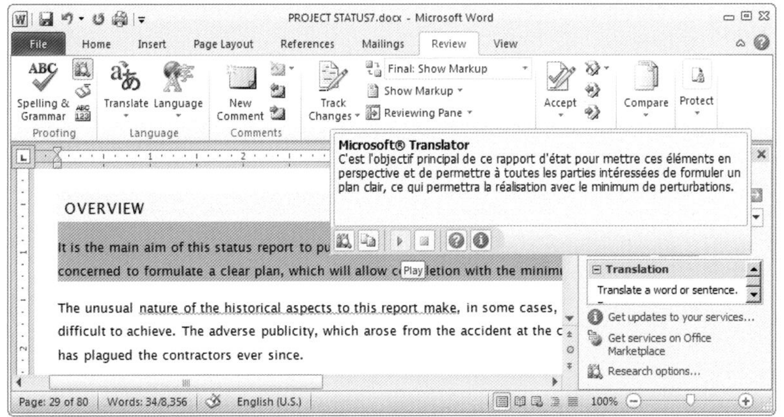
PROJECT STATUS7.docx - Microsoft Word
Microsoft® Translator
C'est l'objectif principal de ce rapport d'état pour mettre ces éléments en perspective et de permettre à toutes les parties intéressées de formuler un plan clair, ce qui permettra la réalisation avec le minimum de perturbations.
OVERVIEW
It is the main aim of this status report to pu
concerned to formulate a clear plan, which will allow c
Play
letion with the minim
Translation
Translate a word or sentence.
The unusual nature of the historical aspects to this report make, in some cases,
difficult to achieve. The adverse publicity, which arose from the accident at the c
has plagued the contractors ever since.
Get updates to your services...
Get services on Office Marketplace
Research options...
Page: 29 of 80
Words: 34/8,356
English (U.S.)
100%

Hot tip

The Bilingual Dictionary can also "speak" the word or text selected. Make sure your computer's audio output is functioning, then click the ▷ icon.

...cont'd

Proofing Language Settings

All text within your document has a specified language, which is used for translation, spelling, and grammar checking. You can set a default language for all new documents, or override the current language just on selected text.

1. Click the Language icon and choose Set Proofing Language

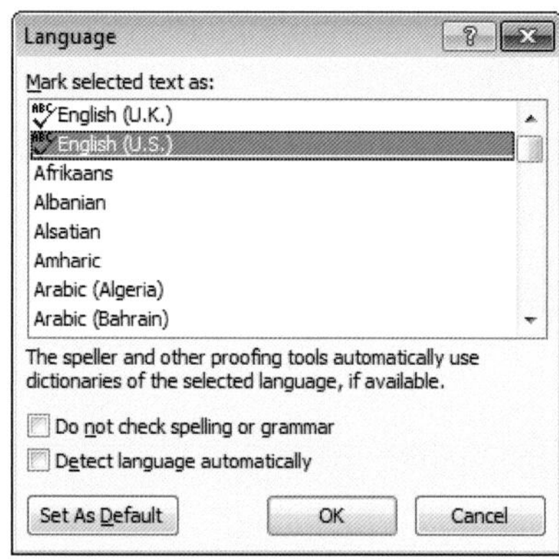

2. Choose the appropriate language for your selected text, or, alternatively, choose a language, then click Set As Default

3. Click OK

Language Preferences

The other option from the Language Tool popup menu is Language Preferences. From here, you can see which languages are installed. You can also decide which language is used for Word's own interface, including buttons, Control tabs, dialogs, and help.

You can also access the Word Options screen by choosing the File tab and selecting Options.

Comments

Adding a Comment

New Comment
Delete
Previous
Next
Comments

1. Select the text you'd like to add the comment to
2. Click the New Comment icon in the Comments area

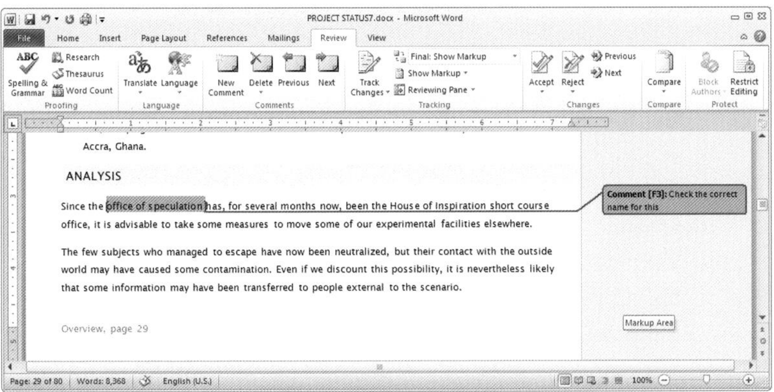
PROJECT STATUS7.docx - Microsoft Word
File
Home
Insert
Page Layout
References
Mailings
Review
View
Research
Thesaurus
Spelling & Grammar
Word Count
Proofing
Translate
Language
New Comment
Delete
Previous
Next
Comments
Track Changes
Final: Show Markup
Show Markup
Reviewing Pane
Tracking
Accept
Reject
Previous
Next
Changes
Compare
Block Authors
Restrict Editing
Protect
Accra, Ghana.
ANALYSIS
Since the office of speculation has, for several months now, been the House of Inspiration short course office, it is advisable to take some measures to move some of our experimental facilities elsewhere.
The few subjects who managed to escape have now been neutralized, but their contact with the outside world may have caused some contamination. Even if we discount this possibility, it is nevertheless likely that some information may have been transferred to people external to the scenario.
Comment [F3]: Check the correct name for this
Overview, page 29
Markup Area
Page: 29 of 80
Words: 8,368
English (U.S.)
100%

3. Add the comment text in the Markup Area at the right
4. Repeat this process to add more comments

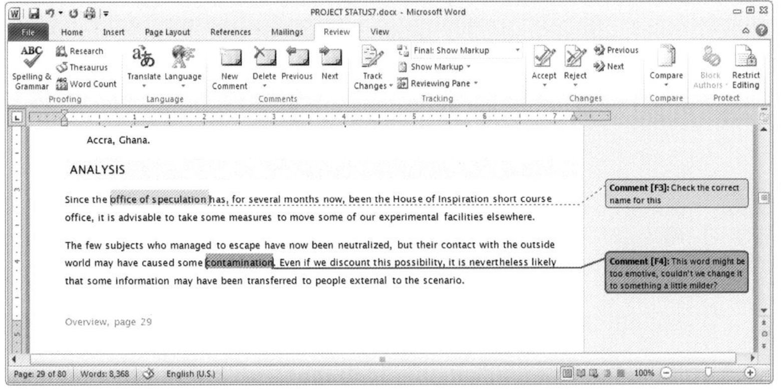
PROJECT STATUS7.docx - Microsoft Word
File
Home
Insert
Page Layout
References
Mailings
Review
View
Accra, Ghana.
ANALYSIS
Since the office of speculation has, for several months now, been the House of Inspiration short course office, it is advisable to take some measures to move some of our experimental facilities elsewhere.
The few subjects who managed to escape have now been neutralized, but their contact with the outside world may have caused some contamination. Even if we discount this possibility, it is nevertheless likely that some information may have been transferred to people external to the scenario.
Comment [F3]: Check the correct name for this
Comment [F4]: This word might be too emotive, couldn't we change it to something a little milder?
Overview, page 29
Page: 29 of 80
Words: 8,368
English (U.S.)
100%

5. To delete a comment, click anywhere within it and then use the Delete icon
6. You can move through the comments in your document by using the Previous and Next buttons

Hot tip

Comments are automatically renumbered as you add and delete them from your document.

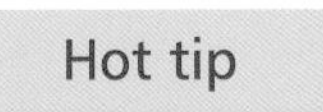
Hot tip

If you allow your mouse to rest over a commented piece of text, the comment will appear as a ToolTip. This is useful if you cannot see the Markup Area (if you are working in Draft mode, for example).

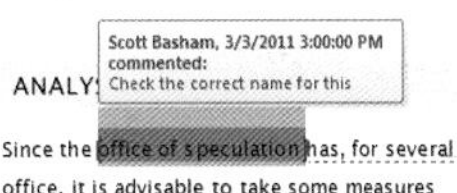
Scott Basham, 3/3/2011 3:00:00 PM commented:
Check the correct name for this
ANALY
Since the office of speculation has, for several
office, it is advisable to take some measures

Tracking

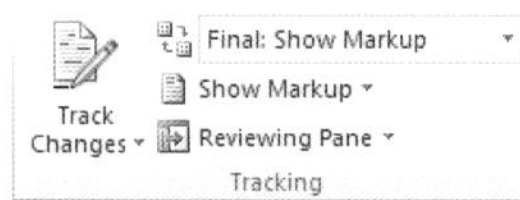

Sometimes it's useful to track changes you make to a document, so that someone else can see exactly what you have done. It may even be necessary for someone to approve or reject those changes, before they become permanently incorporated into the document.

Don't forget

Deleted text is shown in red, with a horizontal line running through it. New text is also in red, and underlined. A vertical line in the margin indicates that changes have been made in this area.

1. To activate change tracking, click the Track Changes icon in the Tracking area

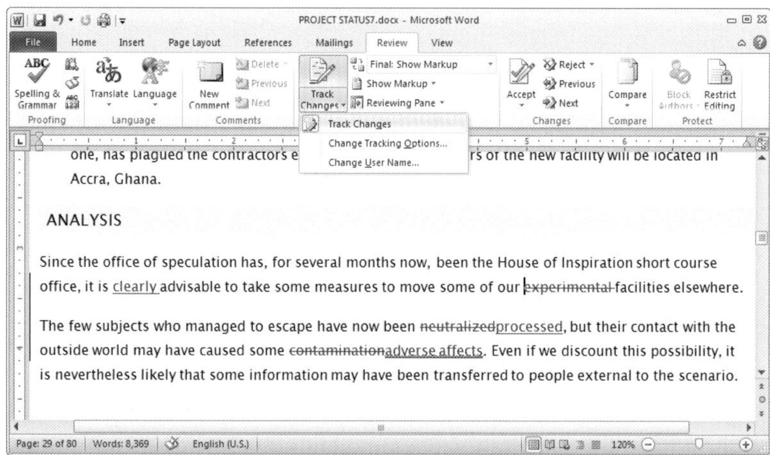

2. Now your edits will be shown visually. Experiment by deleting some old text, adding in some new text, editing some existing text, and then, finally, use copy and paste to move a phrase, sentence or paragraph to a different part of your document

Don't forget

If you move text (for example, by using Cut and Paste), then the moved text is shown in green, with a double underline. If you rest your mouse over any changed text, then the name, type of change, and date/time appears as a ToolTip.

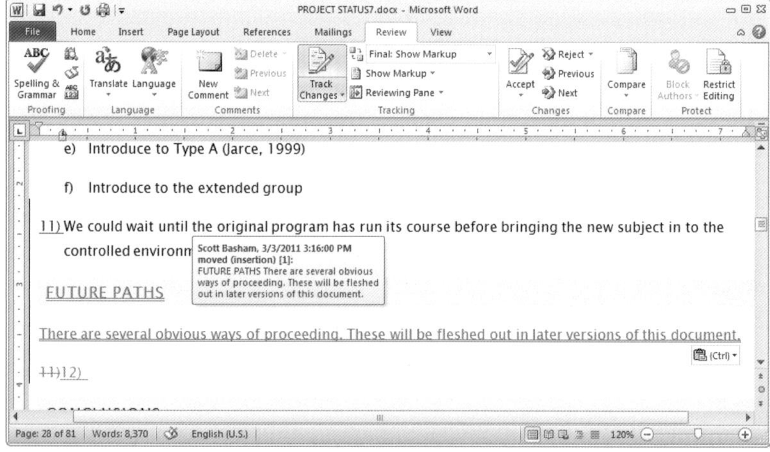

3 Click on the Show Markup icon in the Tracking area, choose Balloons and then "Show Revisions in Balloons" to see all the revision details in the Markup area

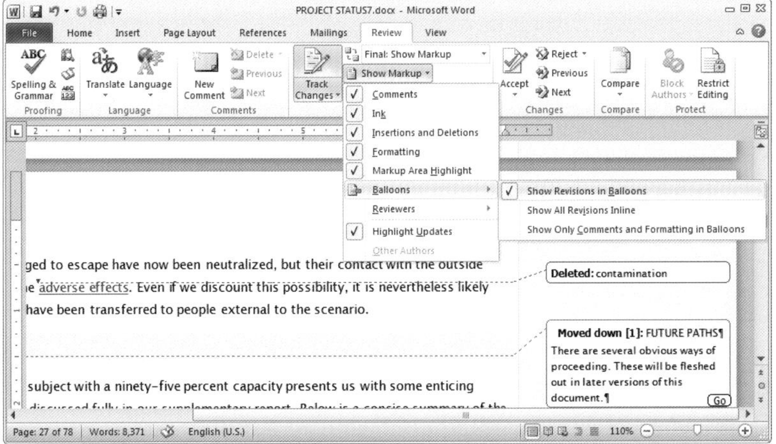

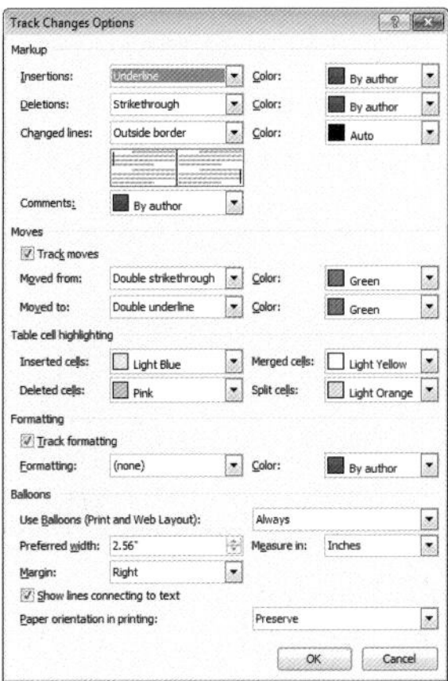

4 Click on the Reviewing Pane icon in the Tracking area, and choose one of the two options (Vertical or Horizontal) to make it visible

5 Make some more changes to your document, and watch what happens in the Reviewing Pane

The Reviewing Pane contains a comprehensive summary of all the revisions made, plus all the added comments.

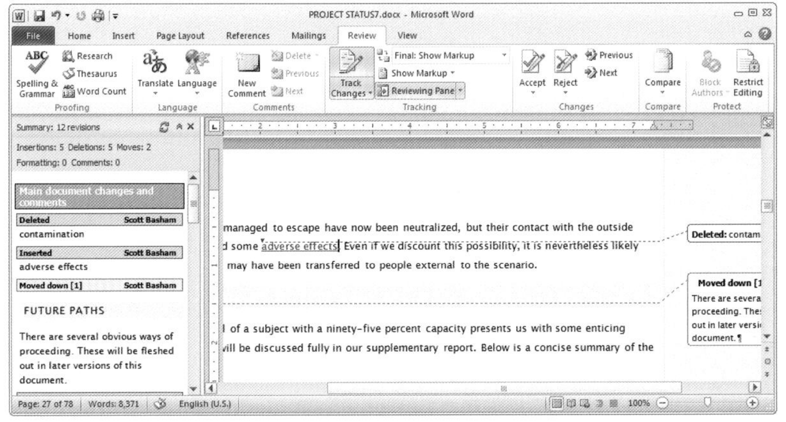

The Tracking tools also allow you to change the way your document is displayed. You can show the final or original version, with or without the changes marked up. You can also customize which types of changes will be displayed as markup.

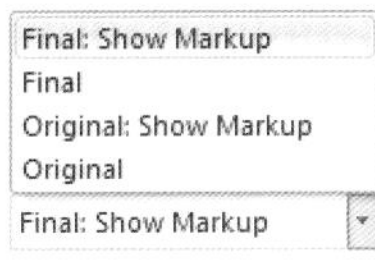

Changes

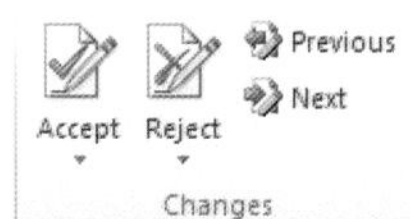

Now, if there are some changes in your document, you can take on the role of someone who reviews these changes. The tools in the Changes area let you work through your document, looking at each change in turn – using the Previous and Next icons.

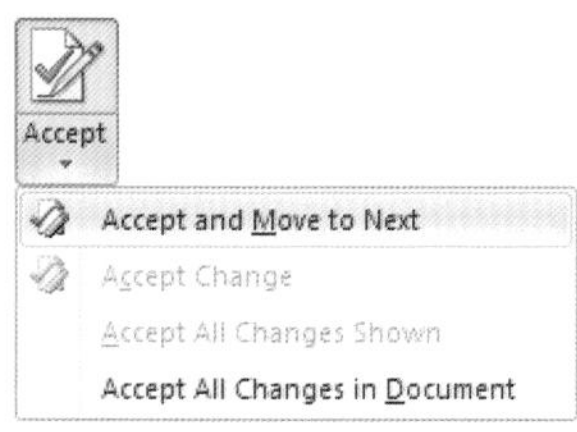

If you click the Accept button, then the change is permanently applied to the document.

If you click Reject instead, the change is removed and the text reverts to its original state.

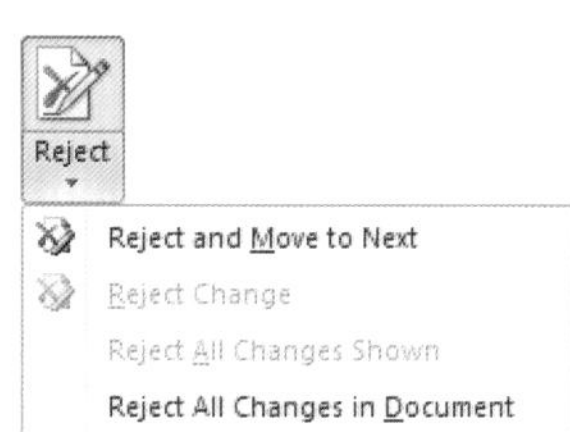

Hot tip

Sometimes the logged changes make it difficult to read a document. If you want to read the text without being distracted by the edits, go to the Tracking area of the Review Tab and choose Final, instead of Final Showing Markup. When you have finished, you can always switch back again.

Comparing Documents

Word allows you to divide the screen into a number of panes, so that you can quickly see the differences between versions of the same basic document.

1. Click on the Compare tool in the Compare area, and choose the first option

2. This dialog appears. Choose two documents to compare and then click OK

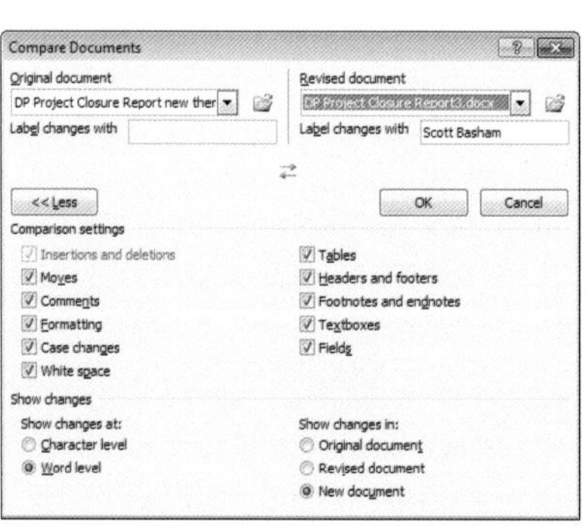

3. If either of the documents contains tracked changes then the following dialog will appear. Click Yes to proceed

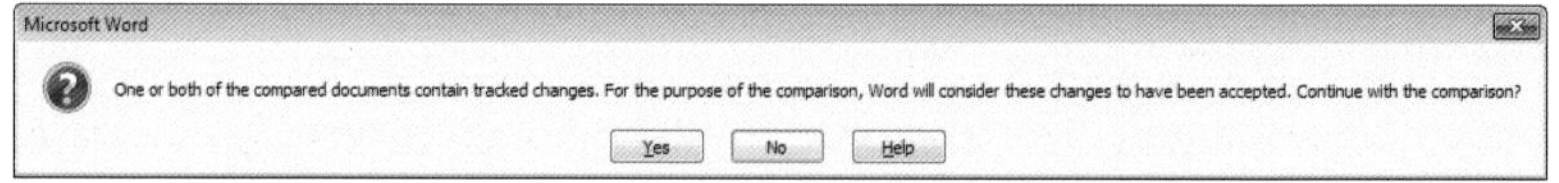

4. The screen will now divide into panes that depict the two source documents (at the right-hand side in this example), with a third larger pane that illustrates the comparison between the two

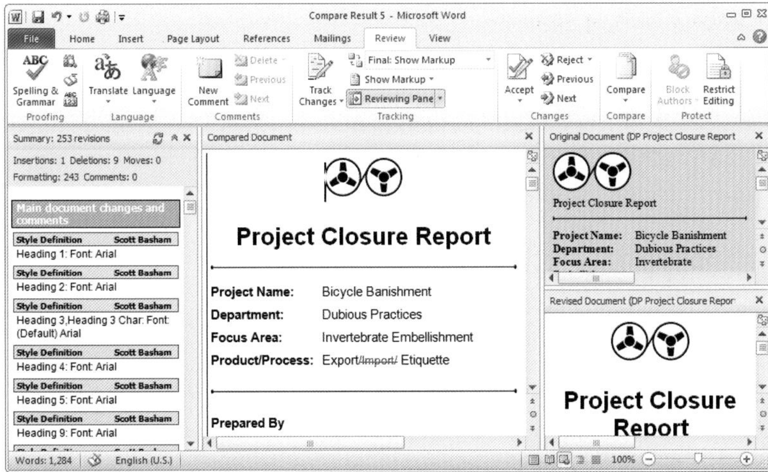

5. As before, the Reviewing Pane lists changes – this time it's the changes between the two documents. Word regards the first document you specified as the "original". It scans through the second document, and registers any differences it finds as revisions to be listed

6. Use the tools in the Changes area to move between changes, and click the Accept or Reject button, either to apply the second document's revisions, or to revert to the state of play in the original document

7. If you don't need to see the source documents, then click the Show Source Documents icon and choose Hide Source Documents

8. As part of this process, you have created a new document called "Compare Result" with a numeric suffix. If you are happy with the accept and reject decisions you have made, then save this document under a different name

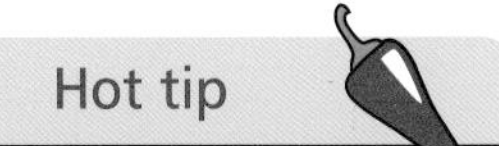

You can also use the Show Source Documents icon to show just one of the source documents, as well as to show both or to show neither.

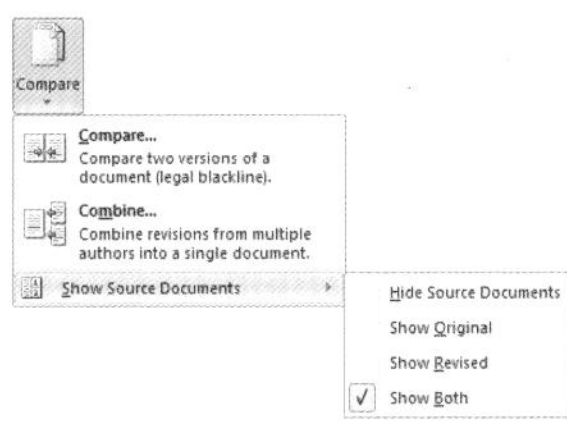

Protecting a Document

Word allows you to protect your document in a number of ways. You can control which aspects may be edited – for example, you may allow a user to add comments, but not to edit the text directly. If you are sharing your document, you can also restrict permissions to certain users.

Opening a Document From the Web

1. Download a document from the Web page, a shared repository (such as Windows Live's SkyDrive) or an email attachment. When you open this in Word, you'll see the following message:

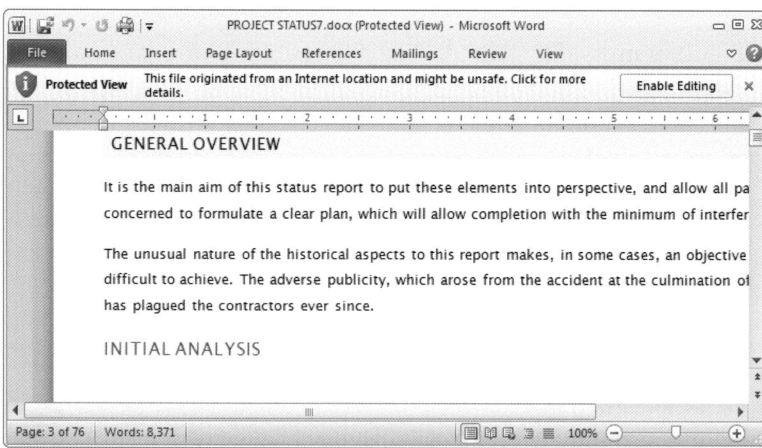
PROJECT STATUS7.docx (Protected View) - Microsoft Word
File
Home
Insert
Page Layout
References
Mailings
Review
View
Protected View
This file originated from an Internet location and might be unsafe. Click for more details.
Enable Editing
GENERAL OVERVIEW
It is the main aim of this status report to put these elements into perspective, and allow all pa
concerned to formulate a clear plan, which will allow completion with the minimum of interfer
The unusual nature of the historical aspects to this report makes, in some cases, an objective
difficult to achieve. The adverse publicity, which arose from the accident at the culmination of
has plagued the contractors ever since.
INITIAL ANALYSIS
Page: 3 of 76
Words: 8,371
100%

2. It's possible for Word documents to contain a virus. Most viruses are only active if Word's editing features are enabled, so, if you're not sure of the source of the document, then keep using Protected View – this will give you read-only access, which is relatively safe

3. If you're sure of the document, then click the Enable Editing button

4. You'll now be able to work with the document in the normal way. Once you've saved it locally in this state, Protected View will not be used

Beware 

Always make sure you have a Virus Checker utility running, and that its definitions are regularly updated. Doing this will minimize your risk of acquiring a virus.

Restricting Formatting and Editing

1. Click the Restrict Editing tool on the right hand side of the Review Command Tab. The Restrict Formatting and Editing pane appears

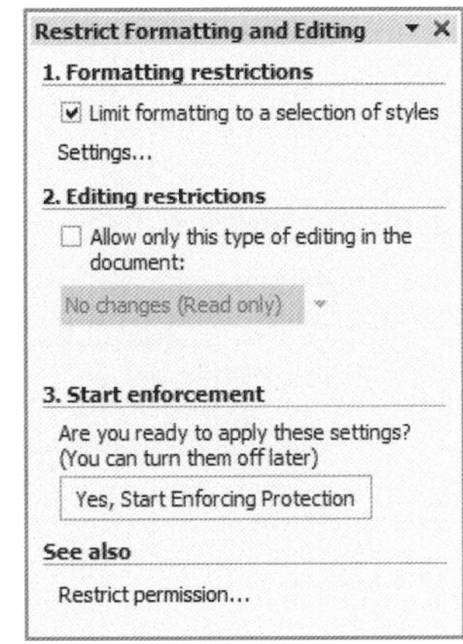

2. Switch on "Limit formatting to a selection of styles", then click on Settings

3. From this dialog, you can choose which styles will be allowed. By default, they're all enabled, so either review each one, or, if you want to use just a few, click "None" then reselect the styles you wish to allow. Click OK to return to the main page

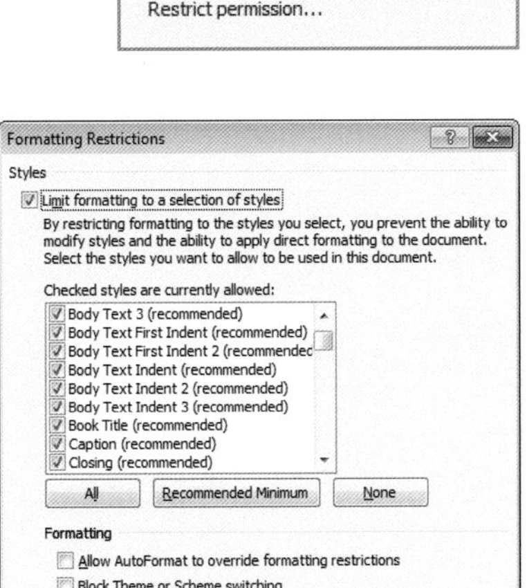
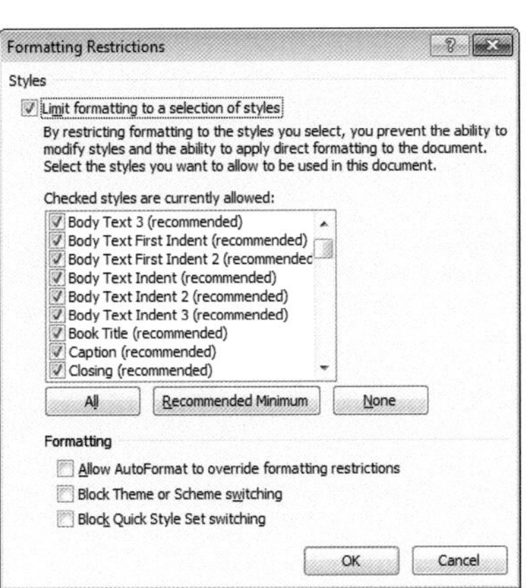

4. As well as formatting, you can also restrict editing capabilities. Select "Allow only this type of editing in the document" and then choose from the popup list. In this example, users will only be able to edit if their changes are fully tracked – they will not be allowed to switch off the Tracking feature

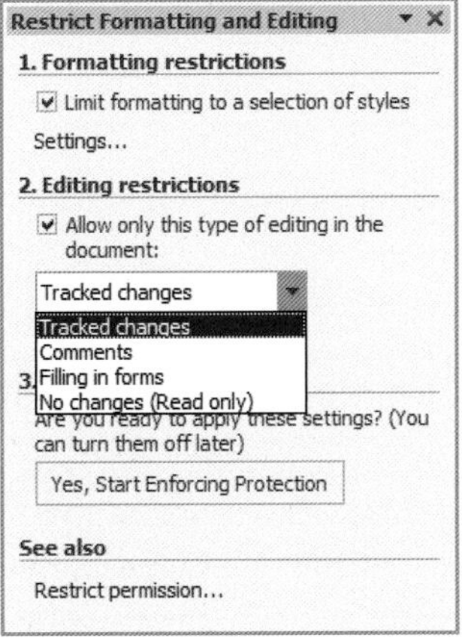

If you drag on the title bar of this pane, it becomes a free-floating window. Double-click on its title bar to restore it to the normal position. This technique works for most panes.

...cont'd

5 When you're happy with your settings, click the "Yes, Start Enforcing Protection" button

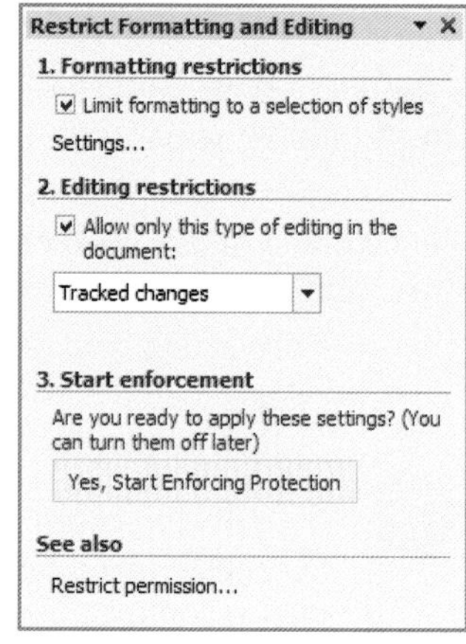

Don't forget

...your password.

6 The above dialog appears. Although optional, it's a good idea to enter a password, or the whole business of protection may become rather pointless

7 Your document is now protected according to your specifications. To remove the restrictions, click the Stop Protection button and enter your password. Your document will return to normal

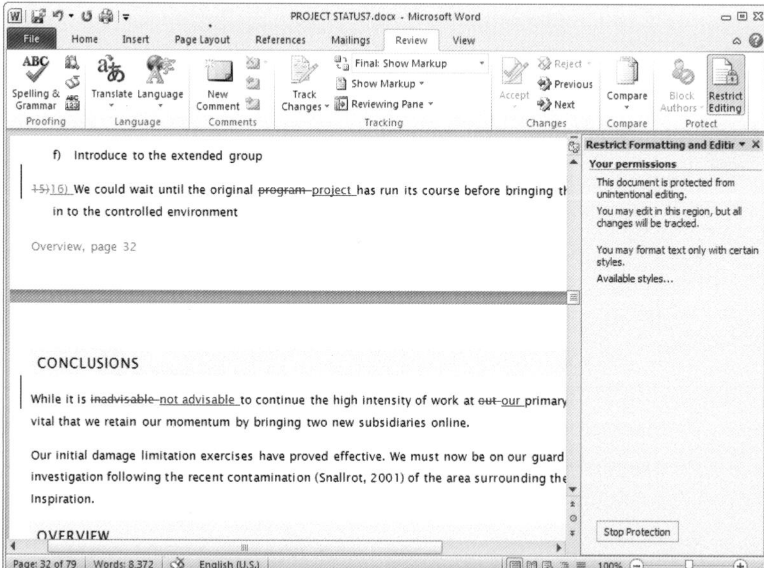

Restrict Permission

Another way to control and protect your document is to restrict the people who are allowed to read from and write to it. For this to work, you need to be set up for sharing. One way of doing this (illustrated here) is to make sure that all participants have their own Windows Live account.

1. Make sure the Restrict Formatting and Editing pane is visible (if not, then click the Restrict Editing button)

2. At the bottom, click "Restrict permission". If this is the first time you've used this feature, you'll need to set up the Information Rights Management (IRM) Service. Word will automatically guide you through this process

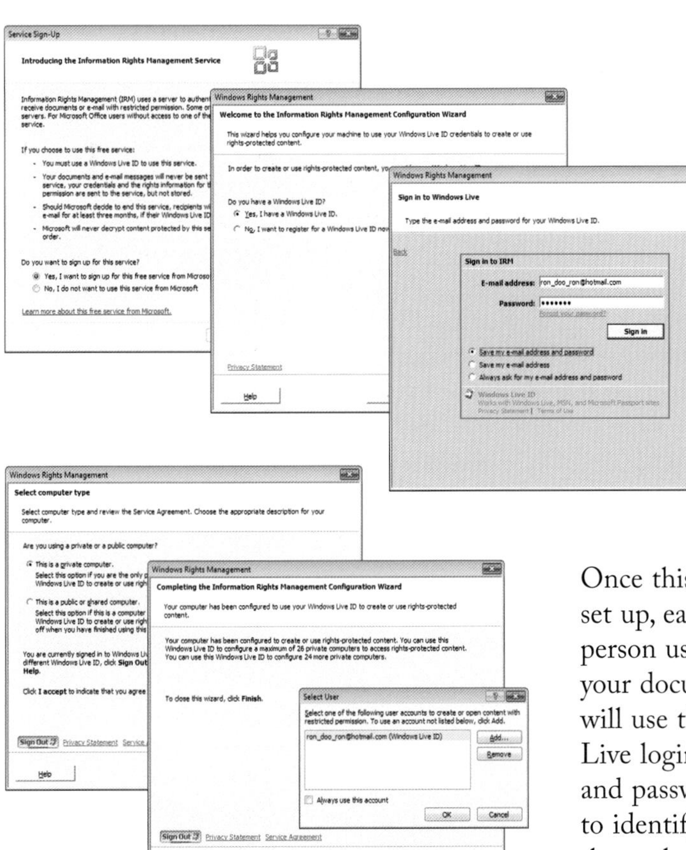

Once this is set up, each person using your document will use their Live login and password to identify themselves.

Hot tip

You can set up your own Windows Live account for free. If you're already a Hotmail user, then your Hotmail login is your Windows Live Account. If not, then it's easy to set one up. See www.home.live.com for more details.

...cont'd

3. If Information Rights Management is set up correctly, you'll see this dialog. Select "Restrict permission to this document"

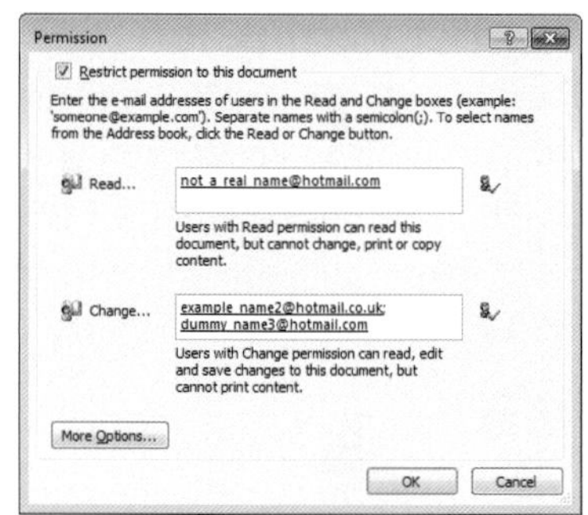

4. Click More Options for additional settings

5. Use the Add button to select users with either Read only or full Change permissions for your document. You can access users from a variety of sources, including your Hotmail contact list, or you can manually enter their login name

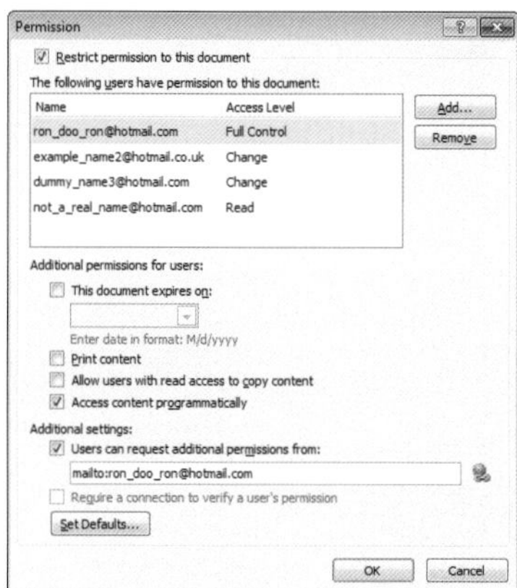

6. Click OK, to dismiss all dialogs, then save your document. The users specified will now be able to use it within the restrictions you specified

Hot tip

To remove the Restricted Access, click the Change Permission button and deselect "Restrict permission to this document". You will only be allowed to do this if you yourself have sufficient permission.

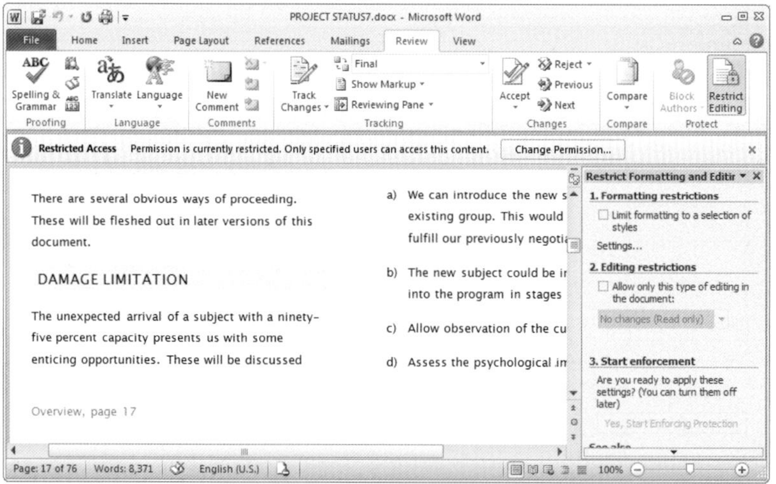

9 The View Tab

The View Tab gives you a range of controls for looking at your document in different ways.

Document Views

Print Layout | Full Screen Reading | Web Layout | Outline | Draft
Document Views

Full Screen Reading View

1. Make sure the View Command Tab is active. In the Document Views area, click the Full Screen Reading icon

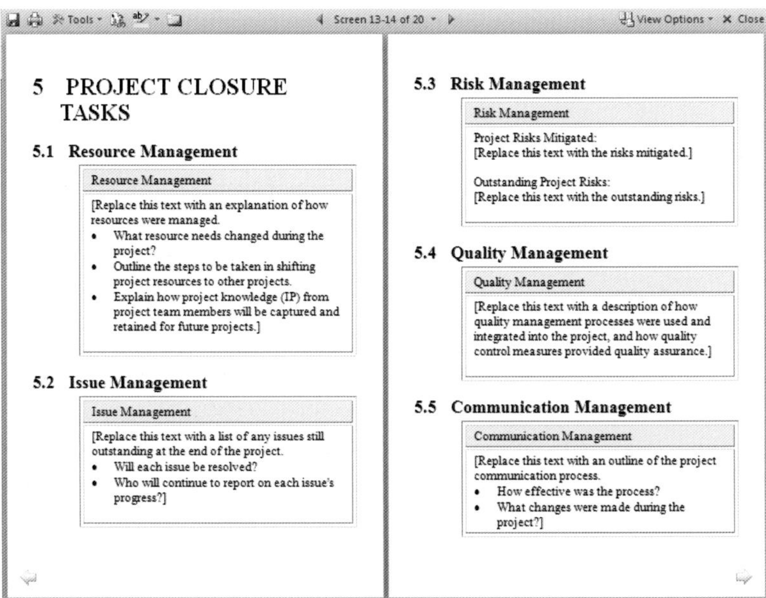

Tools · Screen 13-14 of 20 · View Options · Close

5 PROJECT CLOSURE TASKS

5.1 Resource Management

Resource Management

[Replace this text with an explanation of how resources were managed.
- What resource needs changed during the project?
- Outline the steps to be taken in shifting project resources to other projects.
- Explain how project knowledge (IP) from project team members will be captured and retained for future projects.]

5.2 Issue Management

Issue Management

[Replace this text with a list of any issues still outstanding at the end of the project.
- Will each issue be resolved?
- Who will continue to report on each issue's progress?]

5.3 Risk Management

Risk Management

Project Risks Mitigated:
[Replace this text with the risks mitigated.]

Outstanding Project Risks:
[Replace this text with the outstanding risks.]

5.4 Quality Management

Quality Management

[Replace this text with a description of how quality management processes were used and integrated into the project, and how quality control measures provided quality assurance.]

5.5 Communication Management

Communication Management

[Replace this text with an outline of the project communication process.
- How effective was the process?
- What changes were made during the project?]

2. The screen will look similar to the example above – designed to maximize space available for reading, or for adding comments. Use the "previous page" and "next page" icons in the bottom corners to navigate

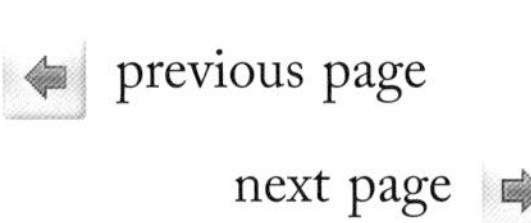
previous page
next page

3. You can customize this screen using the View Options menu in the top right corner. If you use the options to Increase or Decrease Text Size, this will only affect the current view, so will not permanently change your text

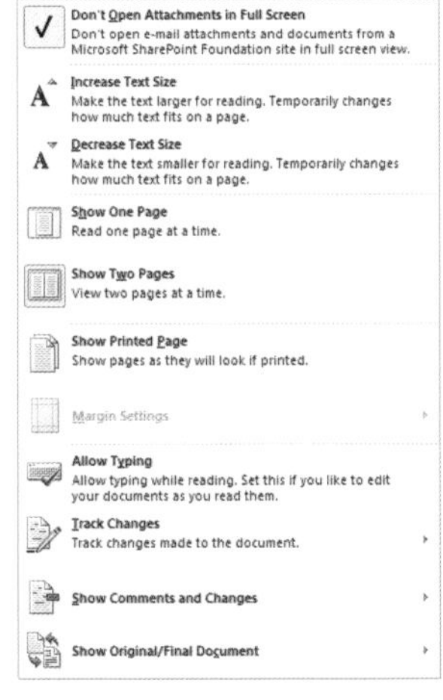
View Options
Don't Open Attachments in Full Screen
Don't open e-mail attachments and documents from a Microsoft SharePoint Foundation site in full screen view.
Increase Text Size
Make the text larger for reading. Temporarily changes how much text fits on a page.
Decrease Text Size
Make the text smaller for reading. Temporarily changes how much text fits on a page.
Show One Page
Read one page at a time.
Show Two Pages
View two pages at a time.
Show Printed Page
Show pages as they will look if printed.
Margin Settings
Allow Typing
Allow typing while reading. Set this if you like to edit your documents as you read them.
Track Changes
Track changes made to the document.
Show Comments and Changes
Show Original/Final Document

Hot tip

Word's Full Screen Reading View uses fonts that are specially designed for easy reading on your computer's screen.

4. The indicator in the center, at the top of the screen, shows you the current page number. It's also a pop-up menu, containing a range of navigational controls. From here, you can also invoke the Navigation Pane

5. Although most of the controls seen in other views are absent, you can access a shorter list of familiar features from the Tools menu at the top left of the main page area

6. When you're finished with Full Screen Reading View, click the Close button in the top right corner of the screen

Web Layout View

1. In the Document Views area, click the Web Layout icon

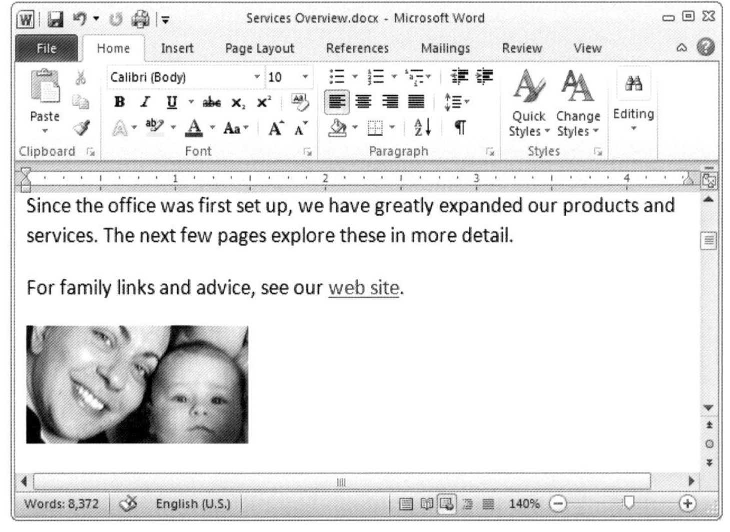

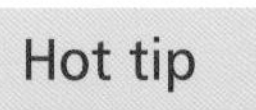

Web Layout View gives you a good idea of how your document would look if saved as a web page and then viewed in a browser, such as Internet Explorer. See Chapter Eleven, "Advanced Features", for more on this.

...cont'd

Outline View

In the Document Views area, click the Outline icon

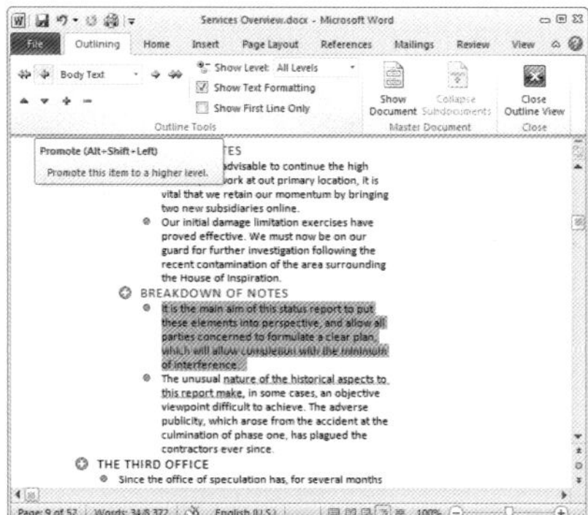

Outline view is useful if you structure your document using headings and subheadings allocated to indented levels. The Outlining Tab controls let you change levels, move lines up/down, or "collapse" items, so that lines on lower levels are temporarily hidden from view.

Beware

Outline view is only suitable if your document uses at least two levels of heading and subheading – otherwise, there is not enough structure for it to add any real value.

Draft View

In the Document Views area, click the Draft icon

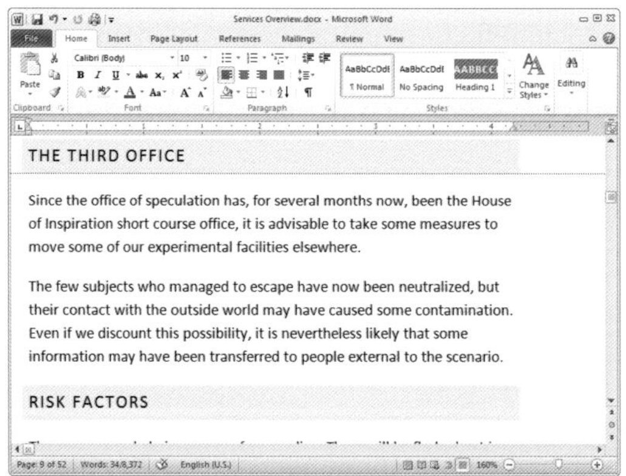
THE THIRD OFFICE
Since the office of speculation has, for several months now, been the House of Inspiration short course office, it is advisable to take some measures to move some of our experimental facilities elsewhere.
The few subjects who managed to escape have now been neutralized, but their contact with the outside world may have caused some contamination. Even if we discount this possibility, it is nevertheless likely that some information may have been transferred to people external to the scenario.
RISK FACTORS

The screen now shows a simplified view of your text, with elements, such as headers and footers, not visible.

2. This view is useful if your computer is slow, or if you just want to concentrate on the text with no distractions

3. You can continue to edit your text in this view. However, if you wish to see how your document will look when printed, make sure that you return to Print Layout view by clicking the appropriate icon in the Document Views area of the View Command Tab (or in the Status Bar)

Gridlines

Defining and Customizing Gridlines

Gridlines are useful for helping you to align objects, and to resize them in a regular way.

1. When you're working with a drawing element, the Drawing Tools appear automatically. Make sure the Format Tab is active, click the Align icon in the Arrange area, and then choose Grid Settings

2. Here you can set the size of the grid, using "Grid settings". You can also control how many visible vertical and horizontal lines will be displayed. For example, if you set "Vertical every" to 2, then a visible line will appear for every second actual gridline. This is useful if you don't want your page cluttered with too many gridlines

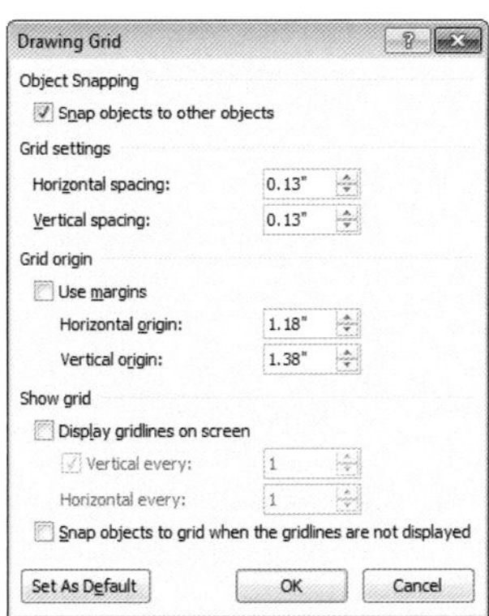

3. Select "Display gridlines on screen" and then click OK

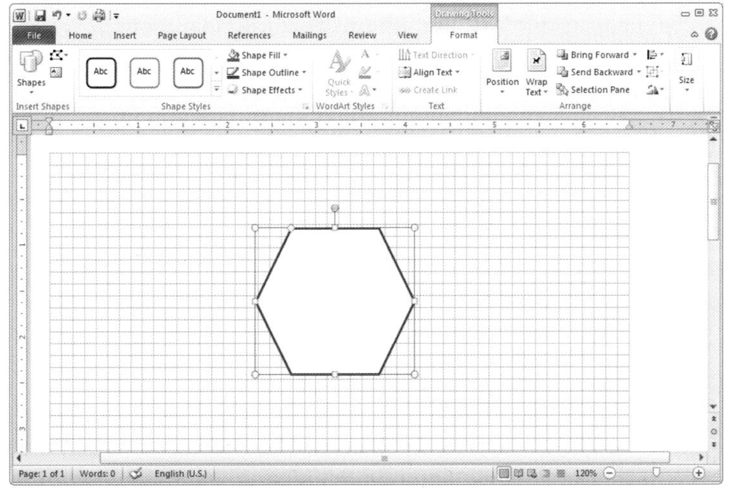

Hot tip

Gridlines can be easily switched on and off from the Show Controls in the View Tab. To customize your grid, however, you need to follow the instructions on the left.

Ruler

Gridlines

Navigation Pane

Show

Don't forget

Gridlines do not print – they are just there to help you arrange items on the page. When the grid is active, objects will "snap" to the nearest gridline, as if it were magnetic.

The Navigation Pane

The Navigation Pane can use the headings in your document to create a structured list, located to the left of the main page area. This can be used to navigate easily through a long document.

Activating the Navigation Pane

1. In the Show area of the View Command Tab, click the Navigation Pane checkbox to switch it on

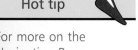

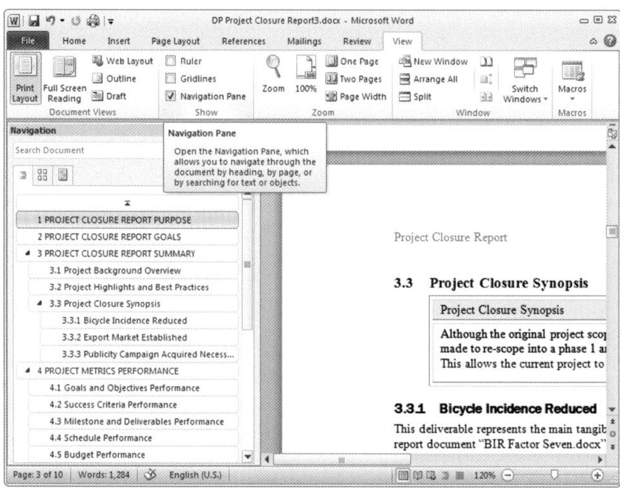

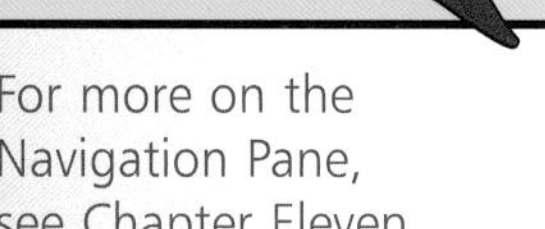

For more on the Navigation Pane, see Chapter Eleven, "Advanced Features".

2. The Navigation Pane appears, with its own scroll bars. It has three tabbed pages, so make sure the first of these is active. This will list any headings, or subheadings. If you click on one of these, then the main document window will automatically move to this line, scrolling if necessary

3. The second tabbed page will display the pages in your document as Thumbnails (small images), so you can scroll visually through the document

4. The third tabbed page allows you to search, based on text or objects, such as pictures, tables or equations

5. When you're finished with the Navigation Pane, either click the close icon in its top right corner, or switch off the option in the Show area of the View Command Tab

Windows

Sometimes it can be useful to view a document in several windows simultaneously – for example, you might want to zoom and scroll differently in each window.

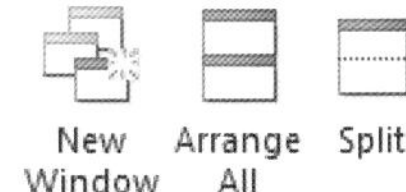

1. Click New Window in the Window area of the View Command Tab. A second window opens in front of the first. You now have two windows for the same document

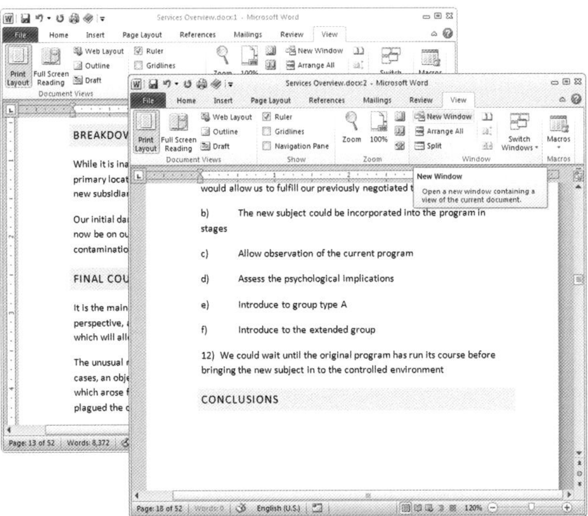

2. Another way of looking at your document in two ways is to split the main window. Click the Split tool

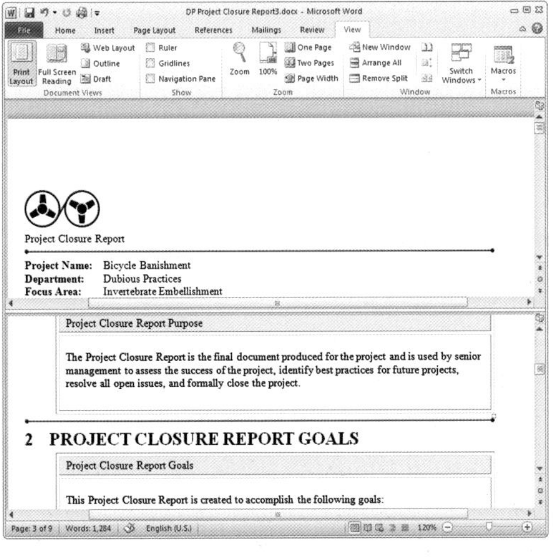

The window splits into an upper and lower segment – you can drag the boundary up and down to make them unequal sizes. You can now scroll each segment independently of the other.

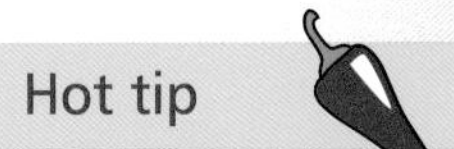

Split windows can be recombined by clicking on the Remove Split tool

...cont'd

Arrange All

1 With Word, you can have many documents open at the same time. This is useful, but it can be confusing trying to keep track of them. To see all your Word windows simultaneously, click the Arrange All button

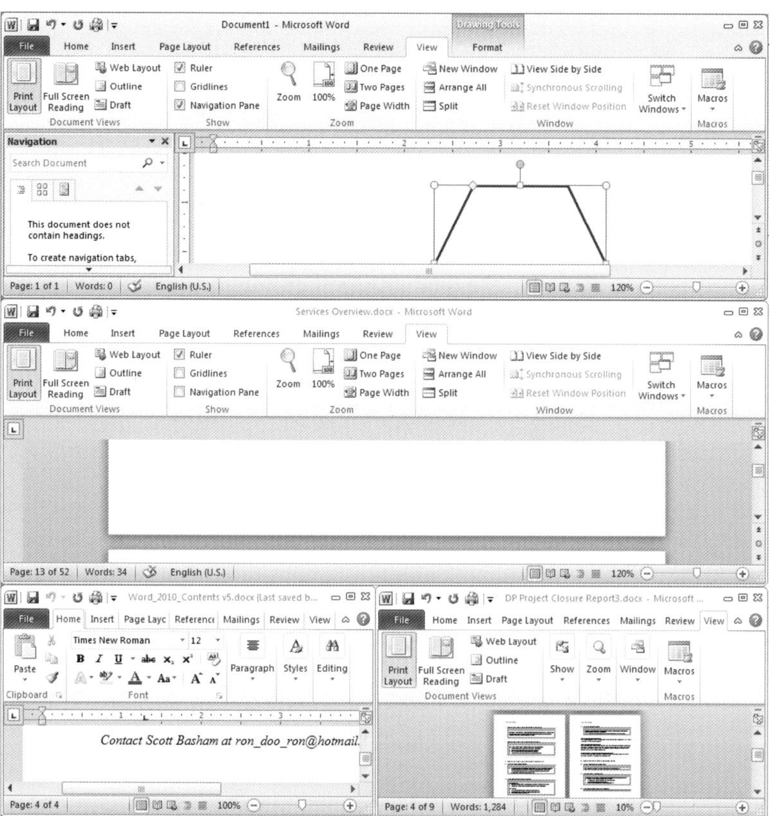

2 Word will divide up the entire screen between all open windows. You can still move, resize, maximize, or minimize them in the normal way

3 If you decide you don't need some of these documents, close them. Then, if you click the Arrange All button again, Word will have an easier time dividing up the screen area amongst the documents which are still open

View Side by Side

1. Make sure you have at least two documents open

2. Click the "View Side by Side" tool. The following dialog will appear

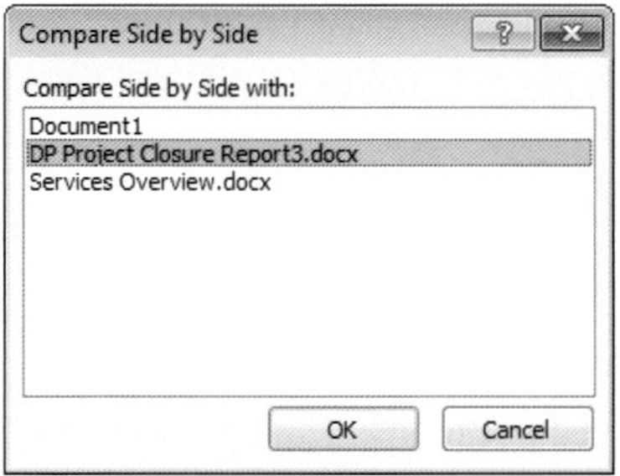

3. Word will compare (side by side) the current document with whatever you select here

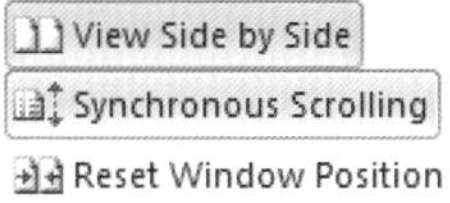

4. The two tools below now become active. Synchronous Scrolling allows scrolling one window to control the other as well. If you've moved or resized either window, then Reset Window Position will size them equally once more

Switch Windows

1. You can switch from one document to another by using any of the normal Windows methods, e.g. the Taskbar, Alt+Tab, or the Task Manager

2. Another way is to click the Switch Windows tool, and then select the desired document from the popup menu that appears

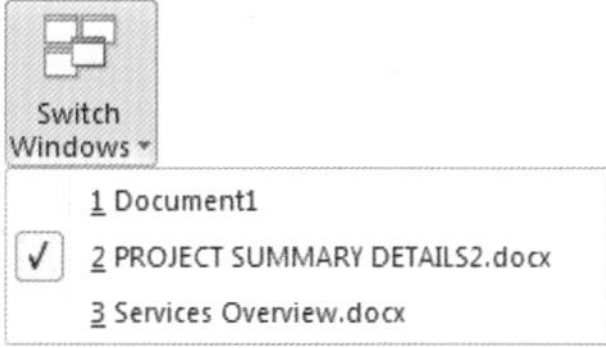

Macros

Macros are recordings of common activities. You can record your own macros, and then play them back whenever necessary. If you understand Microsoft Visual Basic, you can even open existing macros and edit them.

Recording a Macro

1. Make sure the View Command Tab is active, click on Macros, and choose Record Macro

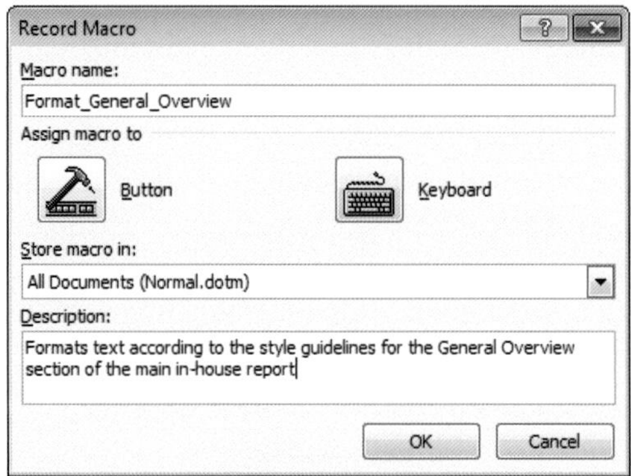

2. The Record Macro dialog appears. Enter a name for your macro, and decide where you want to store it. If you choose "All Documents (Normal.dotm)", then the macro will be available in all normal new documents from now on. Alternatively, you could decide to store the macro locally in the current document

3. Enter some text in the Description field. This will help you remember what the macro does later on

4. If you want to assign the macro to a keyboard shortcut, click the Keyboard button

5. In this example, rather than using a keyboard shortcut, we'll assign the macro to a button in the Quick Access Toolbar. To do this, click the Button icon

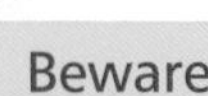

A macro name must be a whole word, so it cannot contain spaces or special characters. You are allowed to use the underscore character, so macro names like Format_Overview are allowed.

6 The Word Options Customize dialog appears. Your new macro appears in the list on the left. To add it to the Quick Access Toolbar, select the macro and then click the Add button

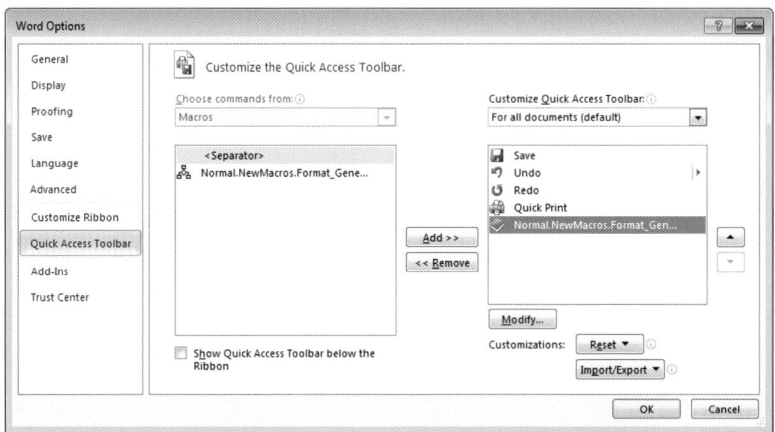

Click the Modify button to customize the icon to be used

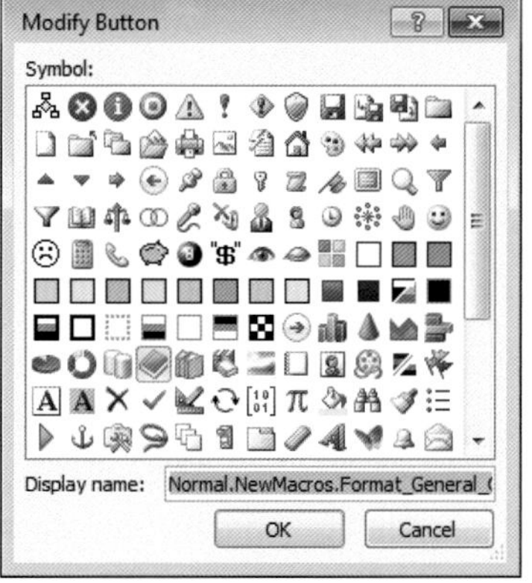

You have not yet finished recording your macro, but, ultimately, it will appear in the Quick Access Toolbar as the icon you selected. Its full name will appear as a tooltip, if you hover over the icon in the Toolbar.

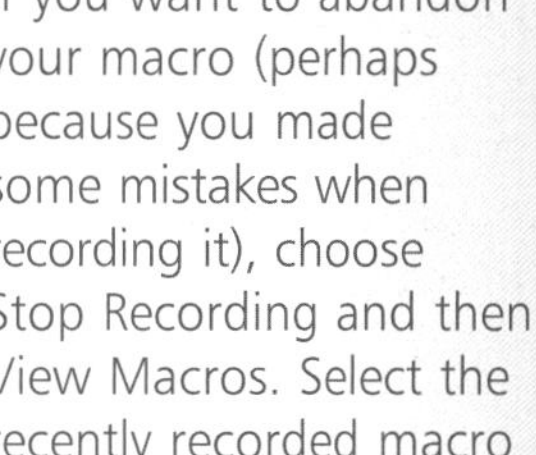

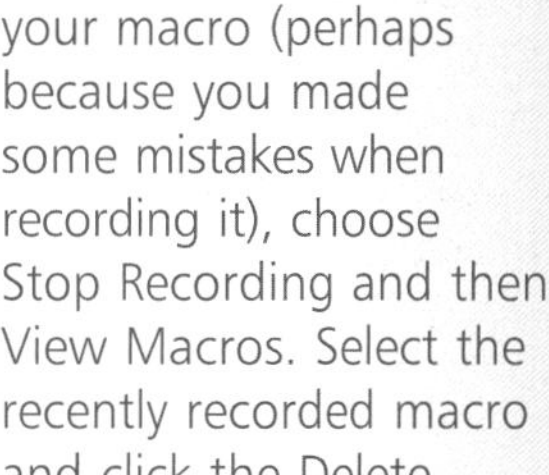

Hot tip

If you want to abandon your macro (perhaps because you made some mistakes when recording it), choose Stop Recording and then View Macros. Select the recently recorded macro and click the Delete button.

7 Step through the actions you want to record, then click the Macros button and choose Stop Recording

8 Your macro has now been saved. You can now run it from the Quick Access Toolbar, or via a keyboard shortcut. Another way is to click the Macros tool and select View Macros

...cont'd

Viewing and Editing Macros

Don't forget

Macros are a standard feature of Microsoft Office applications. The underlying language used is Visual Basic. Some Visual Basic commands are universal, and some apply only to a particular Office Application.

Click the Macros icon and select View Macros. The Macros dialog box will appear

Here you can select a macro and read its description, before deciding to run it. You can also create, edit, or delete macros.

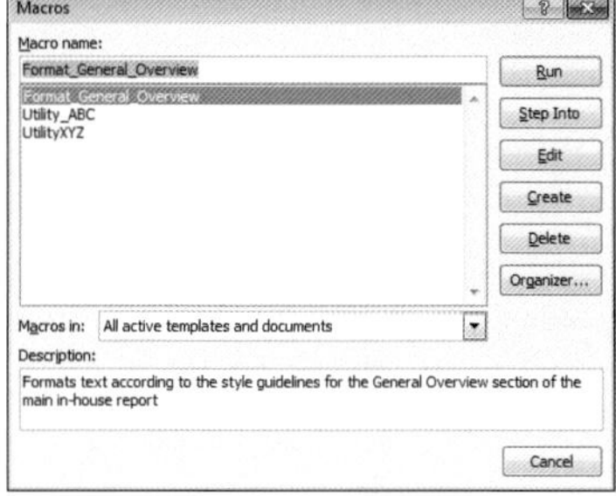

Choose a macro and click Edit

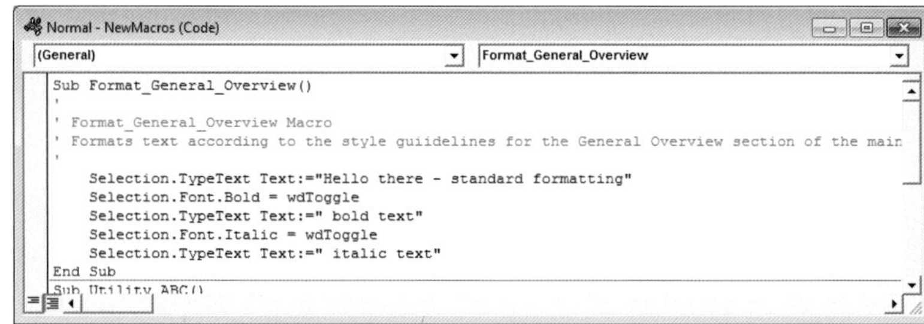

A Visual Basic editing window appears. If you're familiar with this language, then you can add to, edit, or delete the commands already recorded within the macro.

Don't forget

For security reasons, you can't save macros as part of a normal Word document (a .docx file). To save a document, together with its macros, choose Save As and select the file type Word Macro-Enabled Document (.docm).

Close the Visual Basic window, then return to the Macro dialog (click the Macros button and choose View Macros) and click the Organizer button

Here you can copy your macros between documents and templates. A macro embedded in a template is available to any document based on that template.

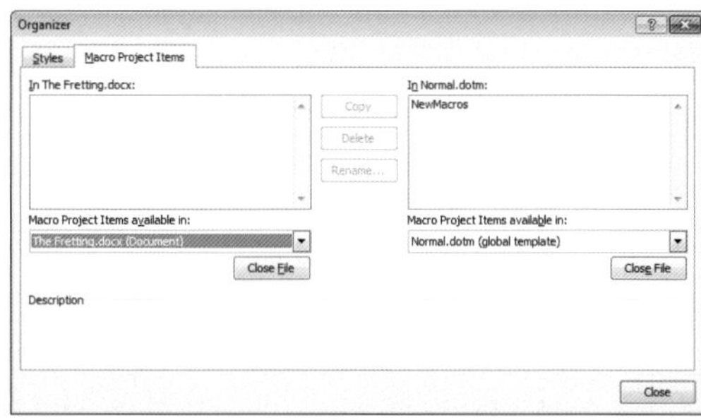

10 Backstage View

Backstage View is a new addition to Word 2010. It contains many settings and controls for operating on (rather than within) documents.

Info

1. Activate Backstage View by clicking on the File Tab

2. By default, you see the Info screen. This gives you a useful summary of your current document's properties – listed along the right hand side

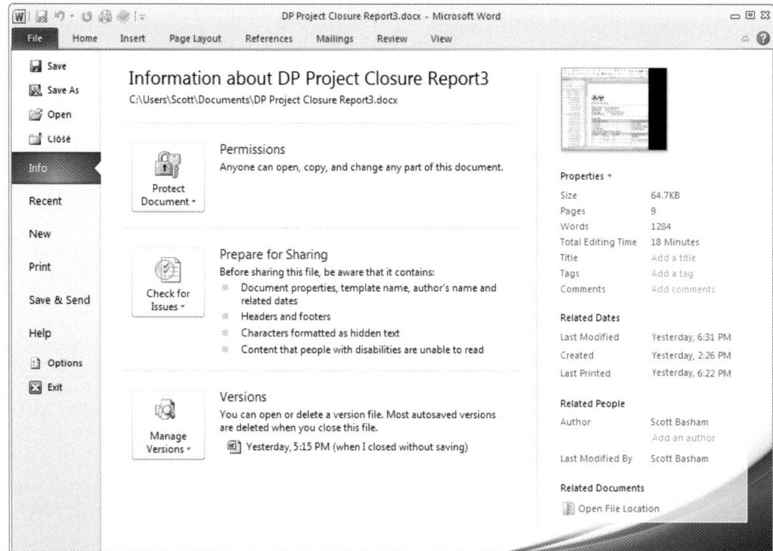

3. In the central part of the screen, there are controls for changing the permissions, checking for issues before sharing or distributing, and clearing up any draft versions of your document, which may have been created automatically

4. If your current document is in a format for an older version of Word, you'll be missing out on some of the new features. If you want to upgrade it to the latest format, click the Convert button:

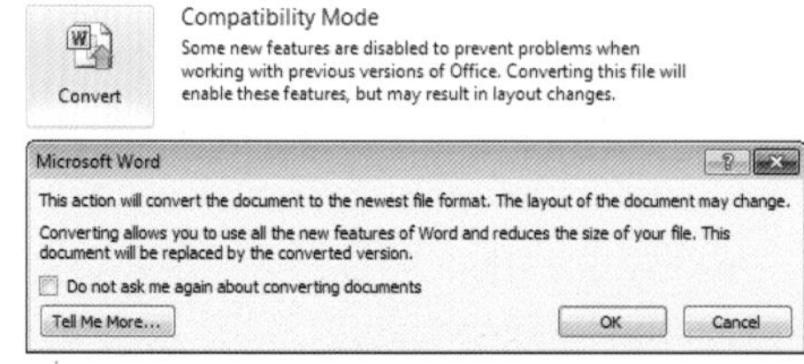

Beware

If you do convert your document to Word 2010 format, others using earlier versions may not be able to open it. If you need them to work on your document, use Save As and select "Word 97 - 2003 Document" as the file type (see next page).

Save and Save As

1. Choose Save As to see the following screen

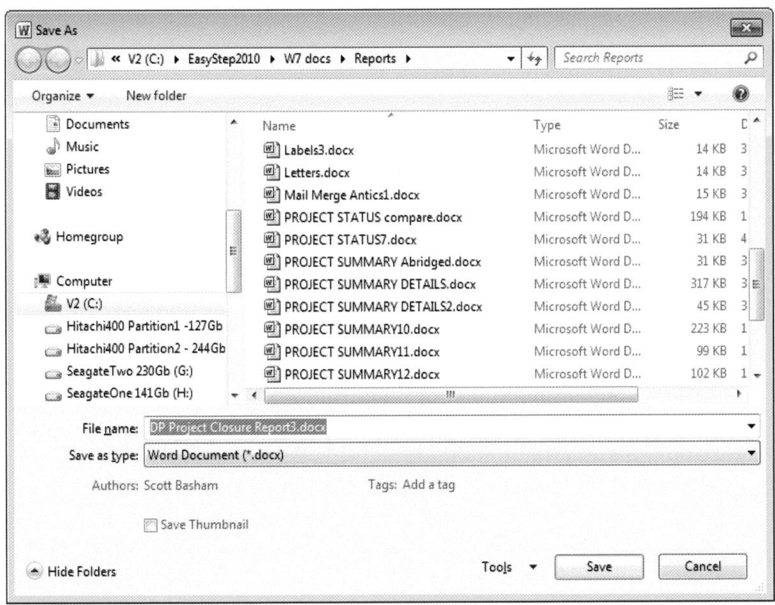

2. Open the "Save as type" popup to see the types available

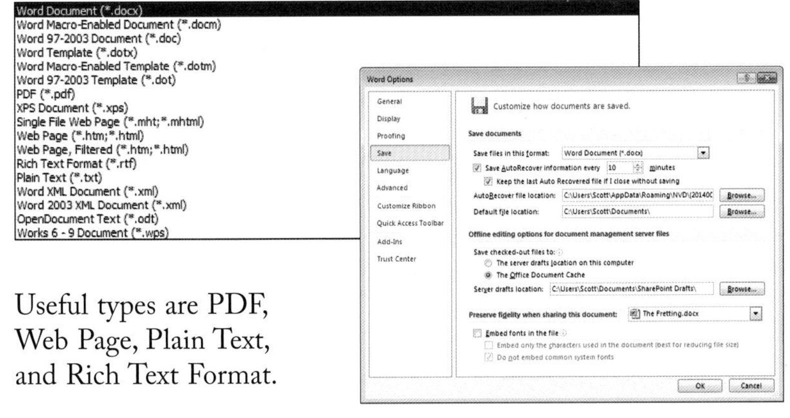

Useful types are PDF, Web Page, Plain Text, and Rich Text Format.

3. Click on Tools and choose Save Options to control default settings, such as file format and locations

4. When you are finished with this dialog, click OK and then Save to save your document

Hot tip

Plain Text is the simplest type – there's no formatting, but your file will be readable on virtually any system.

Map Network Drive...
Save Options...
General Options...
Web Options...
Compress Pictures...

Recent

Click on Recent. You'll see a list of the most recently-accessed documents

The Open option in the File Tab was covered in Chapter One, under "Working With Files".

Any of these documents can be opened easily, with just a single click.

If you select the small pin icon to the right of an item in the list, it will become a permanent list item, even if it hasn't been used particularly recently.

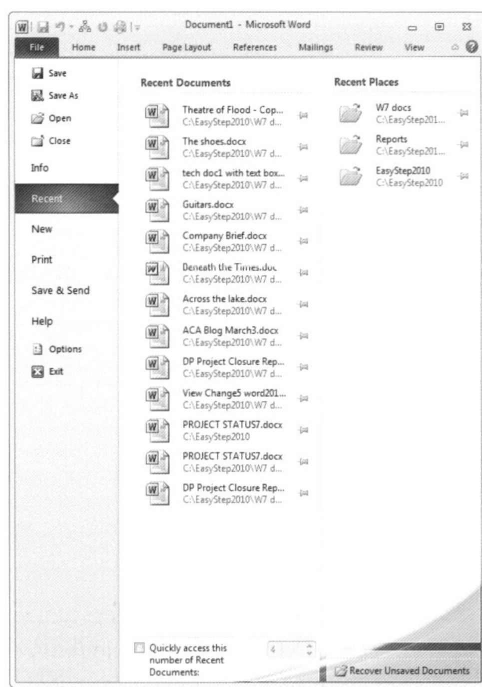

2 Near the bottom is an option "Quickly access this number of Recent Documents". If you select this, then a shorter list of recent documents will always be directly available in the File Tab list of commands. This is a handy way of making it easy to open your most important files

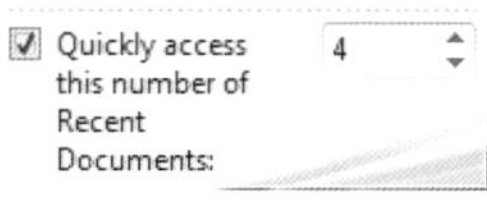

3 If you don't want to open any of the recent documents, simply move to another Tab

Using Templates

1. Click on New. In this screen, you can create a variety of new documents based on many designs, ranging from the simple to very complex templates

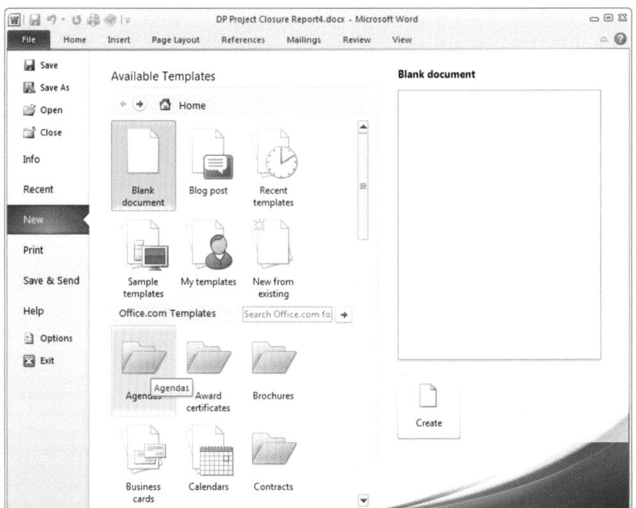

2. Under the Office.com Templates section, open the Agendas folder. There may be a slight delay while the remote files are accessed

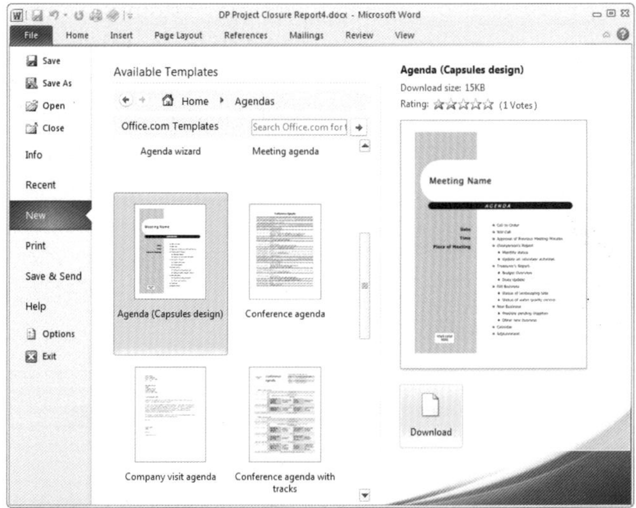

3. Select any Agenda template, then click Download

To start off working with a single blank page, simply double-click the "Blank document" icon

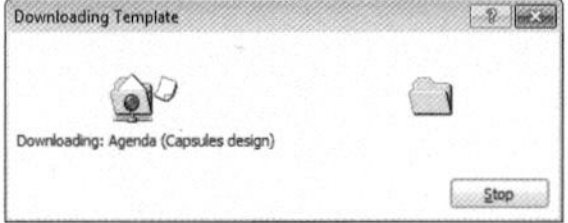

A new document is created, as a copy of the Word Template. It uses example text, already formatted, so all you need to do is replace it with your own.

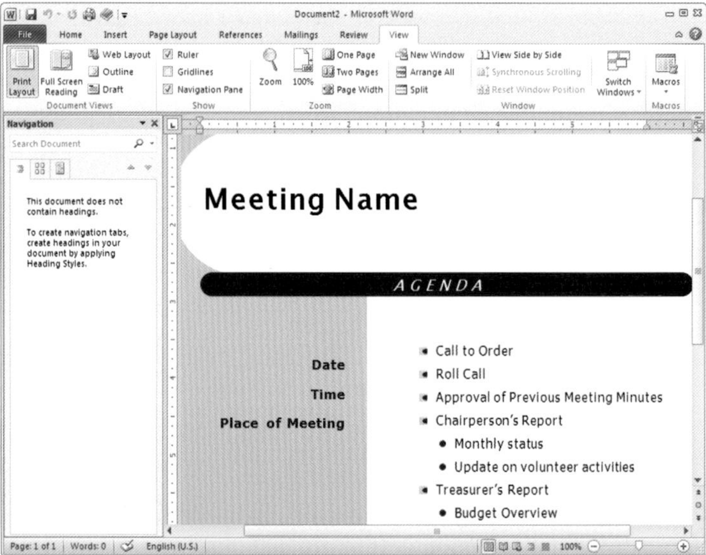

4. Select the text "Meeting Name" and type in your title. Fill in the other details by replacing the template text

5. When you're finished, save the new document

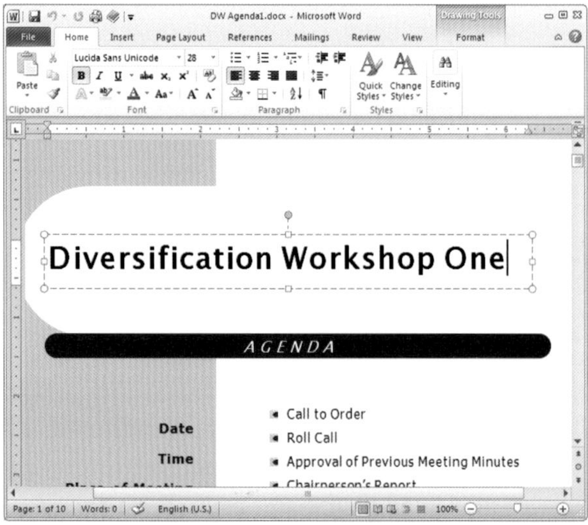

Creating Your Own Templates

A template is just an ordinary Word document saved as a special file type, and is usually in a special location.

1. Create your document in the normal way. You may want to use dummy placeholder text. When it's ready, choose Save As from the File Tab

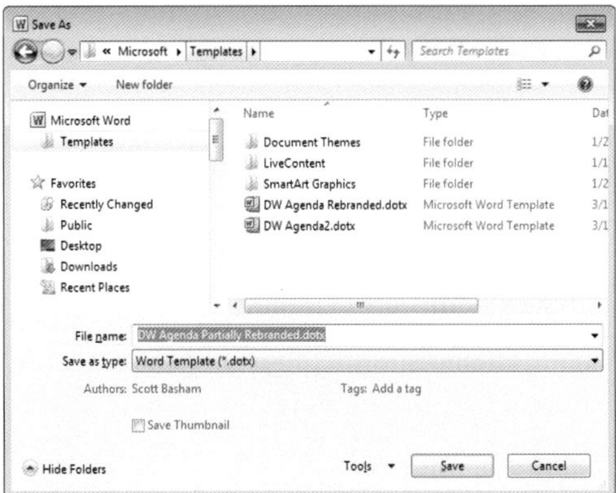

In the top left of the Save As dialog, select Microsoft Word, Templates for the file location.

Make sure you choose "Word Template (*.docx)" as the file type.

2. When you're ready to use your template, choose New from the File Tab. In the Available Templates section, click on "My templates". Any templates saved in the special location will be listed. Select one and click OK

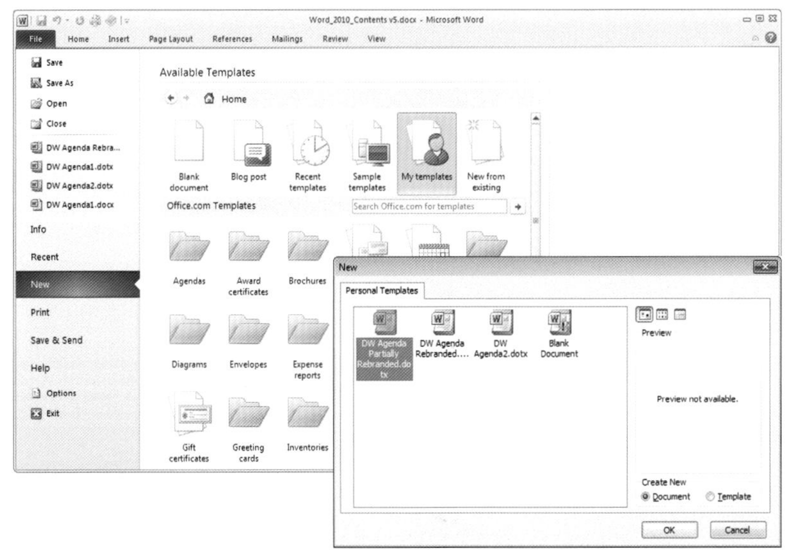

Hot tip

Even if you haven't prepared templates according to these instructions, you can still achieve similar results by choosing New, then clicking on the "New from existing" icon in the Available Templates section.

Print

1. Make sure you have an open document. Choose Print from the File Tab

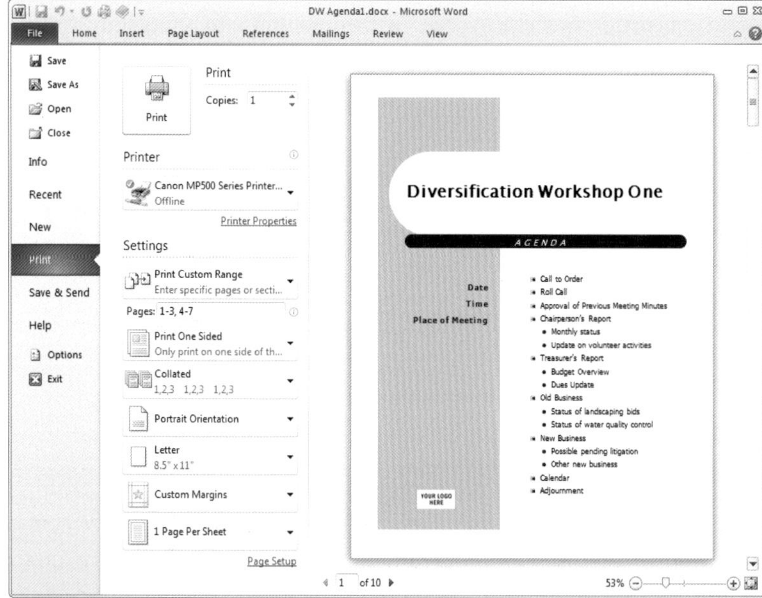

2. You'll see a preview of the current page, which is useful for checking margins and text flow. Click on the forward and back arrows at the bottom, to move through the pages of this preview version

3. Make sure the correct printer is selected, and that it is online. If your printer isn't listed, choose Add Printer

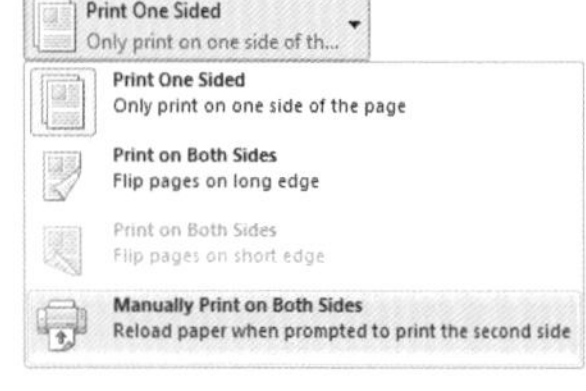

4. Review the other Settings listed. If you don't want to print all pages, then there are a number of other options available. In the example above, a discontinuous range has been chosen (pages 1 to 3, followed by 4 to 7)

5. You can click on the Printer Properties link, or Page Setup, to access more detailed dialogs

6. Finally, go back to the top of the dialog, check the number of desired copies, and then click Print

Save and Send

1 Make sure you have an open document. Choose "Save and Send" from the File Tab

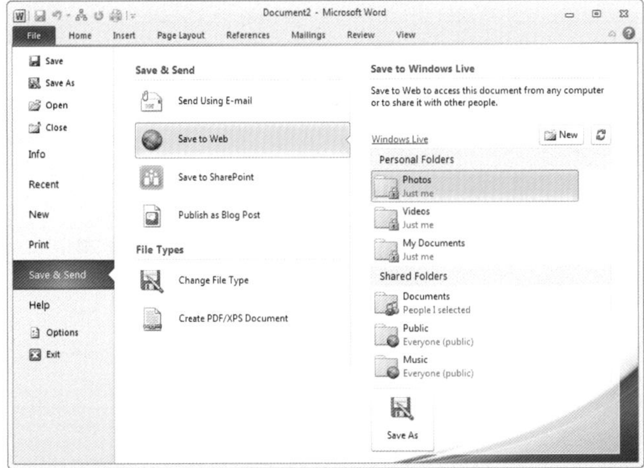

When saving to the Web, you'll be asked to sign into your Windows Live account, if you're not already connected.

2 You can save to the Web (Windows Live's SkyDrive), to a SharePoint site, or publish to a Blog. You can also create a read-only portable document (such as PDF or XPS), or send your document via E-mail

3 To try out Blog publishing, click "Publish as Blog Post". Read the instructions on the right of the dialog, then click the second "Publish as Blog Post" icon underneath

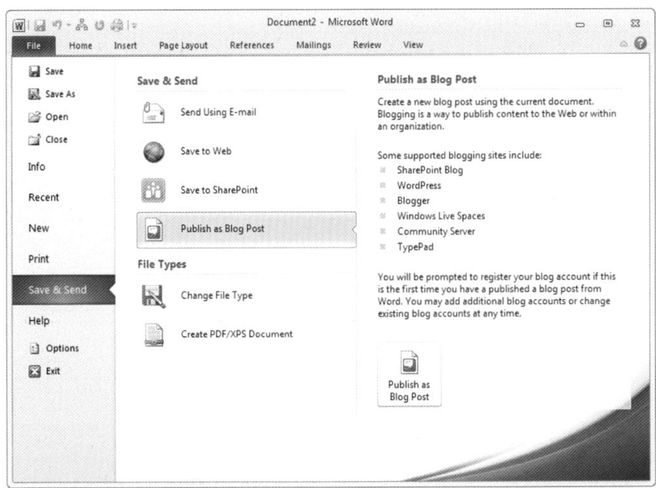

...cont'd

4. A new copy of your document is now generated, reformatted so that it's suitable for publishing to a Blog. Note that there are some new Blog tools in the left side of the Command Toolbar. Also, the other available tools are a subset of Word's normal features

Another way to write a Blog entry is to start a new document from scratch. To do this, choose New from the File Tab, then select "Blog post" from the Available Templates.

5. Make any necessary changes to your Blog entry, then click the Publish icon. In the popup, you can opt to publish normally or just as a draft

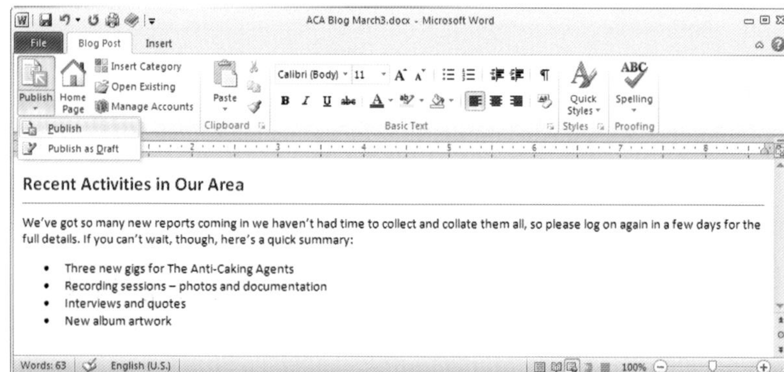

6. If you haven't set up your Blog Account, you'll be prompted for the necessary details before your post is sent

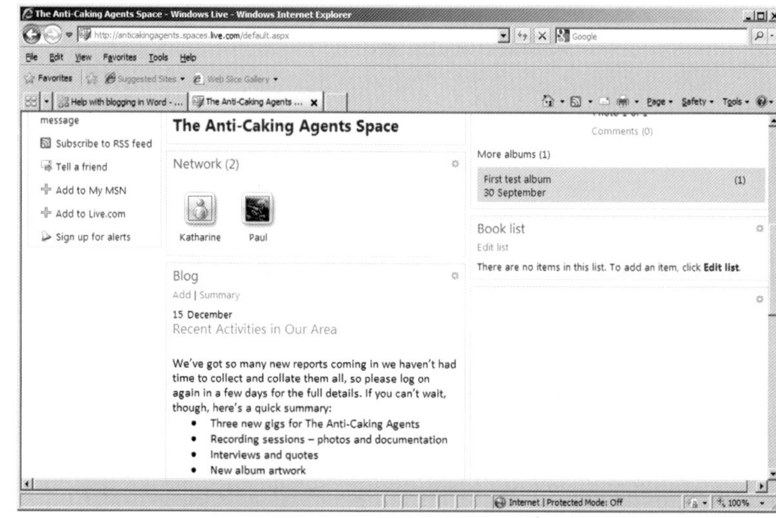

Options

We've already seen how to change certain options in earlier chapters (e.g. Customize Ribbon in Chapter One). All these options, and many more, are available in one place, via the File Tab.

1. Make sure the File Tab is active, then click Options. The Word Options dialog opens. It's organized into ten sections, with General options displayed first

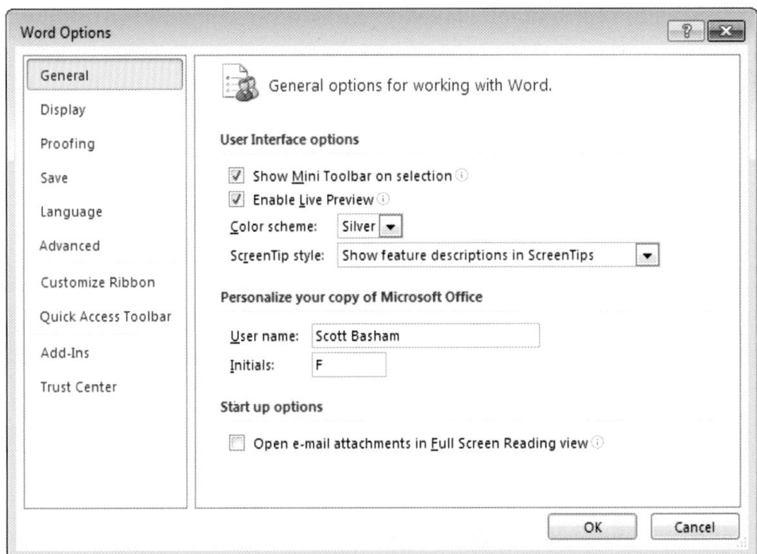

2. Unless your computer is very slow, keep on the options "Show Mini Toolbar on selection" and "Enable Live Preview". The latter controls what happens when you hover over a formatting feature, for example, hovering over a Style in the Style Gallery will temporarily show selected text in that format

3. Click on the Trust Center section. This gives an overview of security and privacy settings. There are links to more information, and a Settings button to let you change how Macros are handled

...cont'd

4 Click on the Display section to control whether Word displays non-printing characters, such as Tabs and Paragraph marks

5 This dialog also has Printing options so you can, for example, elect to print without drawings created in Word. This will speed up printing, and save on printer ink – simple blank boxes will be printed in place of the graphic

Many of the settings in the Word Options dialog have a small letter "i" in a circle next to them. If you hover over this, you'll see a popup explaining what the setting does.

Show highlighter marks

Show highlighter marks
Turn off this option to hide any highlighter marks, both on the screen and when printing.

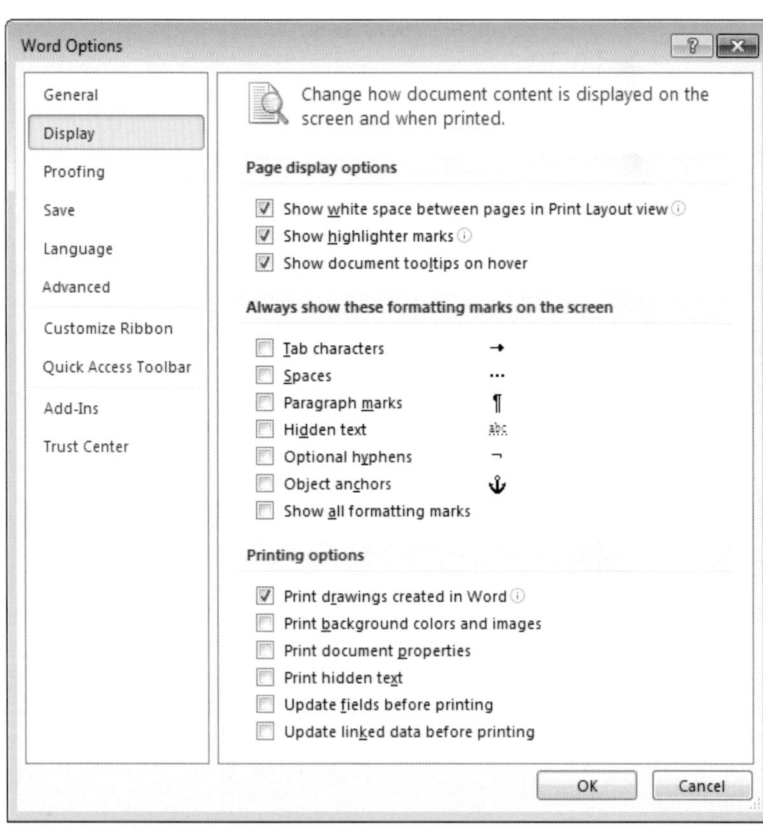

6 Have a look at the other sections. The largest of these is Advanced, which contains extra settings for editing, display, printing, and saving. There are also general compatibility options, which allow you to set certain aspects of Word (e.g. spacing, table manipulation) to behave like they did in earlier versions

11 Advanced Features

This chapter examines some of Word's more advanced features and tools, building on techniques you've seen in earlier chapters.

The Document Inspector

Before distributing your document to others, it's a good idea to check its content carefully. Sometimes your document might contain hidden information, or details you'd rather not include. The Document Inspector can help you with this.

1. Activate Backstage View by clicking on the File Tab

2. The Info screen should appear by default (if not, click on Info). Click on the "Check for Issues" button, then select Inspect Document from the popup

The Document Inspector dialog appears. It lists six categories of content worth checking, most of which is hidden to you at the moment, but would be readable by someone who knew how to operate Word.

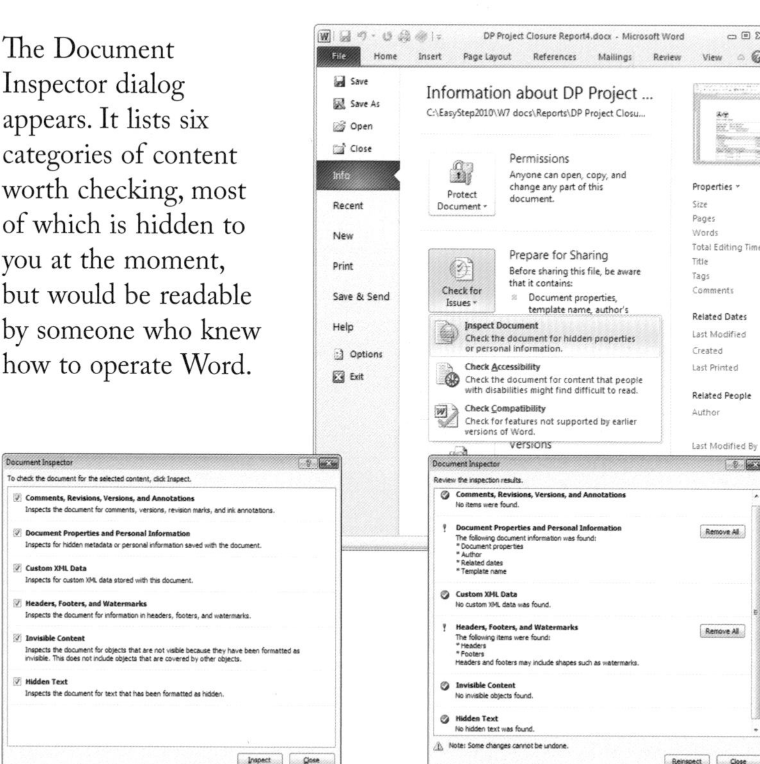

3. Click the Inspect button. The Results window appears

4. If you have any found items, you can get rid of them by clicking on the Remove All button. Click on Reinspect to verify the current state of play, then Close when you've finished

Navigation Pane Features

We looked briefly at the Navigation Pane in Chapter Nine. Here we'll see some advanced examples of it in use.

Browsing Headings

1. Make sure the Navigation Pane is visible. If not, select the View Tab and click on the checkbox labelled Navigation Pane

2. Make sure the first of the three icons is selected at the top of the Pane. This lists just the headings in your document

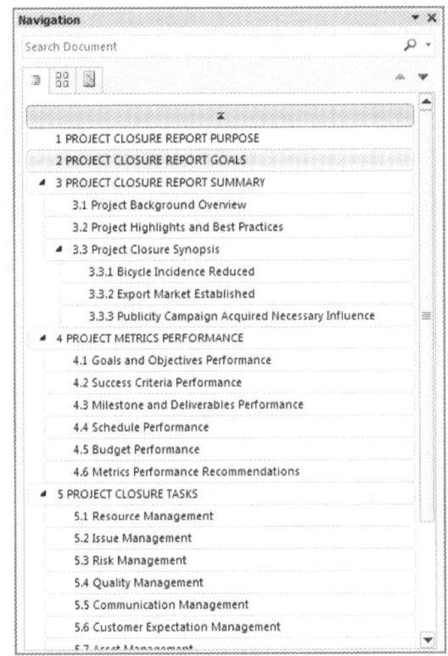

3. The network of headings and subheadings is displayed as a "tree" structure. If you click on the small triangle in this area, the sub-structure beneath this line will be collapsed (hidden) and revealed in turn

4. You can drag headings up and down to a different location, effectively restructuring your document very easily

5. Right-click on a heading to see options for adding, deleting, promoting, demoting, selecting, and printing headings

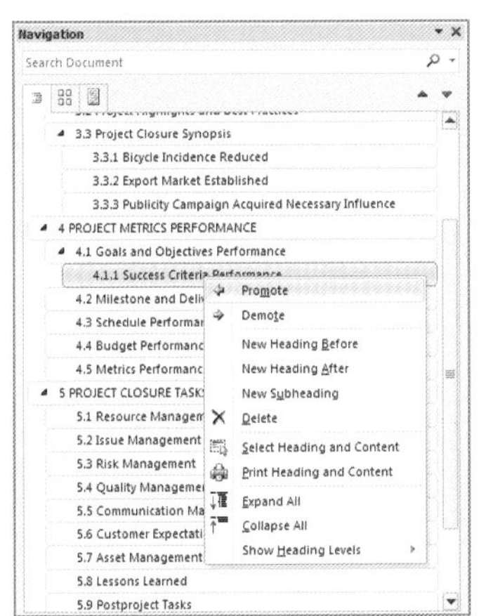

Hot tip

If your document has no headings, then there's nothing to display in this part of the Navigation Pane. Instead, you'll see a message explaining this, suggesting that you should apply some Heading Styles to your text.

Browsing Pages

1. Make sure the Navigation Pane is visible, then click the second icon near its top. This allows you to browse by scrolling through small thumbnail images of each page

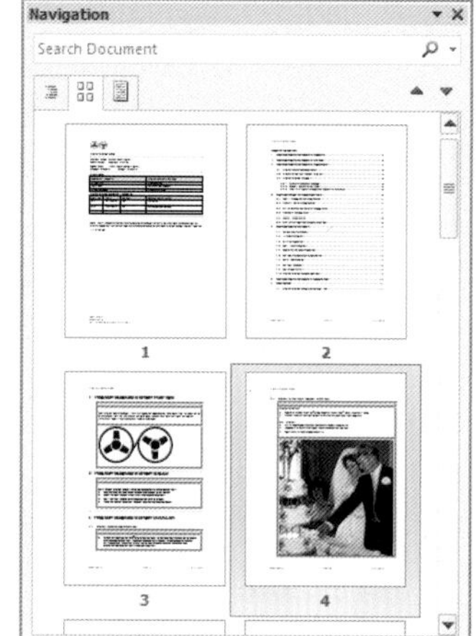

2. You can resize the Navigation Pane by dragging horizontally on the vertical border between it and the main page. Also, you can drag on its title bar to make it a free-floating window

3. If you click on any page icon, the main window will scroll to that page

Browsing Search Results

1. If you click the small triangle beside the hourglass at the top of the pane, you can browse through objects, such as graphics, tables or equations, as well as text

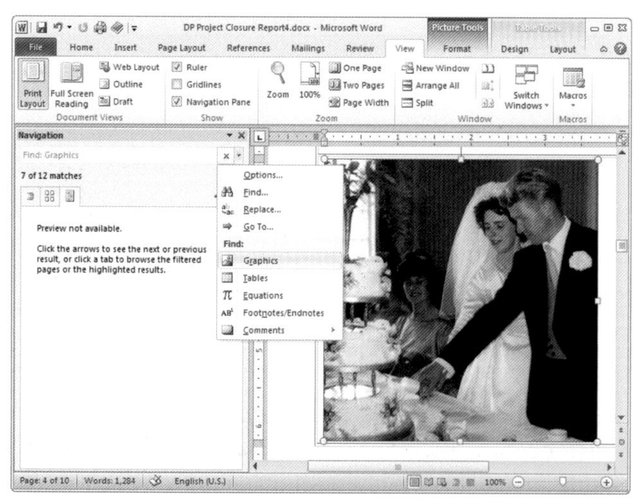

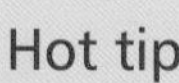

Hot tip

If you click on the third icon at the top of the pane, you can see your search results in context. Click on one of these, and the main page will scroll to the appropriate location.

Word on the Web

An exciting new feature of Word 2010 is the ability to view and edit documents directly on the Web, even if Word isn't installed on your computer. This means you'll be able to work on your documents from any machine with internet access, provided you've saved your document to a shared area, such as a Microsoft SharePoint server or Windows Live's SkyDrive.

Saving to a Shared Area

1. Make sure your document is open, then go to the File Tab and choose Save & Send

2. Select "Save to Web". Once you're signed in, you'll see your online folders. Double-click on one of these

There may be a delay while the remote directory structure is accessed.

You might also be prompted for your Live login name and password.

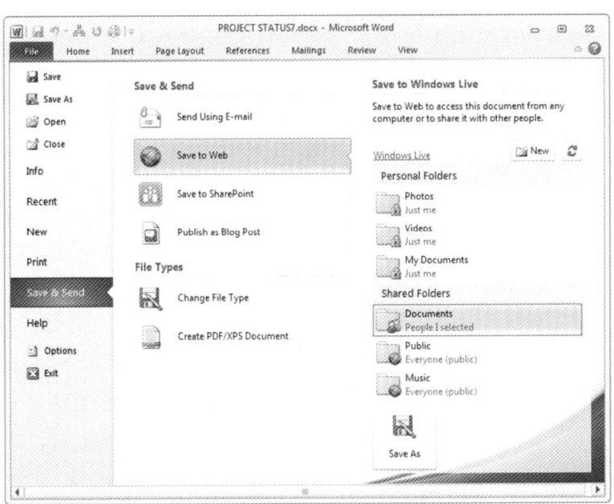

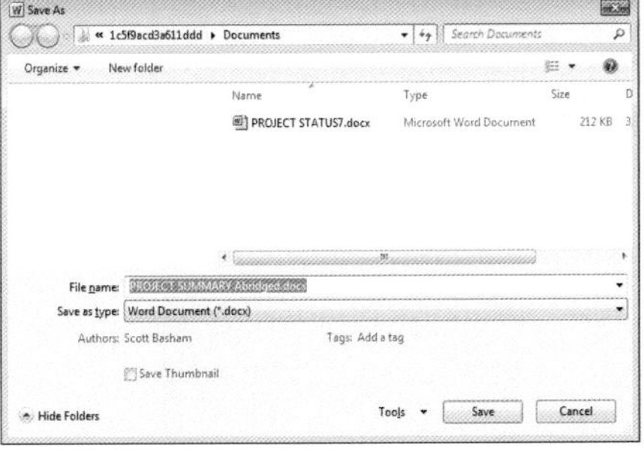

3. You'll see the standard Save As dialog. Make sure the name and file type are ok, then click on the Save button

Your document is now in your SkyDrive shared area. Note that you can also upload and download documents directly from SkyDrive on the Web.

...cont'd

Working Directly on the Web

1. Login to Windows Live at http://home.live.com
2. From the More menu at the top of the screen, choose SkyDrive. You should see your folder structure on the main screen

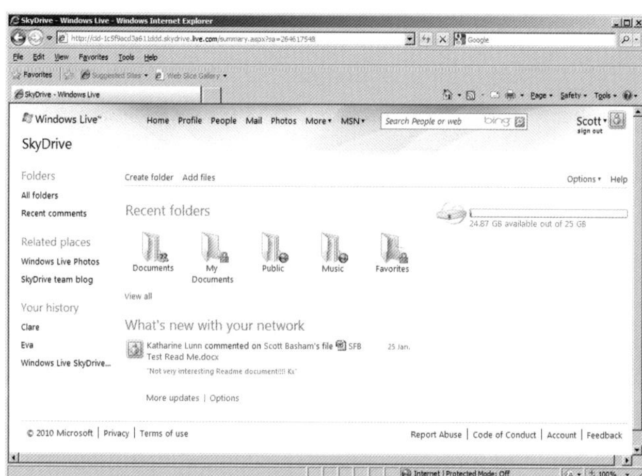

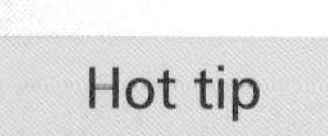

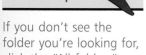

Hot tip

If you don't see the folder you're looking for, click the "All folders" option at the left of the main window.

3. Click on the relevant folder to see its contents

4 Click to select your file. You'll see the file information, any comments, and options to View, Edit, Download, Delete, and Move

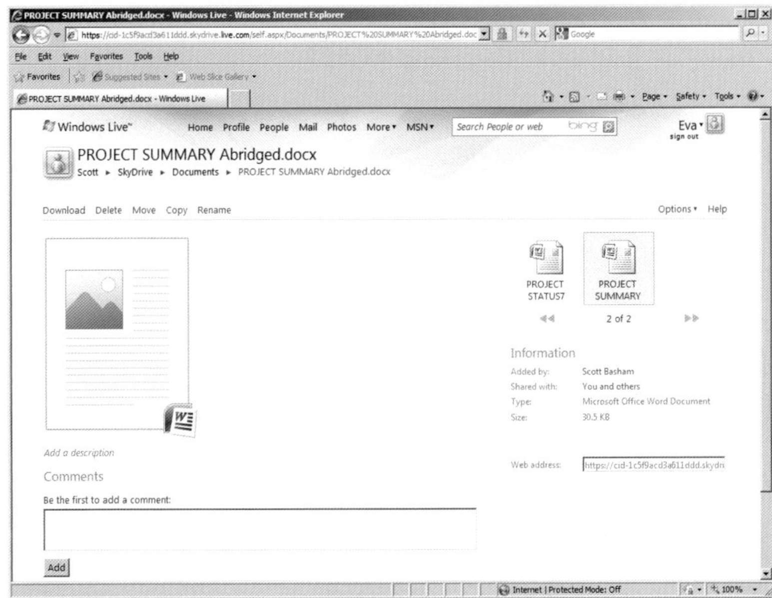

5 Click Edit to start working on your document

The View option is also useful, in that it gives you a full screen preview of your document, including controls for Find, Zoom, and Page selection.

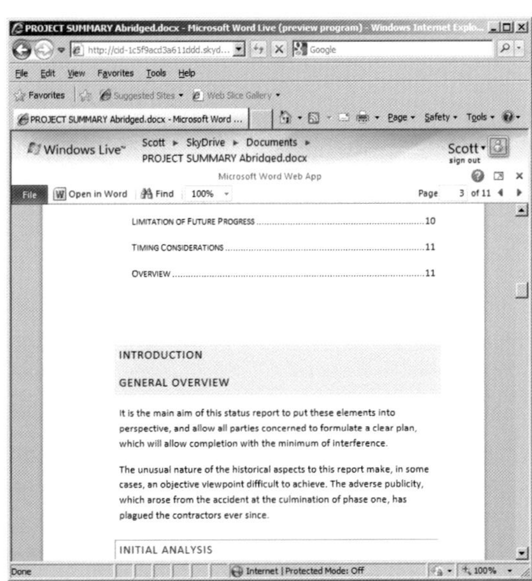

Style Management

We looked at Styles in Chapter Two, “The Home Tab”. Styles are saved along with the document, so it’s worth knowing that there’s a special template file “Normal.dotm” that is used to create all new documents. If a Style definition is stored in “Normal.dotm” then that Style will be available to all new documents.

Styles
Clear All
Body Text
Body Text 2
Body Text 3
Body Text Indent
Bracketed Template Ins
Show Preview
Disable Linked Styles
Options...
Manage Styles

Importing and Exporting Styles

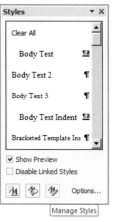

1. First, make sure the Home Tab is active, then click on the icon in the bottom right corner of the Styles area to access the Styles Pane (pictured on the left)

2. Click on the Manage Styles icon to see this dialog box

3. In the lower left corner, click on the Import/Export button

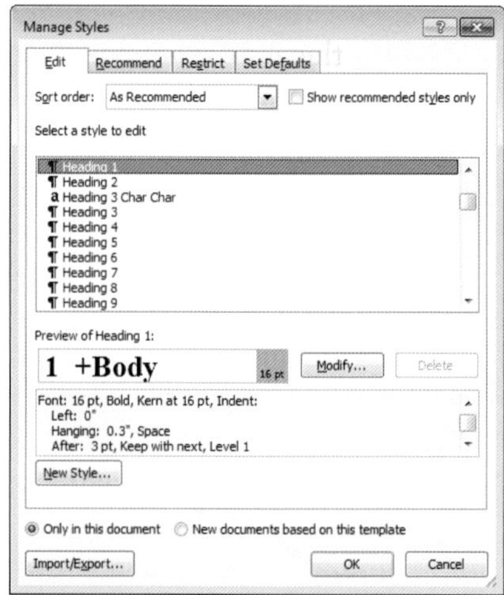

4. The Organizer dialog allows you to freely copy Styles from the current document to and from Normal.dotm

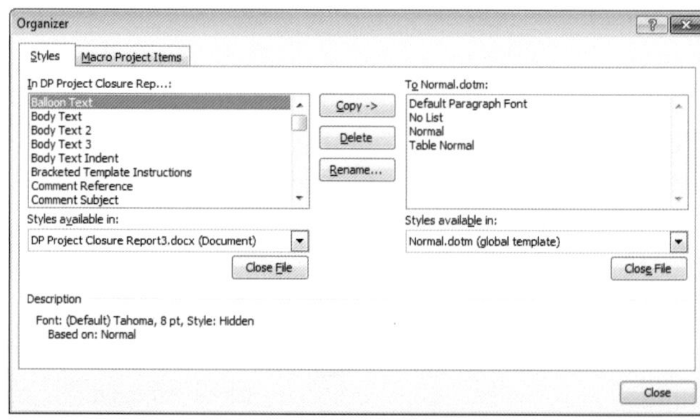

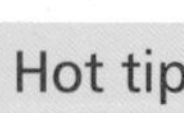

Hot tip

You can use this dialog to copy Styles between any two documents. For either the left or the right side, simply click the Close File button, and then click on the Open File button that appears in its place.

Artistic Effects

We saw many of Word's features for manipulating pictures in Chapter Four, "Special Tabs". In addition to these, Word has an interesting range of artistic effects, normally only found in a photo editing application.

1. Make sure you have an imported photograph to work with. It's a good idea to use copy and paste to create some duplicates – that way it's easier to see the affect of the different options

2. Select one of the images. The Format Tab will appear

3. In the Adjust area at the left side of the Format Tab, click on the Artistic Effects tool

4. A popup gallery of effects appears. As you hover over one, you'll see a preview in your main image. You can also click on the menu item "Artistic Effects Options" to see a dialog with extra controls

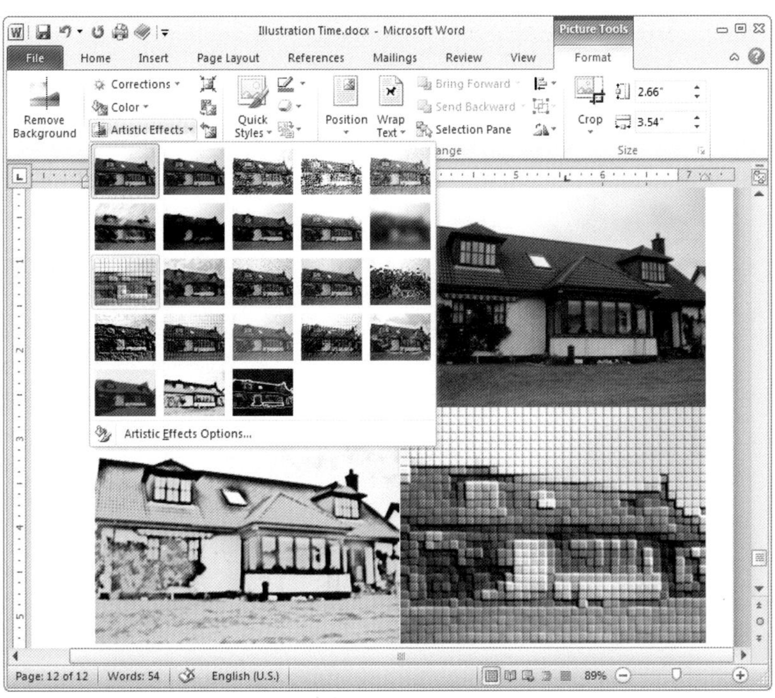

Hot tip

If you can't see much difference in your picture when the effect's applied, check its resolution. If this is quite high, then the effect will be very subtle, unless you zoom right in. Remember, you can lower a picture's resolution by clicking on the Compress Pictures icon in the Adjust area of the Format Tab.

Document Passwords

In Chapter Eight, "The Review Tab", we saw that you could set a password to restrict users from certain types of editing. It's also possible to set a password at the document level – this means that users are effectively locked out of the entire document, if they don't know the password.

1. Make sure your document is open

2. Select Info from the File Tab. Click the Protect Document icon and choose "Encrypt with Password" from the popup menu

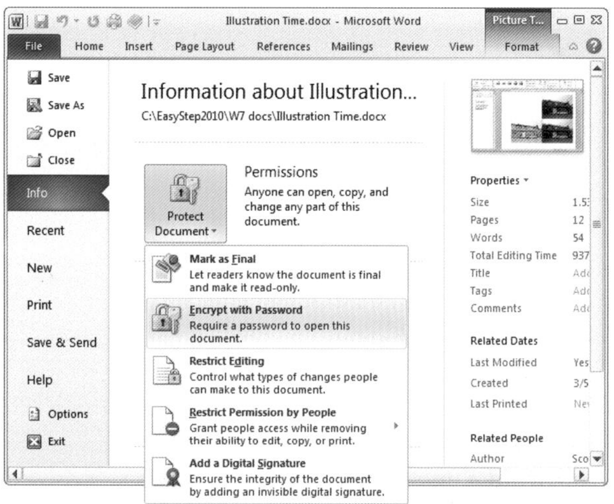

3. You'll be prompted for a password. Make sure it's something you can remember, so you don't lock yourself out of your own document. Click OK

4. Next you're asked to enter the password a second time, to confirm it's correct

5 If you now return to the Info page on the File Tab, you'll see that there's a Permissions message reminding you that the document is password protected

6 Save your document

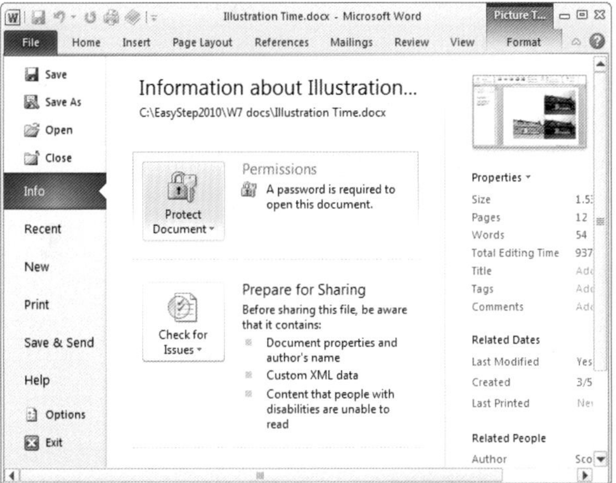

7 Close and then try re-opening your document. You'll see this prompt for the password. Enter the password carefully, then click the OK button

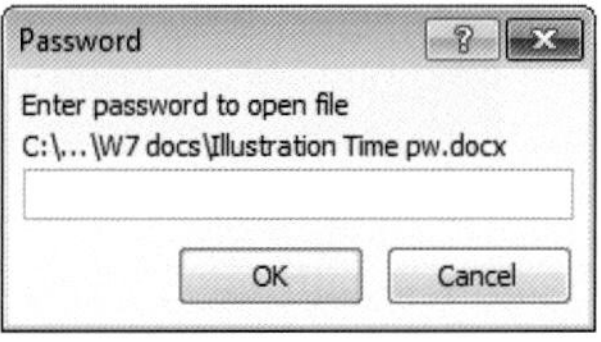

If you enter the password incorrectly, you'll see this message. Remember that passwords are case-sensitive, so a password of "Avocado123x" is different to "avocado123X".

Creating Web Pages

Although not the first choice for dedicated HTML designers, Word is provides a very reasonable range of features for creating web pages. You can easily include text (with formatting), graphics, and hyperlinks, using the tools you've seen in previous chapters.

1. Create your document in the normal way, but make sure that Web Layout view is active, by clicking on the icon in the Status Bar at the bottom of the screen

2. You'll now see a preview of how the document will look on the Web. Add and format your text, and import or create any graphics

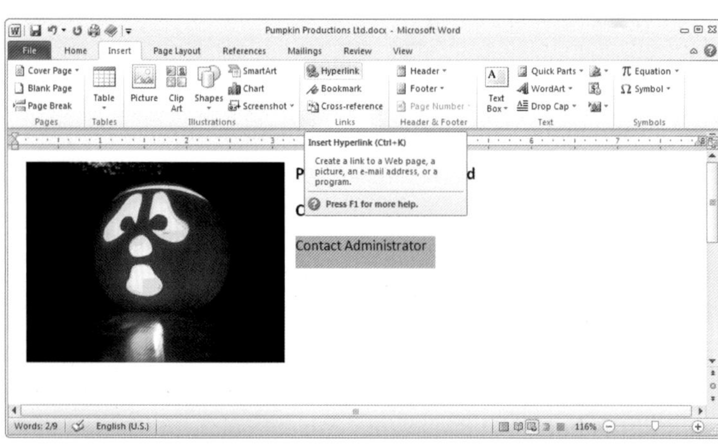

3. In this example, we wanted to make the text "Contact Administrator" into an email hyperlink. Select the text, click Hyperlink, then, in the following dialog, choose Email address and fill in the email details

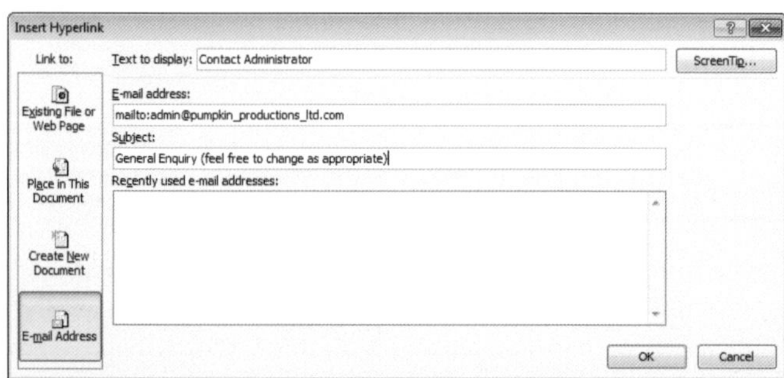

Hot tip

HTML stands for HyperText Markup Language, and is the essential format for virtually all web pages. It's a text-based language, so it's relatively easy for Word to generate HTML files.

4 If this user clicks on this hyperlink, their email client (if configured on their computer) will open automatically. In this example, three more hyperlinks have been added: these examples link to other parts of the document

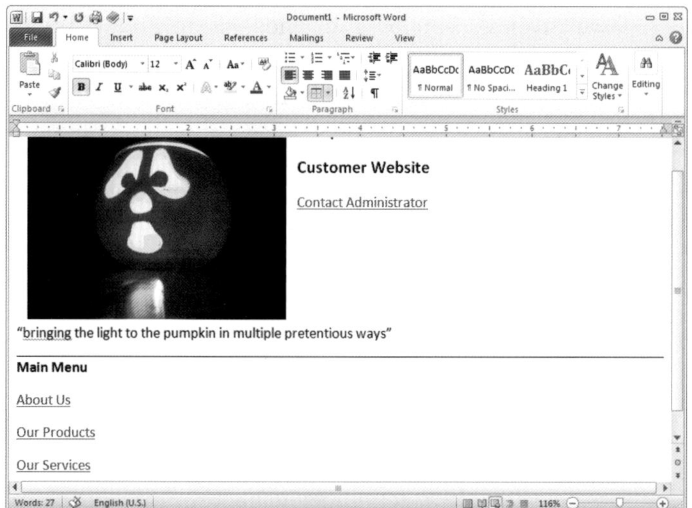

5 When you're happy with the document, go to the File Tab and choose Save As. Select the directory, enter the file name and make sure you choose "Web Page (*.htm; *.html)" as the file type. It's also worth clicking on the Tools button and choosing Web Options, to review compatibility with different browsers

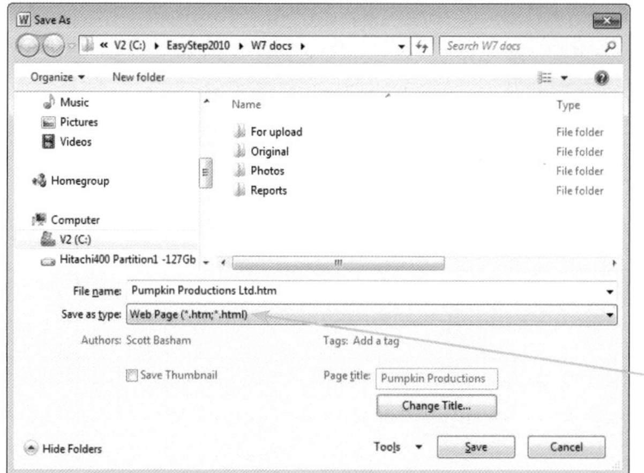

save as type "Web Page"

Don't forget

Hyperlinks can also point to other web pages. For this to work, you'll need to know their URL (Uniform Resource Locator). This is simply the web address, normally entered into the address bar of the Web Browser.

...cont'd

6 Web pages have titles that usually display in the title bar of the browser. By default, this is blank, so click the Change Title button and enter your text

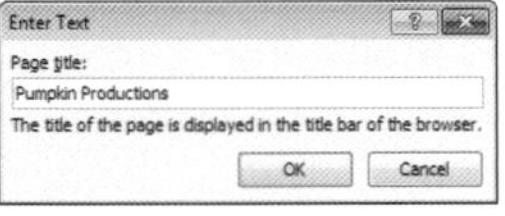

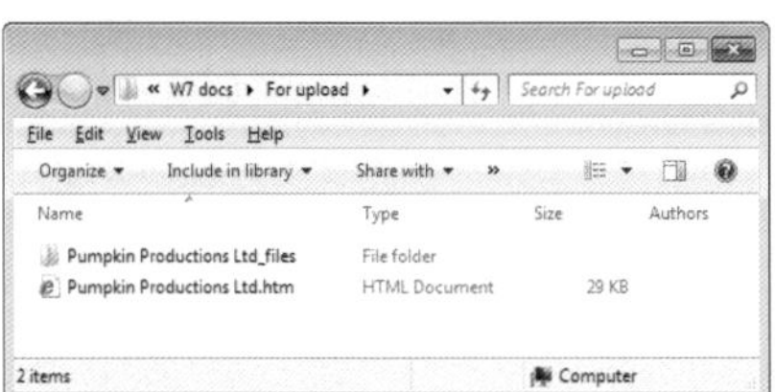

When you save only, the main text is stored in the .htm file. Graphics, some formatting, and other resources, are kept in a separate folder. It's important to make sure the folder always stays in the same location as the .htm file, or your document will display incorrectly.

7 Finally, quit Word and locate your .html file in one of the Windows file views. If you double click on it, a browser window will open and you'll see your web page

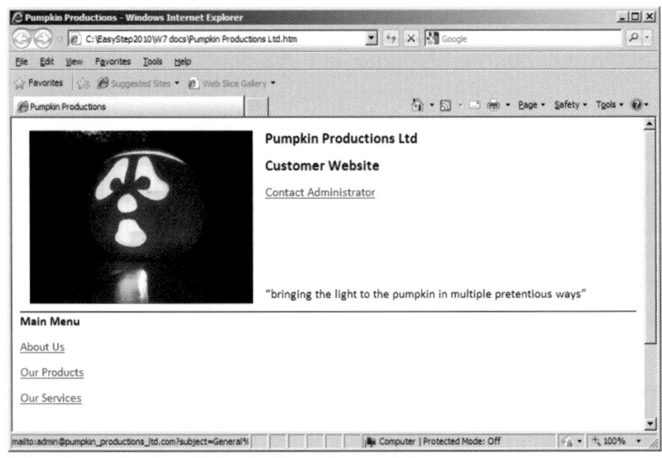

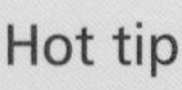

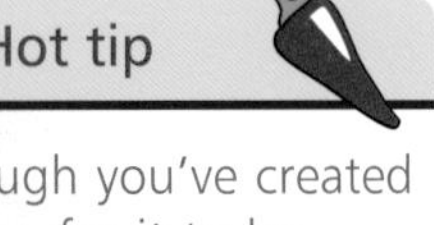

Hot tip

Although you've created a page, for it to be available on the Web it must be copied onto a server provided by a web hosting service, or Internet Service Provider. If you have an account with one of these, then the company will be able to give you instructions on how to upload your files to their site.

8 If you need to make changes to your page, start up Word again and open the document

Index

A

B

C

D

E

F

G

H

I

J

K

L

M

N

O

P

Q

R

S

T

U

V

W

X

Y

Z